WORLD PRESSURES ON
AMERICAN FOREIGN POLICY

WORLD PRESSURES ON AMERICAN FOREIGN POLICY

Edited by Marian D. Irish

Henry B. Mayo
Roy C. Macridis
William S. Livingston
Merle Fainsod
Frederick M. Watkins
Gwendolen M. Carter
Federico G. Gil
Lucian W. Pye

PRENTICE-HALL, INC. *Englewood Cliffs, N.J.*
A SPECTRUM BOOK

Preface

Each year the Department of Government at the Florida State University sponsors a series of public lectures and guest seminars which brings a group of distinguished scholars to the campus. In the academic year 1962-63 eight professors from other universities were invited to examine the outer limits of American foreign policy. Each from the vantage point of his special competency in comparative government and international relations contributed to an over-all view of the United States in the dynamic context of contemporary world politics.

It was my happy assignment to act as chairman for the lecture series and as editor of the resultant essays. On behalf of the Department of Government, faculty and students, I thank our whole company of visiting scholars for an experience that was personally delightful and professionally rewarding. The essays speak for themselves, attesting to the interest and concern of political scientists with the awesome range of external problems that press upon our policy makers.

As I retire from a long-time headship of the Department of Government, I take this occasion to publish a note of appreciation to my colleagues at Florida State University. We have shared many endeavors, including the Government Lecture Series, to bridge the gap between the development of our discipline and the public knowledge. Last, though certainly not least, I acknowledge the encouragement and continuing support of James Murray, Social Science Editor at Prentice-Hall, Inc.

M.D.I.

Table of Contents

WORLD PRESSURES ON
AMERICAN FOREIGN POLICY

INTRODUCTION

Marian D. Irish

A month or so after he had been in office, Secretary of State Dean Rusk made an informal talk to the policy-making officers of the Department of State on how to think about problems in foreign policy. "The problem . . . begins to take shape as a galaxy of utterly complicated factors—political, military, economic, financial, legal, legislative, procedural, administrative—to be sorted out and handled within a political system which moves by consent in relation to an external environment which cannot be under control." [1] The essays in this series cover a "galaxy of utterly complicated factors," observed from diverse vantage points in that "external environment" where American foreign policy must be implemented.

Charles Burton Marshall, who served as a member of the Policy Planning Staff of the Department of State during the 1950's, stresses "the obvious but often overlooked externalness of foreign policy." In his experienced outlook, "The fundamental circumstances giving rise to

---

[1] Selected Papers, prepared by the subcommittee on National Security Staffing and Operations, 87th Cong., 2d sess. *Administration of National Security* (Washington, D.C.: Government Printing Office, 1962), Committee print, p. 23. Informal remarks made to the policy-making officers of the Department of State, February 20, 1961, by the Honorable Dean Rusk.

MARIAN D. IRISH, *Professor of Government, Florida State University, is co-author (with James Prothro) of* The Politics of American Democracy, *editor of* Continuing Crisis in American Politics *(an earlier Symposium in this series), and a frequent contributor to professional journals.*

foreign policy is that most of the world is outside the United States." [2]
This is the recurring problem in all eight essays—to search the outer
limits of American foreign policy. To give a common theme and some
coherence to the volume as a whole, all of the essayists were asked to
give some consideration to the same question: *What ideologies, forces,
events, and persons over which the United States has no jurisdiction are
none the less influential in determining the role of the United States in
the changing world scenes?*

Because of the popular tendency to reduce the whole spectrum of international relations to one highly charged issue, Americanism versus Communism, we asked Henry B. Mayo, a political theorist, to examine some
of the ideological factors that condition our foreign policy. *Theory,
Ideology, and Foreign Policy* raises some crucial questions and offers some
myth-shattering answers in a discourse that is both rational and persuasive. Mayo believes that abstract theory may be relevant, but that as
a political and social force it is never enough to control policy. He
observes that the decision makers in the Kremlin have, "on the record,
adjusted Marxist ideology to their practice rather than the other way
round." Over the years, Soviet foreign policy has been directed chiefly
to strengthening the Soviet Union and only secondarily at achieving the
Marxist class revolution throughout the world. Mayo sees Western political theory as essentially nonideological, but he notes also that a world
power like the United States is condemned to have an ideology. We are
made to stand for more and something other than "national interest,"
both by public opinion at home and by expectations abroad. Actually,
however, we, along with our Western allies, have no agreed definable
ideology except perhaps a belief in diversity. As Mayo states, "Democracy
is a kind of supraideology, a tacit recognition of the right to disagree
and also that this right is basic to all other rights."

If, then, the underlying facts belie the notion of "a cosmic ideological
struggle to the death"; if Soviet foreign policy is not wholly shaped by
revolutionary Marxism but includes a great deal of pragmatism; and if
Western foreign policy is not motivated by a crusading counter ideology,
both sides may still move from perspectives and standpoints closer to
reality. As a professional political theorist, Mayo is not likely to minimize
the effectiveness of ideas and beliefs in the political arena. Nevertheless,
recognizing that a variety of factors other than ideological ones must
enter into the total assessment, he foresees reasonable prospects of "a
détente and, in time, perhaps a *rapprochement*" between the United
States and the Soviet Union." [3]

[2] Charles Burton Marshall, *The Limits of Foreign Policy* (New York: Rinehart &
Winston, Inc., 1954), p. 15.

[3] See also *United States Foreign Policy*, prepared under the direction of the Committee on Foreign Relations, United States Senate, 87th Cong., 1st sess. (Washington,

The conceptual framework of foreign policy in the 1950's—a bipolarization of world politics provoked by opposing monolithic ideologies—turns out to be fairly unrealistic in the 1960's, if indeed it ever applied to the 1950's. Perhaps even more outdated is our representation of power politics—the United States and the free world versus the Soviet Union and the satellite bloc. Charles Lerche, in a recently revised edition of *Foreign Policy of the American People,* points out that "the process of breaking up the two-power world began almost as soon as the Cold War was well underway." [4] The development of multiple independent power centers has radically changed the factual situation in international relations and compels basically different approaches in American policy. Europe, which had been the main focus of our immediate postwar concern, has achieved an economic miracle; it is now not only self-supporting, but on its own has also become extremely prosperous. Earlier, we had counted on a unified Europe, a NATO bloc which would as a matter of course and necessity accept American leadership. But—partly due to Gaullism and partly to a continental suspicion of the Anglo-American alliance—Europe has divided itself, with both power blocs beginning to resent and to slip out from under our control. (Moreover, as William S. Livingston intimates in his essay in this volume, the Anglo-American alliance is not nearly so strong as it appears to the Europeans.) [5]

Roy C. Macridis, in *Western Europe: Promise and Dilemma,* raises some fundamental questions about the emerging nature of Western Europe, which we helped to reconstruct. As Macridis sees it, the political and economic integration of Western Europe poses a basic dilemma for American foreign policy: Shall we recognize and accept the Western bloc as a political and economic rival, an independent third force in international power politics? Or shall we bid for a genuine partnership in an Atlantic Community? Macridis, who has recently spent a considerable amount of time in Europe, much of it in France, discusses the brutal and dramatic changes in the European system which call for a radical overhaul of American foreign policy. The subtitle of his essay,

---

D.C.: Government Printing Office, 1961). The Committee was authorized to "use the experience, knowledge, and advice of private organizations, schools, institutions, and individuals. . . ." The result was a compilation of thirteen important research studies. Study No. 10, "Ideology and Foreign Affairs," was prepared by the Center for International Affairs, Harvard University.

[4] Charles Lerche, *Foreign Policy of the American People* (Englewood Cliffs, N.J.: Prentice-Hall, Inc., 1961), p. 443. See also Cecil V. Crabb, Jr., *American Foreign Policy in the Nuclear Age* (Evanston, Ill.: Harper & Row, Publishers, 1960); and Paul Seabury, *Power, Freedom and Diplomacy* (New York: Random House, 1963).

[5] See *United States Foreign Policy, op. cit.,* Study No. 3, "Western Europe," by the Foreign Policy Research Institute, University of Pennsylvania.

"Promise and Dilemma," suggests both optimism and anxiety as he appraises the several alternatives still open to the United States.

Change is the dominant theme in all the essays. Everywhere in the world today we are confronted with fundamental and far-reaching changes that we can neither stop nor slow down. Even the seemingly most solid and stable foundations in our external environment have crumbled under increasing strains and unpredicted pressures. The disintegration of the British Empire and the delimitations of the Commonwealth are obvious examples. Professor Livingston, in *British Politics and American Policy*, reminds us that for most of our history the foreign policy of the United States was shaped not so much by American aspirations or capabilities as by the position of Great Britain in the power structure of the world. Even in his contemporary analysis he finds that "what Britain is, wants, and does is also part of the environing circumstances that shape American policy."

Livingston's assessment of the continuing Anglo-American alliance in the postwar period is perceptive for its realistic appraisal of mutual interests, its frank recognition of sources of friction, and especially for its forthright value judgment. He states: "The possession of common traditions, values, language, institutions, aspirations, and objectives will, because it must, overcome the divisive influences." The United States needs allies, specifically Great Britain. "One need not perhaps belabor the obvious point that America is even more important to Britain." In some respects, British and American roles have been reversed since the war; the United States has inherited many of the tasks that British diplomacy once performed. Livingston, like Macridis, notes the thorough and continuing change in the European political system. What was formerly Britain's prime responsibility—to keep the balance of power in Europe—is one role, however, which the United States is not expected to assume today. Western union has replaced the old balance of power.

In the formulation of foreign policy, several processes must occur simultaneously. Even while identifying the problem, the policy maker must be gathering his data and thinking about the facts that surround the problem. At the same time, as Dean Rusk pointed out to his policy officers, one must begin to "box the compass of alternative lines of action, including doing nothing." This is the manner in which Merle Fainsod approaches his study, *The Future of the Communist Bloc and American Foreign Policy*. "The aim in this essay is not to predict what will happen, but to project various alternative paths of development and to examine their implications for American foreign policy while recognizing that the actual sequence of events may not conform to any of the alternatives considered."

Fainsod's study is based on a mass of empirical data. What he has to say, especially about the Sino-Soviet rift, is highly significant in its implications for the future of American foreign policy. Like Henry Mayo —though the two arrive at their similar conclusions by quite different lines of scholarship—Fainsod emphasizes the polycentric tendencies within the Communist orbit: "The world Communist movement can no longer be viewed as a monolith subject to Soviet direction and control." He warns us, however, to keep in mind that for all their differences Khrushchev and Mao Tse Tung are both Communists, and if we attempt too flagrantly to drive them further apart, we may end up by bringing them closer together. On the whole, he advocates policy that is both flexible and firm. We should keep open the channels of communication with the satellite countries, reinforce their aspirations for independence, and at the same time maintain our own capacity for instant and full retaliation.

The restraint in style and the moderation in tone that characterize Fainsod's essay must not be mistaken for appeasement in any degree. He indicates that "only Western strength will serve to dampen Communist messianism," and he declares that the principal problem in American foreign policy is "countering and, if possible, reversing the expansion of Soviet power and influence in the world." [6] With the other essayists, he shares a profound faith in Western values: "If the non-Communist nations can hold out the prospects of freedom and welfare for their peoples, they need fear no Communist threat within, and by pooling their strength and resources they may reasonably expect to ward off any threat from without." He believes it "an act of total despair" to assume that thermonuclear war—or ultimate Communist victory—is inevitable.

Soviet-American relations seemingly underwent a change in attitudes and emphasis during 1963. To some people the turn of events on the diplomatic front—notably mutual agreement to an atmospheric nuclear test ban and also the willingness of the United States to sell its surplus wheat to the hungry Soviets—signaled the beginning of the end of the Cold War. President Kennedy, however, speaking at the University of Maine in October 1963, advanced the same lines of caution that we find in Professor Fainsod's essay. Observing that the United States and the Soviet Union "still have wholly different concepts of the world, its freedom and its future," President Kennedy gave fair warning of continuing crises "both in areas of direct confrontation—such as Germany and the Caribbean—and in areas where events beyond our control could involve us both—areas such as Africa, Asia and the Middle East."

More than a billion human beings living under non-Communist rule and nearly another billion within the Communist bloc are in the complex

---

[6] See also *United States Foreign Policy, op. cit.,* Study No. 11, "U.S.S.R. and Eastern Europe," by a Columbia-Harvard Research Group. (Professor Fainsod was a member of the panel that planned and drafted this study.)

process of "transition from life in the setting of a traditional society to life in a modern setting." [7] Here is probably the most overwhelming single factor in international relations today. Lucian Pye, in *Transitional Asia and the Dynamics of Nation Building,* observes that most social scientists deliberately try to avoid the pitfalls of normative studies and tend to concentrate on explaining the "realities of the contemporary scene." Hence they are inclined to shy away from such issues as "cultural relativism" implicit in studies of underdeveloped or developing countries.

The essay of Frederick Watkins, *Colonialism, Dictatorship, and the American Political Tradition,* takes a look at the emerging nations in the light of traditional political assumptions. The hypothesis of the author may be controverted, but no serious student of political science and no American foreign policy maker can ignore the core question which he poses: "Why is it that totalitarianism, rather than democracy, has provided the model for so many of the more successful revolutionary regimes of the twentieth century?" Whatever the answer, the conventional wisdom of political science and traditional foreign policy practices are bound to be sorely shaken.

Watkins finds that liberal colonialism has not generally promoted democratic government, that colonial independence has usually been won under conditions of extreme tension, and that constitutional government can not function normally in crisis situations. As he views it—and his evidence is impressive—"the prospects of constitutional democracy in ex-colonial areas are in general rather slim." On the other hand, while he foresees dictatorship as the probable form of government among the newly liberated nations, he surmises that most of the new governments are likely to become fascist rather than communistic. Americans may well be disappointed that our encouragement of national self-determination now results in a world that largely repudiates or fails to accept our traditional beliefs in constitutional democracy as a way of life for all men. Watkins puts it bluntly. "This is one of the many unwelcome but important facts that America will have to learn to live with in the contemporary world."

The most dramatic and the least anticipated change in the international environment was effected by the emergence of newly independent countries in Africa. The year 1960, when sixteen African states were admitted to membership in the United Nations, marked a turning point in the history of the world. [8] The Afro-Asian states have now become a

---

[7] See *United States Foreign Policy, op. cit.,* Study No. 12, "Economic, Social, and Political Change in the Underdeveloped Countries and Its Implications for United States Policy," by the Center for International Studies, Massachusetts Institute of Technology.

[8] *The United States in the United Nations, 1960—A Turning Point,* Report to the Committee on Foreign Relations, United States Senate, by Senator George D. Aiken

bloc with enough votes among them to control decision making in the international organization on important questions of substance. The United States can no longer count on a comfortable majority of votes to support its proposals for Pax Americana; thus it faces the dilemma which Britain had encountered earlier when its own disintegrating empire and a changing Europe did away with Pax Britannica.

American policy makers have recently found it difficult to steer between Scylla and Charybdis, between loyalties to our NATO associates (who were recently the colonial powers of Africa) and between strategic interest in the many new states (which have become such important variables in the power politics of the Cold War). Hitherto the United States has developed no positive or particular policies toward Africa. Suddenly it finds itself caught in a maelstrom of racist and socio-economic problems, both at home and abroad, that are crucial to its relationships with the African nations. The impact of African nationalism upon the Western bloc, and especially upon the United States, can easily be exaggerated. Issues charged with emotionalism tend to be magnified by the demagogery of extremists. Nevertheless, the African preoccupation with anticolonialism and with racism poses serious problems for American foreign policy in terms of our political alignments, national security, and economic interests.

Gwendolen M. Carter's essay, *United States Foreign Policy Toward South Africa,* focuses on African desires and American aims at the principal point of conflict—the imposition of sanctions against South Africa. The Union of South Africa epitomizes the racial issue, because there *apartheid* (apartness), is "buttressed and sanctified by statute." As Miss Carter points out, South Africa embodies in its acutest form one of the most sensitive problems of the twentieth century: the relationships between a dominant white minority and an increasingly assertive nonwhite majority. At the heart of the problem is the issue of human rights and dignity of the individual to which the Western World is committed in principle. Miss Carter reports the inequitable conditions in the Union of South Africa in the dispassionate language of scholarship, but the problem which she discusses is a major headache for our policy makers, the more so because it ties in with the most violent and one of the most crucial domestic issues in current American politics. Her essay suggests the immense difficulties in dealing both diplomatically and effectively with a situation which arouses intense emotionalism and bitter resentment among all the colored peoples of the world, a situation which she perceives, however, to be so carefully stabilized at the moment that no normal "threat to the peace" seems applicable.

---

and Senator Wayne Morse, 87th Cong., 1st sess. (Washington, D.C.: Government Printing Office, 1961), Committee reprint.

The revolution of rising expectations" is the central theme of our times —revolution now rampant in all the underdeveloped countries of the world. Anticolonialism and wars for national independence are nothing new in history. The United States knows this kind of revolution from its own experience. The contemporary process of revolution, however, is much more drastic and complex. The whole society is involved at every level and in all aspects. The immediate objectives are social justice, economic development, and a civilization based on Western technology— in short, a "modernized" nation.

The dynamics vary. The emerging nations cannot all be lumped together as backward or underdeveloped; they have enormously different kinds of potential in terms of their traditional cultures, their material resources, and their psychological motivations. All these differences call for policies on our part which reflect the varying dynamics—policies tailored to the individual countries to help them pass through the extremely complex phases of their development.

Only recently have we realized that our Latin American neighbors in the Western Hemisphere belong to this world in popular upheaval. Over many years we had come to regard Latin American revolutions as routine political phenomena that demanded no great changes in our relations with a succession of personal and military dictators. Thus we were totally unprepared to recognize, much less cope with, Fidel Castro's really "modern" revolution, just 90 miles off the coast of Florida.

Federico G. Gil, a native Cuban, has titled his essay *Latin America: Social Revolution and United States Foreign Policy*. He regards the Alliance for Progress as "a major turning point in the history of the hemisphere." Through this plan the United States has assumed a "novel role as a champion of social revolution," a role that has "forced the United States to develop a new kind of diplomacy, the diplomacy of social revolution." Gil's analysis of the changing Latin American environment points up the extraordinary complexity of formulating, programming, testing, and reviewing policies under the Alliance for Progress.

The implementation of the Alliance is all the more complicated because the input represents multilateral cooperative efforts, whereas the output affects exceedingly diverse situations in each of the countries involved. As Gil sees it, Cuba's incorporation into the Soviet bloc shattered the traditional structure of the Western Hemisphere. The success of the Soviet offensive in the hitherto closed system of the American republics has provoked the United States into sponsoring counter social revolution in all of Latin America on financial and economic terms that shake the very foundations of our long-time dealings with those countries. Gil concedes that the issues and problems are innumerable and "portend a long, hard road ahead," but he believes "there is solid ground for

optimism concerning the outcome of the revolutionary crusade undertaken by the Alliance."

The final essay by Lucian Pye, *Transitional Asia and the Dynamics
of Nation Building*, holds particular insight for the social scientist seeking some kinds of manageable hypotheses for understanding the problems of nation building. Nowhere is the "galaxy of utterly complicated
factors" more confusing and frustrating to scholars, as well as to policy
makers, than in the modernizing but very old countries of Asia.[9] In
what he describes as "the crisis approach to political development,"
Pye organizes his analysis of nation building in Asia around five basic
generalizations: the crises of identity, integration, penetration, participation, and distribution. Within this orderly intellectual context, we
begin to comprehend the tremendous range of variables that occur in
the dynamics of nation building.

Professor Pye is somewhat dismayed by the gap between popular concern and policy involvement in Asia. This is a problem that inevitably
confronts our representatives in all areas of policy making, but especially
in foreign policy. As Pye insists, public policy in the long run must rest
upon popular sentiments. "No matter how clever or ingenious the policy
ploys, the work of officials must reflect popular convictions if they
are to have sustaining consequences." The lectures from which these
essays were written were intended to serve this very function—to help
bridge the gap between the public views and the official policies—
through informed analyses of the ideas, institutions, and processes in
the external environment which in large measure shape American foreign policy.

The essays may appeal most to those students of political science who
are interested more in the substance of public policy than in professional
methodology. Here students will find systematic analysis of political
behavior all over the world, but the shiny new tools of analysis are not
on display—game theory, model building, opinion surveys, or simula-
tions.[10] The reader, however, who looks for quick answers and pat
solutions may be somewhat disappointed. As Secretary of State Dean
Rusk recently put it to a congressional committee, it has been many
decades since the conduct of American foreign affairs was relatively
simple or easy. All these studies bear out Rusk's official observations—
"the breathtaking pace and baffling complexities of our modern society"

---

[9] See *United States Foreign Policy, op. cit.*, Study No. 5, "Asia."

[10] For theoretical approaches and scientific studies, the interested student might see
George Modelski, *A Theory of Foreign Policy* (New York: Frederick A. Praeger, Inc.,
1962), and Richard C. Snyder, H. W. Bruck, and Burton Sapin, *Foreign Policy Decision Making* (New York: The Free Press of Glencoe, Inc., 1962).

and "an almost unparalleled transformation in the world beyond our borders." [11]

These essays cover a world in turbulent transition. The shape of the period ahead is still unknown but it will in large measure be determined by the ideologies, forces, events and persons observed, analyzed, and to some extent appraised in this volume. Political and economic realignments both within the Free World and the Communist Bloc, the continuing upsurge of racial and nationalist aspirations and everywhere the pressures of accommodation among peoples of different races and cultures, world-wide demands not only for political independence but for economic and social improvement and technical advancement—the range of issues is obviously much too vast for studies in depth in a volume of this sort. All the essays, however, include *Suggestions for Further Reading* and also footnotes which provide valuable guidance to documents and authoritative materials on both general and special aspects of the problems discussed.

In one small volume it is clearly impossible to cover the whole area of current international relations; some omissions are inevitable. The most notable, of course, is Germany, especially Berlin, which admittedly is the most critical commitment in American foreign policy today. President Kennedy's statement with respect to Berlin in the crisis of July, 1961, is exceedingly impressive: "For the fulfillment of our pledge to that city is essential to the morale and security of West Germany, to the unity of Western Europe, and to the faith of the entire free world." But within the context of external environment, we note that American policies toward Germany and Berlin are still not made in Bonn and Berlin as much as they are in Paris, London, and Washington—a fact made rather clear during President Kennedy's European tour in June, 1963. Other areas also are unfortunately omitted from specific consideration: Italy, Greece and Spain, the Middle East, the Scandinavian bloc, East Germany, Yugoslavia, and Poland. In the over-all picture the factual situations in these countries too have important ramifications in world politics, but we did not think it wise to attempt an encyclopaedic compendium in a single volume.

The essayists are highly knowledgeable in the areas they discuss. They write from personal and professional experience as well as from a scholarly background. All are recognized as experts, and most of them have served officially or informally as government consultants. The authors do not share identical values; their views separately expressed do not

[11] Hearings before the Subcommittee of the Committee on Appropriations, United States Senate, 87th Cong., 1st sess., Departments of State and Justice, the judiciary and related agencies for the fiscal year ending June 30, 1962 (Washington, D.C.: Government Printing Office, 1961), p. 88.

always fit together into a consistent composite. All of them, however, have made searching inquiries into critical areas. None has tried to offer specific prescriptions for action, but all have put forward some fresh ideas and have made some fruitful proposals. Each in turn has counselled the practicality of alternatives in decision making and the wisdom of flexibility in the formulation and execution of grand policy.

THEORY, IDEOLOGY,
AND FOREIGN POLICY

Henry B. Mayo

Our tragedy today is a general and universal fear so long sustained by now that we can even bear it. There are no longer problems of the spirit. There is only the question: when will I be blown up? [1]

Political theory and international relations are not, on the whole, very closely integrated subjects of study. With a few notable exceptions, political theorists have dwelt far more upon national than upon international politics, upon internal order and justice rather than upon peace and war. This neglect has been particularly marked in the political theory of the English-speaking world.

The historic gap between political theory and international relations is being filled today by many hands, largely because events are forcing us to do so. The really great problems facing us today appear at the

[1] William Faulkner, in Speech of Acceptance upon the Award of the Nobel Prize for Literature, Stockholm, Sweden, December 10, 1950.

HENRY B. MAYO *is Senior Professor of Political Science and Head of the Department at the University of Western Ontario, London, Canada. He has also been a member of the faculty at the University of Alberta and a visiting professor at McGill University, Duke University, and the University of South Carolina. He is the author of* Introduction to Democratic Theory *and* Introduction to Marxist Theory, *and is a frequent contributor to professional journals. He has been a civil servant and still serves as occasional consultant for Canadian provincial governments.*

12

international level. If these problems are solved, all else is manageable; if they are not solved, nothing else is worth worrying about.

We have been living for almost twenty years in what is called—unhappily I think—a "Cold War"; its nature and possible outcome have been our chief political preoccupation. Although most of the popular writing on this subject has been highly partisan (understandably enough, given the spirit of our times), it is regrettable that much of our scholarly writing and research has also been marked by the same spirit of party and the same rigidity of thought.

Still, there has been recently a gratifying amount of first-rate political theorizing directed at international politics. So many talented minds are at work in this field today that one gets the impression of an *embarras de richesse*. We have systems theory, mathematical and game theory, cybernetics, group dynamics, role analysis, philosophical anthropology, and many more theories brought to bear on the chief problems of our times. I do not propose to take the reader on a journey up those heights, nor to explore such great unifying concepts as equilibrium, or power, or the national interest, and relate them to world politics. My aim is pitched much lower: to conceive of political theory in a simple fashion; to put a few questions and examine a few tentative answers; and, by this means, to try to order some of the complexities of the present-day international scene.

THE POLAR CONFLICT OF IDEOLOGIES
IN INTERNATIONAL RELATIONS

There are, at the present time, two great nations in the world, which seem to tend towards the same end, although they started from different points: I allude to the Russians and the Americans. Both of them have grown up unnoticed; and while the attention of mankind was directed elsewhere, they have suddenly assumed a most prominent place among the nations; and the world learned their existence and their greatness at almost the same time. . . .
Their starting-point is different, and their courses are not the same; yet each of them seems to be marked out by the will of Heaven to sway the destinies of half the globe.[2]

Although these (perhaps familiar) comments sound so up-to-date, they were in fact written more than a century ago by the French statesman and author, Alexis de Tocqueville. Many people believe that this prophetic diagnosis of de Tocqueville can be applied to the current bi-

---

[2] Alexis de Tocqueville, *Democracy in America*, World's Classics ed. (New York: Oxford University Press, Inc., 1946), pp. 286-87.

polarization of the world; and that this bipolarization is the main fact of international politics today. The picture is of two Titans, two superpowers, each the head of a powerful bloc of satellites or allies. These two hold the fate of the world in their hands, and particularly with them rests the fateful decision whether or not to plunge the world into war. Outside these two great blocs lie a number of neutral or uncommitted states, which each of the Titans tries to win to its side, but the uncommitted, for all practical purposes, do not count.

This picture of the essential facts of international politics today is one standpoint from which to look at the foreign policy of the great powers. One may call it a framework of theory. It is a very simple theory, more in favor among neutrals than in either the United States or Russia.

As sober facts—that there are two superpowers and that they are opposed—this picture of the world is accurate, so far as it goes. But as a theory it does not explain very much. For example, why are the two superpowers in opposition? What are they both after? What is the relation of each to its satellites and allies? What is the role of neutrals?

A second picture of the world scene, though with interesting variations, is similar, and even more well-known. The protagonists on each side are the same: the United States and Russia. In this picture of international politics today as a battle for men's minds considerations of power politics are played down, and the emphasis instead is on opposing ideologies locked in mortal combat. On one side is the ideology of communism with all that it entails, while on the other we are somewhat more vague and certainly not monolithic. We stand for freedom, democracy, capitalism, religion, or for whichever set of values we select from the smorgasbord of the Western historical tradition.

Whereas the first picture, of equally selfish superpowers, tends to be favored by neutrals, the second picture, of ideologies in conflict around the globe and even in space, seems to be held by the superpowers themselves. To be more precise, we should say that this view of ideologies in conflict is held only by a section of public opinion in the West, whereas in the Soviet Union the conviction is held by the rulers and is thus official. The global conflict, as these two powers see it, is between "Socialism" and "Capitalism," one or the other of which will eventually triumph. It is a view that seems to lift the Cold War above a mere power struggle, to endow it with meaning and an almost cosmic purpose. A drama of good and evil is being played under our very eyes to the predestined judgment.

It is this picture or theory of international relations today, with some of its implications, that I wish to examine. Other pictures of the world scene can of course be composed. It is possible, for instance, to see the present Russian-American friction as essentially temporary and short-run, and to say that the deeper and more significant division is along "racial" lines or is between the rich nations and the poor nations. One could also argue that with the establishment of a united, quasifederated Europe and with the rising power of China, the bipolarization and the bi-ideological divisions are already almost obsolete. Other perspectives have been constructed, but they will not be examined here.

COMMUNIST "IDEOLOGY" AND SOVIET IMPERIAL POLICY

The meaning of the word "ideology" is so broad today that it can cover almost any grouping of beliefs or ideas, but in the Marxist usage it came close to meaning a rationalization of bourgeois class interests—the set of beliefs, or theory, by which class interests were justified. Today, it may roughly be described as a mixture of normative and empirical political and social theory—a general theoretical set of beliefs about man, society, and the state which purport to explain and justify particular political ideals and systems. In this sense Marxism is itself an ideology, with a theory of history and society that also includes ideals for the future. And, of course, where Communist states exist, the ideology is used to justify their institutions and their practice.

The first interesting question which arises is: What is the relation of the Marxist theory or ideology to Russian foreign policy? By Marxist (or Communist) theory, I mean of course the corpus of Marxist doctrine through Marx, Engels, Lenin, Stalin, to Khrushchev, and (occasionally) others. Clearly, even this is a large and amorphous question. It is, however, just the sort of question to which nearly everyone seems to have a ready answer. There is something about Marxism and Soviet policy that engenders dogmatism even among experts, that makes them fanatical about their own diagnoses, and that causes them to see visions or dream nightmares. The truth is that no one really knows for sure how Marxist theory influences Soviet foreign policy. To find out, we should have to read the minds (conscious and subconscious) of those in the Kremlin. There are in fact no experts on this, but only varying degrees of ignorance and prejudiced guesswork. Hence "Kremlinologists" disagree, and offer a potpourri of theories in search of reality. Hence, too, what I have to say on the subject can only be a thesis, depending for its plausibility on the evidence put forward.

In order to approach an answer, I shall first put a smaller, more manageable question: What has the original Marxist theory, in the works of Marx and Engels themselves, to say about foreign policy? Marxism, of course, is a many-sided system of thought, which consists of philosophy, political theory, economics, history, strategy, and tactics. The whole theory, while containing some elements of partial truth (very few theories

are wholly wrong), will not I think stand any sustained logical or historical analysis.[3] But the point here is that there is not much on foreign
policy in this classic Marxism. Underneath the main theme, however,
there is a little that is *related* to foreign policy. That little consists of
two points:

1. As capitalism spread its tentacles around the world, national wars
(so Marx thought) would be replaced by an international class war of
united proletarians on one side and bourgeoisie on the other. Now,
nineteenth century liberalism of the free trade or Manchester variety
also used to argue that national wars would cease as trade and commerce
knit the world together. As it turned out, this was a great mistake on
the part of economic liberalism. (Mercantile communities, from the
Italian city states onward, have generally been inclined to optimism and
to the belief that since commerce thrives on peace, peace is virtually inevitable.)

Marx argued along the same line, in a reverse kind of way, and he was
equally optimistic and wrong. In both cases that force, which we call
nationalism in other countries and patriotism in our own, has proved
so much stronger than international ties, whether these are economic,
class, religious, or any other kind.

2. Where would the revolution happen first? In the most industrialized
countries, Marx believed. Given the revolution in these countries first,
and more or less simultaneously, Marx thought that they would dominate the rest of the world by their example and power, and so keep the
peace. In time the whole world would tread the same historic path, and
universal peace and the classless society would prevail.

Again, how wide of the mark this forecast has been! We have learned
that revolutions are much easier to make in so-called "backward" lands,
and Marxist parties have come to power chiefly in peasant countries,
while highly industrialized nations are generally strongly inoculated
against Marxism. Latin America, for instance, is on this ground a much
easier prey for Communist parties than the United States or Canada.
We must conclude that there is very little in the original Marxism to
enlighten our understanding of Soviet foreign policy, and still less to
throw light on that of Communist China.

The second specific question to arise is: What did Leninist theory
add to Marxism, up to the Bolshevik Revolution, that might throw
light on Russian foreign policy since then? For our purposes, Lenin's
chief addition was his theory of "imperialism." This theory was invented
to show why Marx's prediction had not come true by the early twentieth

---

[3] H. B. Mayo, *Introduction to Marxist Theory* (New York: Oxford University Press,
Inc., 1960).

century. Industrial capitalism, Lenin argued, had been saved from collapse by resorting to colonial and other imperialist ventures. It had changed into decadent finance-capitalism, which in its scramble for overseas markets, raw materials, and investment would usher in an age of wars *between* the capitalist states, and *then* the international revolution would happen in the resulting crisis conditions. The chief point related to foreign policy in this theory concerns the tactics to be followed by Communists and Communist parties. They should try—according to Lenin—to convert the national imperialist wars into an international class struggle, which in turn should be directed at promoting the revolution in the most industrialized countries. The story of how this was attempted and failed in the Great War of 1914 is well-known, with Marxist parties nearly everywhere falling into line behind their governments and supporting the war—on both sides.

The other part of Lenin's prescription which is related to foreign policy was his emphasis on party tactics in stirring up trouble in colonial territories and overseas spheres of influence, so that the industrial proletariat at home could be made miserable and could thus be given their class-war opportunity. Marx had hinted at the same idea—for instance, in his references to Ireland and India and their relation to Britain —but he could never seem to get clear whether the colonial revolt would force the mother country into proletarian revolution or whether it would be the other way round. Lenin was more definite: first the colonial troubles, then the revolution at home.

Communist tactics today include this agitation in dependent territories, but not I think for the original Marxist or even Leninist reasons. Where the parties are indigenous, they try to seize power and then to industrialize and collectivize the economy; where they are assisted by the Soviet Union, the help is given in order to secure friends and allies for the Soviet Union and to create the nuisance value which such agitation has for the Western powers.

But both these points made by Lenin (concerning "imperialist" wars and colonial rebellions) touch only the fringes of foreign policy. They become increasingly irrelevant as colonial empires dwindle. They give tactical hints, now well understood both in the West and in the Soviet Union, but that is all.

There could not be much on foreign policy in Marx, Engels, and the early Lenin simply because foreign policy occurs between states—by all ordinary meanings of the term. There was no Communist "state" by 1914—that is, no dictatorship of the proletariat—so the question of the relation between Communist and non-Communist states did not arise. The period of worldwide, simultaneous revolution envisioned by Marx and Lenin was also expected to be very short, so they wrote next to nothing about what foreign policy would be like during that stormy interim.

The third question is: How did this position change after the Russian Revolution of 1917-18? Thanks to Lenin and his faction and to the circumstances of the time, the Bolsheviks seized control of Russia, and after the Civil War they were firmly established. A dictatorship of the proletariat, even if not along the original Marxist lines, was set up in practice and was no longer a matter of theory.

Again, at first, foreign policy was negligible. It consisted of negotiating peace with the Germans, of appealing to foreign peoples over the heads of their governments, and of awaiting the revolution elsewhere, while abetting it by means of aid and advice to foreign Communist parties. The Bolsheviks conducted a kind of holding operation in Russia and waited for the revolution in Germany.

Apart from a few short-lived attempts, there was no real revolution elsewhere, and so the Bolsheviks turned their attention chiefly to the Soviet Union. They were determined to rule and to industrialize the U.S.S.R. as a fullfledged proletarian state, and a foreign policy was gradually and seriously developed. But they were faced with the question of whether to encourage world revolution or to build up the Soviet Union. The answer they gave was that they should do both, but that the Soviet Union must come first; and as the 1920's wore on, the emphasis shifted more and more in a nationalist, almost a parochial, direction. Only rarely—as in a brief Chinese episode—did Stalin turn outward. The U.S.S.R. was to be the citadel of world revolution, a citadel that must not be endangered. Once taken, this stand has never been reversed.

World revolution, of a kind, has not been forgotten, but it takes second place to what may be called Soviet imperial policy. My thesis is thus modest enough: A better clue than Marxist theory to Russian policy is the great-power interest of the Soviet Union, as the inner circle in the Kremlin may be imagined to conceive that interest; and they have, on the record, adjusted Marxist ideology to their practice, rather than the other way round. Further, this has taken the form of an obsession with national security, strength, and expansion, not a general expansion of Communist rule everywhere by arms.

A good theory or generalization should explain the facts. It seems to me that this thesis does so. (Logically, this does not prove a theory true, but it is an essential, if not a sufficient, test.) The theory accounts for these important policies:

1. It explains the frequent sacrifice of Communist parties and membership abroad whenever Soviet foreign policy required it. They were treated as expendable, as tools of Soviet foreign policy rather than as agents in a class war.

2. It gives a rational case for the expulsion of Trotsky in the 1920's—making more sense than to interpret this action merely as a case of "thieves falling out" (though the latter may well be explanation enough, and it is true that some of Trotsky's ideas were adopted by Stalin).

3. It explains the emphasis on espionage for the military purposes of the Soviet Union. This has been, for example, the main use of the Party in the United States, and in some of the other Western democracies, without much serious expectation that the Party could ever come to political power. (Every foreigner can understand and sympathize with the American fear of espionage, but no foreigner is ever able to understand why Americans seem to fear ideological subversion by a small Communist Party.)

4. It explains the emphasis within the U.S.S.R. on patriotism, and even at times on Great Russian chauvinism, and it explains the absurd claims for priority in inventions such as the airplane, and the rejection of "cosmopolitanism." How far all this is from the internationalism of Communist thought before 1917!

5. It explains also the Soviet willingness to use any kind of "reactionary" allies, as long as they are anti-Western. How better can we explain Soviet "friendship" with governments like that of Syria, for example, rather than with the "toiling masses" or, in some cases, with the outlawed Communist parties? How better can we explain the extension of "economic aid without strings?" All this is calculated foreign policy, everywhere following considerations of national interest, not proselytizing on behalf of an ideological revolution.

6. It explains the forcing of industrial and military growth within the Soviet Union and the sacrifice of consumer goods to heavy industry (a forced growth we perhaps had reason to be grateful for in the war years of 1941-45).

7. The attack on Finland, and its comparatively limited objective, fits into the pattern of emphasis on national security; so does the more recent move in stamping out the ill-fated Hungarian national rebellion. When satellites were sought, they have been near the Soviet Union and therefore subject to direct control; that is, they have been in East Europe in what would normally be regarded, in power politics, as the legitimate sphere of interest of the Soviet Union.

8. As for national expansion, many people have observed and documented the striking resemblances between Soviet and Tsarist imperial ambitions. Stalin added territory in a way reminiscent of the Tsar. He could even talk in 1945 of having "waited 40 years to avenge the Japanese defeat of 1904." This is nationalism speaking, not the universalist doctrines of Marxism. So marked is this tendency that an observer like Lester Pearson could say:

A study of the lives and times of Russian czars and Chinese emperors is, I think, as valuable for the understanding of our difficulties with Moscow and Peking as an expert knowledge of dialectical materialism.[4]

In the Soviet expansion in Europe, apart from security considerations, there is something close to the idea of "manifest destiny," and like the American version of that aspiration it is nationalistic to the very roots. It is not ideological crusading as Marx, Engels, Trotsky, or the early Lenin believed in it, in spite of the Marxist language which is often used. All national aspirations—with very occasional exceptions like those of Nazi Germany—tend to be clothed in humane and universal ideals: Hypocrisy is the price which selfishness always pays to idealism.

9. People were shocked by the Hitler-Stalin pact of August, 1939. They were also much confused. It is, I think, almost impossible to see this treaty and what followed except in terms of national security and interest, rather than in ideological terms.

10. The thesis explains also the ambiguity of Soviet foreign policy towards the Spanish Civil War. On the one hand, the Soviet Union did not quite dare to fly in the face of the nonintervention policy of France and England (and so alienate possible future allies against Germany), while on the other hand, it was fearful of a nationalist regime in Spain and bound by sympathy to the Spanish government. As a result it tried to ride both horses and failed: The nationalists *did* win in Spain, and the Western European allies were to some extent encouraged by Russian intervention to appease the Nazi and Fascists.[5] After the Munich affair of 1938, the Soviet Union tried its own hand at bargaining with Germany, and secured substantial territorial gains from the Hitler-Stalin agreement of 1939.

Can we then conclude that a provisional thesis has been confirmed? If so, we could say that Soviet foreign policy has been directed chiefly at strengthening the Soviet Union, and only secondarily at the Marxist class revolution throughout the world. I think we can safely say this, while noting that it is a question of emphasis: Where the choice has been between two mutually exclusive policies, the Soviet Union has chosen the nationalist policy; where nationalist and revolutionary aims coincided, they could follow both policies at once.

The examples given (except for Hungary) scarcely touch foreign policy in the post-Stalin period. There is perhaps some evidence to suggest that Mr. Khrushchev is somewhat more inclined than was Stalin to gamble further afield—pre-eminently in Cuba. But his gambles are, it

[4] Lester B. Pearson, *Democracy in World Politics* (Princeton, N.J.: Princeton University Press, 1955), p. 85.

[5] This general thesis is documented in David T. Cattel, *Soviet Diplomacy and the Spanish Civil War* (Berkeley, Calif.: University of California Press, 1957).

appears, chiefly foreign policy ventures, where the growth of Soviet power and strategic advantage, and not primarily ideological extension, are his aims.

"WESTERN" FOREIGN POLICY AND WESTERN "IDEOLOGY"

Let us turn now to the other side of the question. What is the relation of Western foreign policy to Western ideology? This strikes us as a more peculiar question. It assumes an entity that we describe as "Western," and it assumes that this entity has a unified foreign policy and possesses a unique ideology. Unless these assumptions are valid, it makes little sense to talk of a Western policy or of a Western ideology in conflict with that of Russia.

The only clear meaning one can see for "Western," in this context, is the NATO alliance led by the United States, while on the periphery is another, more loosely knit group of allies and friends of the NATO powers.

Does it make sense to say that the NATO allies have a united policy? (If we cannot say this of NATO then it cannot be said of the wider and looser alliance.) Let us take good intentions for granted and assume that all countries in the NATO alliance are anti-Communist, against Soviet expansion, and against expansion of other Communist states. But this is better defined as an attitude, an aim, or a goal; rather than as a policy. It sheds little light on the policies which may be adopted.

A few examples of how the Western Alliance is divided in its policies and opinions may perhaps lend an air of verisimilitude to the narrative. Shall we recognize the Communist Chinese government or not? Should we admit it to the United Nations? What sort of trade and commerce should we have with what Communist states? How far afield exactly will NATO go in protecting the non-European interests of its members? One need not prolong this tale of diversity—which is of course one of the reasons why NATO always threatens to break apart at the seams whenever there is a lull in the Cold War and the fear of Soviet attack declines. (Some observers have said that the Western nations are divided on nearly every question of world importance, and that we are less united than the diverse nations of Africa or Asia, but I am not sure of that.)[6]

The Western coalition cannot always agree on its over-all *military* policy alone, to say nothing of total policies. Thus, some appear to think that all we need do is rely on massive, nuclear deterrence—the power to retaliate; others think that since we have reached stalemate in this way, limited nuclear arms, and even a conventional army, are more nec-

[6] Ahmed S. Bokhari, "Parliaments, Priests and Prophets," *Foreign Affairs*, 35 (April, 1957), 405-11.

essary now than ever—since only limited wars can now be fought.[7] Some
nations in the alliance want nuclear arms and some—like Canada—
seem to waver from time to time.

Still, in some overriding or fundamental way there exists a policy
adhered to by the United States and its NATO allies. An open attack
on one will be an attack on all.[8] There is minimum agreement that a
stand will be taken at certain places and over certain issues. Perhaps we
should not press too closely some of the debatable points, so let us grant
for the moment a minimum Western or NATO policy, as it is worked
out from time to time by the allies. Could we, however, predict this
foreign policy from "our ideology"? Is there some rigorous logic connect-
ing the two? Is NATO foreign policy designed to spread "our" ideology,
and extinguish that of Russia? That, of course, raises the prior question
of whether or not there is any common Western ideology, and on this
surely we must have many reservations.

To begin with, it is extraordinarily difficult to identify the ideology of
any one country, say the United States. What is Americanism? What
is the American way of life? What is the American dream? I have followed
with fascinated interest—as no doubt others abroad have done—the
flood of self-critical and soul-searching books that have poured from the
press in the last few years trying to identify the American way of life,
the national purpose, national goals, and so forth.[9] I do not know what
others make of it all, but I find it impossible to see any agreed or definable ideology, unless it is that of a belief in diversity. (At the extremely
high and abstract level of ultimate ideals one can find agreement—freedom, individual rights, and so forth—but the level of generality is so
high that the ultimates lack any substantive content, and virtually every
political creed can incorporate them.)

In any case, it would be a brash man who could make any close relation of foreign policy to United States ideology. In what sense is the
ideology of the United States different today from that of its isolationist
phase of the 1930's, or indeed from that of the position of aloofness
adopted in much of its history? Is it not the mood, the attitude, which
has changed? Is not the policy change stimulated by the outside world
and events—for example, the Second World War, the apparently threaten-
ing policies of Russia, the relative decline of other Western powers?

---

[7] Henry Kissinger, "Strategy and Organization," *Foreign Affairs,* 35 (April, 1957),
379-94; and *The Necessity for Choice* (New York: Doubleday & Company, Inc., 1962).

[8] We should recall, however, that under Article Five of the North Atlantic Treaty
there is no automatic obligation to fight. The U.S. Congress, for example, would still
be able to decide to go to war or to refrain. We must go beyond the legal wording if
we are to make the assumption stated in the text above, but it seems fair enough
to do so.

[9] For example, *Goals for Americans,* the Report of the President's Commission on
National Goals (Englewood Cliffs, N.J.: Prentice-Hall, Inc., 1960).

When we speak of the Western ideology, we have in mind, I think, some such idea as a Western "community" or perhaps a Western civilization, with a set of unique values or institutions; and further, we assume that these have some close political reference.

But what sort of ideas or values do we have in common, and can they be grouped together to make up a reasonable facsimile of an ideology? A parade of candidates has been put forward from time to time for the position of unifying concept in the Western ideology. Private enterprise, religion, and even something called "Western values" are three of these, which must, I think, be ruled out for obvious reasons: Either the West is not agreed upon supporting them (as in the case of private enterprise); or else there is disagreement over their fundamental meaning (as in the case of religion); or there is disagreement over their very identification (as in the case of "Western values").

A fourth candidate, the principle of national sovereignty or national self-determination, has something more to be said for it. Yet it is not a strong candidate, and it may not even deserve to be. For one thing, in a world where common action is required to avoid the greatest of all dangers—large scale nuclear war—the most important article in any political creed today is that concerning world peace. The principle of national sovereignty is certainly not a recipe for peace. In fact, there is considerable popular support in the West for merging national sovereignties in regional federations, and even in eventual world federation. For a second thing, if we stand on a nationalist plank, the Soviet Union is then free to stand for internationalism. Marxist theory is, in fundamentals, international and potentially universal. It would be a mistake to allow Russia to pre-empt the high ground of internationalism while our latest word was Wilsonian self-determination.

The strongest candidate is, I think, democracy. The most powerful of the states in the Western Alliance *are* democracies, and enough other countries are with them on this to justify the broad claim that the Alliance stands for democracy.

But the unity of the Alliance is not, so far as I can see, ideological in most of the usual senses of the word. The wide, although not unanimous, agreement on democracy is not so much an ideological unity, but rather a procedural and tolerant agreement to differ, in order that many ideologies may flourish. Democracy is a kind of supra-ideology, a tacit recognition of the right to disagree and also that this right is basic to all other rights. It is possible to speak of many ideologies competing and often conflicting within any given democracy. Freedom is good, but it does not tell us what to do.

Why should we have or seek an ideology? One is forced to conjecture:

1. As in the 1930's when we faced an aggressive Germany, there is a feeling abroad that we *ought* to have some flaming and inspiring faith

to match the zeal of the potential enemy; that we ought to know exactly and inspirationally what we are for, as well as what we are against.

2. Many interested groups have seized the Cold War as an occasion to cry their wares; to put up their pet candidate as *the* Western ideology, an effort which has at times created some friction among the allies. (There is not much doubt that the prestige of the United States declines among both allies and neutrals whenever there is an upsurge in the extreme forms of ideological conservatism or in the attempt to ensure conformity.)

3. There is, I think, an underlying reason of considerably more importance in the twentieth century. A world power is condemned to have an "ideology"; it is made to stand for something other than its own interests, both by the pressure of its own public and the expectations of foreigners, even if the "ideology" consists only of a critique of the opposing ideology. What it stands for must have international appeal, not only appeal for the United States and not only for the West.[10]

The Western world is marked by a variety of social and political systems and theories; therefore it is unwise to insist on conformity and ideological unity where there is no unity. The very fact that we spend so much time and talk on trying to find or define a common ideology is a strong indication that as yet we have none. One doubts whether it is possible to synthesize or adopt beliefs solely because of their social utility, in this case their utility in the Cold War.

I am inclined to think that the search for ideological unity or a political creed of the West is an outgrowth, rather than a cause, of the international conflict. The friction and fears came first; the clash of ideologies was invented later to bolster morale and to give meaning and purpose to the struggle. The temptation for the West to do so was strong, because Russia for its part did have an ideology—the whole corpus of Marxist theory—and the side with the ideology seemed to have the initiative. Moreover, it is a Marxist thesis that there are only two possible ideologies —Capitalism and Socialism—and that the West stands for Capitalism and Russia for Socialism. But this simple dialectical classification is not true merely because the Russians say it is. We fall into the Marxist trap if we put the label "Capitalist" upon the infinite variety of the Western world.

If the argument is sound, then we are left with a simple conclusion that the Western Alliance is almost wholly defensive, inspired by fear of possible aggression. The Western Alliance was chiefly started that way, though not by fear of *imminent* aggression.[11] To some this seems a nega-

---

[10] The few reasons given are merely suggestive; others will readily occur to the reader, and sociological investigations would very likely turn up many more.

[11] This is not an adequate account of the origins of the Cold War, but it will do for present purposes. We armed, as Mr. Churchill said, in order to parley. The Russians

tive sort of union, and it is negative to those who favor crusades on behalf of great principles. The simple lesson is often forgotten that the chief bond between allies is resistance to a common enemy, a classic example being the Second World War itself.

There is a positive side to such an alliance: (1) The Western Alliance stands broadly for the cause of democracy. (2) Moreover, each country in it stands for its own independence (except as it may be voluntarily modified), its own kind of political or economic or social system, and its own way of life or ideals—however these may be defined. This makes the Alliance lively and positive to each participant. (3) In a sense, therefore, the principle of diversity or freedom is being defended—though I should not myself call this an ideology; but whatever it is called, it is not exclusive to the West.[12]

Edmund Burke once said, "One sure sign of an ill-conducted State is the propensity of the people to resort to theories." It is a good thing that we have no agreed ideology and that we are not conducting an ideological crusade to convert the world. Politics, even international politics, is better off without uncompromising ideological principles. The Russians have been bad enough in this field; let us refrain from adding to the aggressive intransigence, from converting every clash of interest into one of sacred principle. Let us refrain, in short, from adopting the Russian definition of the terms of the "East-West" conflict.

In summary, we conclude that although Russia has an official ideology, we can hardly use it as a reliable guide to predicting her foreign policy. And in the case of the West, our foreign policy cannot be rigorously connected with an ideology that does not exist.

RELATION OF POLITICAL THEORY TO FOREIGN POLICY

I should like now to raise a more general point about the relation of political theory, and even ideology, to foreign policy—a point which, if true, is conclusive and makes the foregoing argument unnecessary. It is this: that there is seldom, if ever, any close logical connection between a political philosophy and its political application. Here we raise the great controversy of the relation between philosophy and politics. All I can do is state with almost desperate brevity the central argument in this dispute—an argument which appears convincing enough to settle the question.

---

of course think it was started by "Capitalist" hostility to them. Cf. Robert Osgood, *NATO: The Entangling Alliance* (Chicago: University of Chicago Press, 1962).

[12] Cf. J. P. Plamenatz, "In What Sense is Freedom a Western Idea?" in *Current Law and Social Problems*, ed. R. St. J. Macdonald (Toronto: University of Toronto Press, 1960), pp. 3-18.

A political theory is inevitably general and even abstract. This is true whether it contains *a priori* postulates, or empirically based generalizations, or moral principles, or a statement of ideals. It holds good also for an ideology, which always mixes these various elements. If they were not general, the propositions would not constitute a theory and would correspondingly lack explanatory power. They would not rise above the particular. Just because theoretical propositions *are* general, they have to be interpreted and broken down first into intermediate propositions (if possible). To put them into policies requires very specific interpretation indeed. A policy is a combination of elements: (1) general principles, whether moral or other; (2) a knowledge of the facts of the situation; and (3) the element of judgment, which in turn consists of estimates, forecasts, feasibility, and so forth.

A political act, as in making and carrying out foreign policy, is a matter of prudential judgment; and theory, though relevant, is never enough by itself to determine policy. The policy makers have to figure things out for themselves, taking principles, practical knowledge, and everything else into account. Mr. Justice Holmes had the same idea in mind when he said that general principles do not settle particular cases. There is always room for different policies, even among those who subscribe to the same philosophy and ideals. No way can be found to show beforehand that any one policy is conclusively right or wise; and after the event there is also room for disagreement on the interpretation or effectiveness. There is no infallible philosopher-king.

Let me put the point in another way. It is not possible, by a process of logic, to deduce a policy and its particular measures from moral or other principles (or we should not need the faculty of judgment in the particular). This in turn goes a long way to explain why political philosophers—and *a fortiori* other philosophers—may be very bad as policy makers. Knowing *that* is different from knowing *how* (and this in turn is to say nothing of motivation). The most we can get is a relation of compatibility (or incompatibility) of policy with intermediate or subsidiary principles; and this, while sometimes helpful, does not really take us very far. All philosophies, and most ideologies, are subtle, and only simple people believe they are easy to apply. Hence it has been said that almost "any practical construction can be put on almost any theory." [13]

The only exception to this argument is where part of the theory, particularly in some ideologies, contains some very specific elements, but this is very rare. The common practice seems to be this: When the need

---

[13] If this still does not sound convincing, consider how difficult it is to get any agreed statement of the purposes or "philosophy" of a social institution—say, a university—and how, even if such a general statement *is* agreed on, the battle starts all over again when we try to give the general agreement a unique application.

for altering the specific element arises, it is then demoted to the status of a nonessential, a mere matter of tactics or methods which must give way to the more general articles of faith.

OPPOSING IDEOLOGIES AND CONFLICTING POLICIES?

Thus far, we have discussed world politics organized around a polar conflict of ideologies and engaged in a life and death struggle, the end of which (if there is an end) can only be the defeat of one side or the other, and the corresponding extinction of one of the opposing ideologies. I hope that I have cast some doubt on the validity of this diagnosis, at least from the Western point of view.[14] Let us now pursue the same inquiry by posing two rather different questions: What type of world does the present or Soviet version of Marxist theory envisage, and what type (if any) does the Western world envisage? In answering these questions we are, at the same time, continuing our exploration of the relation between ideology and foreign policy.

As to the aim, the classical theory of Marx's goal for history is familiar to all: a way of political and economic organization that is almost anarchistic, the famous classless society. While the ultimate goal may seem absurdly unrealistic to us, the disillusioned generations, there is surely nothing in this Marxist ideal that need excite us.

Does Moscow today think in these humane terms? Very occasionally such language is used, but in a rhetorical manner. It is comparable to our turning to romanticism and extolling the simple rural life, while crowding into the cities to live. Usually, however, the ultimate utopian ideals of Marx and the early Lenin, of freedom and equality and the end of the coercive state are conspicuously absent today, even from the rhetoric.[15]

Are the leaders then not Marxist? Lenin, Stalin, and their successors are certainly Marxists, but only, it seems to me, in the sense in which Napoleon was a French revolutionary. The final aims are either forgotten or else placed in a remote future, while the holding of power and the more immediate objectives occupy all their attention. The objectives in domestic affairs are such things as increased production; in foreign affairs, the maintenance and (more recently) the expansion of Russian national interests. These are the common, almost legitimate objectives of all great-power policy.

Now we come to the question of methods or policies. A Frenchman once wrote, "The French Revolution is a universal religion which it is

---

[14] Some corroboration of this point is found in a number of recent studies which explore "the end of ideology," "after Utopia," etc.

[15] Cf. Isaiah Berlin, "The Silence in Russian Culture," *Foreign Affairs*, 36 (October, 1957), 1-24.

France's mission to impose upon humanity." Is this, then, the sense in which Marxist theory is interpreted today in the Soviet Union—the forcing of Communist rule of the Russian type upon reluctant countries by armed conquest?

The answer is both yes and no. In the case of the East European satellites (with the possible exception of Czechoslovakia), we must say yes. But we must also say no. As George Kennan pointed out in his Reith Lectures: To take the simple view that the threat (throughout the world) is solely a military one is to make our own response one-sidedly military, and consequently, ineffective in the wider realm of politics.[16] The unexamined assumption of Western foreign policy, particularly that of the United States, has been the threat of Soviet military aggression. Whether such aggression was, or is, a serious danger may be questioned.

The qualifications which must be made to the thesis that the Soviet Union has set out to spread communism by military conquest are supported as follows:

First, there is no intention of seriously risking the Soviet state in any ideological crusade. Since the expulsion of Trotsky, there has been no turning away from this fundamental axiom. In an age of nuclear warfare, with its much greater risks, this axiom appears to be rooted more firmly than ever. (For us to take this as axiomatic assumes rationality on the part of the Kremlin, and a Western willingness to take a stand at specified points against attempted Soviet aggression. Both these assumptions do not seem to be seriously questioned.)[17]

Second, the Soviet Union has done quite well for itself so far, without overt war and the serious risk of total destruction, in seeing a number of states become Communist. Naturally, where it held back or compromised, at times, the U.S.S.R. had its own calculated reasons for doing so. Such calculation is on the whole a nonideological (and certainly a nonfanatical) approach to policy. The main point is clear enough: The spread of communism has been at a rate that must appear quite satisfactory to the Kremlin (count the countries from Czechoslovakia or Outer Mongolia to Cuba); and this must, if anything, reinforce the intentions of the Russians not to risk their rule and their lives in ideological crusades.

[16] *Russia, the Atom and the West* (New York: Harper & Row, Publishers, 1958). The thesis implied in the title of the book by Elliot R. Goodman, *The Soviet Design for a World State* (New York: Columbia University Press, 1960), is I think erroneous. There is nothing in Marxist or Soviet theory that requires a world state dominated by the Soviet Union.

[17] Cf. Frederick C. Barghoorn, *Soviet Russian Nationalism* (Toronto: Oxford University Press, 1956), and his argument on the aversion of the Soviet managerial elite to rash adventures. I should say that the Soviet withdrawal from Iran, the failure to take military action against a deviant Yugoslavia, and the "backing down" in Korea and Cuba indicate rationality in the Kremlin—under both Stalin and Khrushchev.

Third, Marxist theory is like any other scripture in that it can be interpreted quite flexibly. This is indeed a major point. In particular, the Marxist myth of the inevitability of communism can be reinterpreted easily enough in a number of ways to call for a variety of policies. Khrushchev's prediction that our grandchildren will be Communist suggests or permits a very elastic timetable.

Fourth, present-day Marxist theory and Soviet foreign policy are neatly dovetailed to justify a broad, integrated strategy—in some places of military pressure, but more often of political pressure, economic assistance, propaganda, and foreign Communist parties. In the last decade, too, the foreign policy has been much less defensive and much more positive and aggressive in the nonmilitary sense. In thus playing the role of a confident superpower, the double purpose is achieved of strengthening the position of the Soviet Union, and in some countries of helping along the spread of communism.[18]

Now, what kind of world does the West envisage? As to the distant future I do not think we have anything in mind, comparable to the Marxist utopia. Ours is an essentially nonideological kind of political theory. In this respect it is like democracy itself—which is best defined, not in terms of its purposes, but of its methods and procedures. It is a system which can be put to almost any purpose given to it by the people, or worked out in the interplay of politics.

One is not sure that democracy has much to say on the international scene.[19] Woodrow Wilson appeared to think that if all countries became democracies this would ensure lasting peace. This strikes me as a very dubious belief. Similarly, if all the world consisted of Communist states, it is also doubtful whether peace would automatically result. Adlai Stevenson was in a sense right when he said in 1962 that the United States (and by implication other Western powers) stood for the world of the United Nations Charter, a pluralist world, each country being free to develop along its own lines. President Kennedy described the "basic goal" (in his State of the Union address, January, 1962) in similar terms:

> . . . *a peaceful world community of free and independent states—free to choose their own future and their own system . . . for we offer a world of choice—they offer a world of coercion.*

If the first article in a creed is freedom of belief and choice, that will also be the last one. You cannot add more as a condition of belonging,

---

[18] Cf. Charles Grove Haines, *The Threat of Soviet Imperialism* (Baltimore, Md.: Johns Hopkins Press, 1954), Parts I and II.

[19] For example, what shall we take as the unit of democracy—the local municipality? the state? the nation? the region? the world?

or you will violate the first article. Hence we see again why it is no use to expect the West to agree on clear statements of an ideology or of our aims; given choice and freedoms we have variety.

I have said that the Soviet national aims are pursued by a sort of combined strategy—military, economic, political—and that the Russians were, on the whole, quick at learning this competitive game once they decided to move from the defensive and play it. The West has assumed that it must play a similar game, though perhaps for different stakes.

In some cases the Western response has indeed already successfully countered the Soviet challenges, particularly where the threat has been military, as with the Berlin airlift, the Cuban missiles, and progress in nuclear weapons. We have sometimes been rather less successful on the nonmilitary front—for instance, in the Middle East. We have had of course some notable successes: Greece was kept from falling to the local Communists, and there was the Marshall Plan. It is much harder for us to meet the many-sided challenge than to meet a purely military danger. It becomes impossible if we take up a rigid ideological posture, especially when the Russians themselves are often pragmatic enough to unlearn their doctrinal lessons. (They never unlearn them completely. For example, they never seem to get over their *idée fixe* of implacable "Capitalist" hostility, which they support by much evidence. And, of course, the "evidence" makes a strong case, when it is suitably arranged and interpreted.)

Democracies have an almost subconscious aversion to foreign policy; and this is true especially of the United States which withdrew from the wicked world in the 1920's and 1930's and was, so to speak, pitchforked into it again by Pearl Harbor in December, 1941. We have other handicaps in devising and carrying through any kind of concerted American (let alone, allied) policy: Our very freedom and the publicity which they permit, the aspirations of our people for a higher standard of living, and our reluctance to understand that internal politics cannot be isolated from foreign policy. A bomb thrown in Mississippi is heard round the world. It is doubtful whether any country today, even the most powerful, can in fact have an autonomous domestic policy, so complex and overriding are the requirements of foreign commitments.[20] Throughout history, some of the ablest statesmen have found it easier to get their foreign policy past their allies, and even their enemies, than to get it approved by their own countries. The other side of the truth is that foreign policy is *foreign,* and the reactions of foreigners are as important as those of our own citizens. Democracies are extremely sensitive to adverse criticism from outside.

[20] John Hertz, *Political Realism and Political Idealism* (Chicago: University of Chicago Press, 1951), p. 237.

When policy becomes a matter of dealing, not with the Russians, but with many of the "underdeveloped" countries, it is unfortunately true that Communist movements have some advantages. For one thing they are not tainted in the same way with colonialism and racial prejudice. They stand for the overturn of ancient and unpopular regimes, often a necessary condition of social reform. Then again, communism gives the promise of a short cut to industrialization and economic development and higher living standards; it supplies leaders to tell people what to do, and that is what most people have been used to. Democratic methods are different: We do not stimulate high expectations and promise immediate gratification; we ask poor nations to be patient, to remember that economic development is slow, if it is to be sound, and that capital is scarce; and we preach the virtues of private initiative to people who scarcely know what we are talking about. We point out the terrible price paid in terms of freedom for ruthless and total government, for forced industrialization—a price which is high on our own scale of values, but not necessarily on theirs.

All these things we say are true, but they are not what people want to hear. We have not devised (and perhaps it cannot be done) a method of fast industrialization by democratic means. In one sense, we may never win the propaganda contest in much of the world. Great and affluent powers will never be really popular abroad, unpopularity is part of the price paid for greatness and wealth. But even more to the point is the fact that, being composed of prosperous nations, the West will seldom, if ever, be the source of inspiration for social revolutions in the poor countries.[21] If we do not inspire them, however, we should at least not alienate social revolutionaries, thus letting them fall by default into the hands of local Communists. Or even if they do fall into such hands, we should still endeavor to keep them from falling into the Soviet sphere.

The West has, of course, some great advantages in meeting the wide array of Soviet policy challenges. In some countries the nature of Communist rule is too well-known to have any wide appeal, and these countries turn toward the West instead. Because we wear no ideological blinkers, we are able (or should be able) to see the world more realistically, and hence can (or should) be more flexible and adaptive. The blunders made by the Russians have sometimes worked to Western advantage. Because of our belief in diversity, we can also respect the local differences we find everywhere. So far as aid to poor countries is concerned, we are fortunately rich and equipped with technological and other skills. These are great advantages if they are properly used.

---

[21] All the world is desperately copying the Western technology, but the cultural and economic penetration that usually goes with this is nonetheless resented, and, however unjustly, this feeling is focused mostly on the United States.

THE ACCOMMODATION OF FOREIGN POLICIES TO WORLD AFFAIRS

The Western problem is how to harmonize novel, often Machiavellian, foreign policies with the national traditions and experiences of the West. Behind this statement of the problem lies a somewhat different picture of world affairs from that examined earlier.

The earlier picture was of ideologies in conflict, a conflict that is virtually war. If both sides cherish this picture, what follows? The slogans on both sides become "horribly stuff'd with epithets of war." Leaders on both sides will vie with one another as to which will be "harder on communism" or "harder on capitalism." On both sides it means rigidity in foreign policy, when flexibility is needed. It means that public opinion, even in the West, could become so set in one direction that it would be political suicide for leaders to alter direction, even if they believed a change of policy to be in the best interests of the country and the world. It means a population emotionally impervious to argument, to changing its picture of the world when the world has changed. It means a population psychologically prepared for war instead of for the frustrations of an uneasy peace. It means too much priority for the scientific and military side of budgets, and not enough for other programs. It involves using the nonaligned and the underdeveloped countries virtually as tools in the Cold War. The end of the conflict can only come with the defeat or retreat of the potential enemy and with the extinction of the offending ideology which has somehow caused all the trouble. This is the road to *certain* war—the genuine, not the Cold War, kind.

The alternative picture is somewhat more complex, not the simple and satisfying twofold division of the world into Communist and Capitalist which the Russians cherish. This picture is not one of ideologies in mortal combat; it is one without a counterideology on our part, and consequently stimulates no crusading emotions to generate crusading policies. It does not present a "world civil war," but depicts time as our most precious asset, to use to our best to avoid war. It suggests that we look not to defeat of the potential enemy (what meaning would defeat or victory have in a nuclear war?) but to accommodation with him; not to the extinction of an ideology by arms (if it is possible to kill ideas that way) but instead to a possible easing of his crusading spirit. This picture takes into account not only the diversity within the West, but also that inside the Soviet sphere itself, and that between the Soviet and other Communist spheres. The neutrals and the United Nations are closer to the center of this picture, which suggests not only a blurring of the ideological issues, but also a bridging of the gap in the power struggle. The picture reminds us that opposing blocs (and even militant creeds such as communism) are not new in the world. World politics was not invented by Russia or by the United States, since these countries took leading roles on the world stage after World War II.[22]

A word may be in order to prevent misunderstanding. Although the second is a different picture, arises from different attitudes, and will often lead to different policies, there are some things which do *not* belong to it. It does not lead to pacifism, to unilateral nuclear disarmament for the United States, or to any slackening of military effort in other fields. It does not point to any loosening of the Western Alliance. I would say that it is probably the picture held by most of the close allies of the United States—Britain certainly—or by small or medium powers in the Alliance. It is held in countries—Canada, for example—that are in indissoluble and understanding alliance with the United States, that are indeed close enough to question without offense the assumptions of American foreign policy as much as they do those of Russia.

Let us admit at once that there is no way of showing conclusively which of these pictures is more accurate. Any theory or picture of reality is always selective and interpretive. We usually see what our wishes or fears want us to see. When the world is changing rapidly, our picture of it is especially liable to be out of date; great changes often steal upon us unawares. "New occasions teach new duties: Time makes ancient good uncouth."

Is there any reason to accept the more softly shaded picture of the present Western-Soviet relationship? In making the case that the West is not united in an ideological alliance, I have implicitly said that there is. It is possible to go beyond the other previous argument—that the Soviet ideology permits a variety of policies—and to hold that the Soviet Union is less rigidly ideological than formerly.

At times, even Stalin argued—with excessive optimism, I think—that the Western countries would end by fighting one another.[23] There would occur a "self-destruction" of capitalism, and so there would be no need for the Soviet Union to do the job. Or again, the idea has been advanced from time to time that the expanding economic production of the Soviet Union will prove to the world the superiority of their system, and so encourage more and more imitators in many "underdeveloped" countries. Perhaps we shall hear more along this line as the success of Russian nuclear science and space exploration engenders self-confidence.

We have also been offered the theory that communism may come in different ways in different countries. Khrushchev, for instance, has said:

[22] The "friend-foe" relation, as the essential political relationship between men or states, is on the whole false, and is not one which political philosophers have ever subscribed to. The two possible exceptions are of the German school of "Realpolitik," Ratzenhofer; and Carl Smitt.

[23] *Economic Problems of Socialism in the U.S.S.R.*, Moscow: Foreign Language Publishing House, 1952.

*It is quite likely that the forms of the transition to socialism will become
more and more variegated. Moreover, it is not obligatory for the implementation of these forms to be connected with civil war in all circumstances.*[24]

The point is that "deviations" do exist, however they have been caused
or motivated. The first serious rift was, of course, between Russia and
Yugoslavia; the second, with Poland, during which the Chinese seemed to
have played a mediating role between Polish and Russian Communists.[25]
The third, a more serious and high level rift, is between China and Russia.
These divisions have grown steadily wider and deeper since the famous de-
Stalinization process was announced to a startled world.[26]

The Communist images of the Western world are fantastically erroneous. We in our turn should not think of the Communist world in terms
of our own mistaken stereotypes, fixed in our minds by fears and emotions.
Within the Soviet realm itself there are considerably more ideological and
policy differences than we sometimes think. The Soviet form of communism appears less dogmatic and crusading than the Chinese form.
(The Russians appear to have also a much healthier respect for the disastrous results of a nuclear war.) Crusades do, fortunately, have a way of
fading out. It seems impossible for successive generations to keep up the
zeal of the original prophets; disillusion sets in, and a class comes to
power that has a heavy stake in the maintenance of things as they are.
One should not say however that Russia is yet a fully *status quo* power,
nor that the freedom of speech or the noncollectivized agriculture found
in Poland exists everywhere in the Soviet sphere.

Moreover, there seem to be growing signs of "ideological apathy,"
especially among younger people, inside the Soviet Union itself, although
we could hardly expect the authorities to admit it. *Pravda,* for example,
has indignantly denied it. The apathy is concealed by the old language
and slogans still in use. Even when policy becomes more pragmatic and
realistic, there is a typical "linguistic ritual" which marks Communist
debate, and that is why there must always be so much reading between
the lines in interpreting Soviet speeches. Whatever is done, it is done in
the *name* of Marxist theory. Policy differences are always argued in terms
of doctrinal differences. An analogy may show the point: Outsiders are
always impressed by how often American political differences are argued
in terms of the "real" meaning of the Constitution.

No one really knows whether the changes, division, and apathy will

---

[24] Opening speech to the 20th Congress of the Soviet C.P., February, 1956.

[25] Zbigniew Brzezinski, "Communist Ideology and Power: From Unity to Diversity,"
Journal of Politics, 19 (November, 1957), 549-90.

[26] Donald S. Zagoria, *The Sino-Soviet Conflict, 1956-1961* (Princeton, N.J.: Princeton
University Press, 1962).

lead to changes in foreign policy sufficiently marked to break the circle of fear. Yet, as Sir Thomas Browne put it:

What song the Syrens sang, or what name Achilles assumed when he hid himself among women, though puzzling questions, are not beyond all conjecture.

There is this difference about the many conjectures on the results of the changes taking place in the Soviet sphere, or between the Soviet and other Communist spheres: The future (if there is a future) will show which conjectures are right. We have as yet no examples of totalitarian states, and few of dictatorships, that have developed gradually and peacefully into reasonably free societies. The only example which comes to mind is that of Turkey, and perhaps we should study more the lessons of the Kemal Ataturk regime. (It is fair perhaps to add that some one-party states have come to enjoy considerable freedom.)

There is not, I think, anything in Marxist theory which would rule out substantial changes in Soviet internal or foreign policy. In foreign policy, for instance, the Soviet theory since 1956 has envisaged a sort of permanent "coexistence," thanks to an appreciation of the potentialities of nuclear weapons. In any case, theory can always be adjusted to practice; it is being done all the time. This is one of the meanings which can be given to that wonderfully ambiguous Marxist adage "the unity of theory and practice"!

"THE MORAL AND THE END"

We cannot, of course, base our foreign policies entirely on hope or, as now, on fears. Yet, "If hopes were dupes, fears may be liars." We *can* hold our picture of the world as a provisional one, to accommodate changes as they occur; we can take cognizance of different attitudes as they appear, and so frame policies accordingly.

Unless we are willing to face with resignation the prospect of dying together with the Soviet Union in a "reciprocal spasm of mutual annihilation," then we must find a way of living together. It is altogether too dangerous to keep on living on the edge of doom. Peaceful coexistence and ideological belligerence, which we have now, *is* the edge of doom. The Russians say they believe in the coexistence of "social systems," but they keep us on the brink of war with their ideological fanaticism. Until this slackens or weakens, we cannot move far from the edge. The Western powers, however, need not contribute to the tension or push us closer to the brink by trying to find ideological blinkers of their own to wear.

Both sides are propelled toward each other by two powerful forces. One is fear of mutual destruction. At the moment this fear may be the

strongest force at work. It is one of the assumptions that makes sense of
"deterrence." (The other is that the Soviet Union intends war.) The
other force is common self-interest, not only in avoiding war, but also
in the positive gains that peace and a clear future could bring in terms
of living standards by diverting resources from arms to peaceful uses. The
strength of this force has scarcely begun to flow as yet. (It may be that a
third can be added soon: the common interest in a response to the Chinese
eruption.) Three possibilities lie ahead:

   1. We may drift into war.

> *Must then blind man, in ignorance sedate,*
> *Roll darkling down the torrent of his fate?*

To Dr. Johnson's question, all of us want to say no.

   2. We may with great good fortune drift into compromise and a series
of tacit and unwritten understandings without formal agreements, and so
avoid war.[27]

   3. We can seek settlements and accommodation to avoid war.

Neither possibility 2 nor 3 is possible if both sides constantly hold
before their eyes a warlike picture of themselves engaged in a cosmic
ideological struggle to the death. It has been my purpose to suggest that
the black and white picture of Western relations with the Soviet Union
is overdrawn, that the picture is in fact fading, and that the somewhat
modified picture is a closer representation of reality and should replace
the older one. The consequences of acting upon the perspectives and
standpoints of the first will almost certainly be fatal, while those of acting
upon the second hold more prospects—our best prospects—of a *détente*
and, in time, perhaps a *rapprochement*.

Suggestions for Further Reading

Brzezinski, Zbigniew, *Ideology and Power in Soviet Politics.* New York: Frederick
   A. Praeger, Inc., 1962.
Fleming, D. F., *The Cold War and Its Origins, 1917-1960*, 2 vols. Garden City,
   N.Y.: Doubleday & Company, Inc., 1962.
Hahn, Walter F. and John C. Neff, eds., *American Strategy for the Nuclear Age.*
   Garden City, N.Y.: Doubleday & Company, Inc., 1960.
Hoffmann, Stanley H., ed., *Contemporary Theory in International Relations.*
   Englewood Cliffs, N.J.: Prentice-Hall, Inc., 1960.
Knorr, Klaus and Sidney Verba, eds., *The International System: Theoretical
   Essays.* Princeton, N.J.: Princeton University Press, 1961.

---

[27] Like formal agreements, these can be broken—for example, the breaking by Russia
in the autumn of 1961 of the tacit agreement on unclear tests.

London, Kurt, ed., *Unity and Contradiction: Major Aspects of Sino-Soviet Relations*. New York: Frederick A. Praeger, Inc., 1962.

Mayhew, Christopher, *Co-existence Plus*. London: The Bodley Head, 1962.

Mayo, Henry B., *Introduction to Democratic Theory*. New York: Oxford University Press, 1960.

———, *Introduction to Marxist Theory*. New York: Oxford University Press, 1960.

Modelski, George, *A Theory of Foreign Policy*. New York: Frederick A. Praeger, Inc., 1962.

Schuman, Frederick L., *The Cold War: Retrospect and Prospect*. Baton Rouge: Louisiana State University Press, 1962.

Spanier, J. W., *American Foreign Policy Since World War II*. New York: Frederick A. Praeger, Inc., 1960.

WESTERN EUROPE:
PROMISE AND DILEMMA

Roy C. Macridis

The problems we face today in Western Europe are very different from those in the years immediately after liberation. Dean Acheson may lecture the French and British on their atomic inferiority, and close associates of President Kennedy may show the courage, for the first time, to tell the governments of Western Europe that American nuclear power provides them with the only real security against Soviet threats. The United States Secretary of Agriculture shakes his finger at the French farmers who now seem to produce more than they ought, while the Secretary of the Treasury can do little but watch the French and the Germans increase their dollar and gold holdings. Many Americans, including President Kennedy and Congressional leaders, feel that Western Europe, notably the Six of the Common Market, are strong enough to assume the burdens of foreign aid and military preparedness; yet they express dismay the moment de Gaulle asserts his intention of doing it in his own manner.

Roy C. Macridis *is Chairman of the Department of Political Science at the State University of New York at Buffalo. He has also been a member of the faculties at Harvard, Northwestern, and Washington University. He has been a Ford and Rockefeller fellow and Fulbright lecturer at the University of Paris. He is the author of* Study of Comparative Government, de Gaulle Republic—Quest for Unity *(with Bernard E. Brown), and editor of* Foreign Policy in World Politics, Modern Political Systems: Asia *(with Robert E. Ward), and* Modern Political Systems: Europe *(with Robert E. Ward).*

In the NATO councils our problem is to maintain our leadership and initiative.

In 1945 our concerns were as different as they were urgent: reconstruction of the individual economies and political systems of our former friends and some of our foes in Western Europe, and revival of the idea of a European unity that kept smoldering under the ashes of the destruction wrought by the war. Our task then was to infuse strength and confidence in place of despair and humiliation, to create some reality of military strength so that, with our support, Western Europe could face, or even appear to be in a position to face, the Soviet danger and the vastly changed balance of forces in Europe.

The European scene had changed so brutally and dramatically that the United States was also compelled to make a radical shift in its foreign policy. First in Germany, then through the Marshall Plan, finally through NATO arrangements, no doubts could be left—though they were never entirely dissipated—of American intentions not to return to isolationism. We offered Western Europe what appeared to be a partnership in economic, social, and military reconstruction, but it was a partnership fraught from the very beginning with suspicion and even resentment. One partner was so overwhelmingly strong that he dwarfed all the others and retained for himself initiative and the freedom to make all decisions. Western Europe was put in a state of tutelage. The necessities of the period immediately after the war naturally made it difficult for European resentments to be translated into overt acts, but nevertheless they constituted a strong ingredient of growing anti-Americanism.

The Europeans held and still hold a number of pervasive ideas about the United States. It was a country that, in the last analysis, could not be trusted to pursue a well-defined foreign policy; its political leaders did not have the sophistication and the know-how to conduct diplomacy; and its peoples were prey to military and ideological crusades that threatened the peace of the world at the very time when peace was indispensable for European economic and social reconstruction. The European intellectuals and political leaders shared the feelings Georges Bidault had expressed: "If we only had their power; if they only had our wisdom!" Early manifestations of French, Italian, and even British and German neutralism were based in great part on a deeply embedded distrust of the American character, as well as a distrust of the American political and economic system. All efforts made by American Presidents since 1945 to dissipate these fears were undermined by the European memory of what happened to Woodrow Wilson's Versailles Treaty in the United States.

Now that Europe (particularly the Six) is strong again and now that our efforts to rebuild its strength have succeeded in what is generally considered to be the most fruitful American postwar plan, it is time to reassess not only our relations with Europe, but also all our foreign policy objectives. This paper discusses the promise that West Europe symbolizes today and the dilemma it has created for the United States. I shall conclude with the challenge that it offers for a radical overhaul of American foreign policy.

THE PROMISE OF EUROPE: POLITICAL AND ECONOMIC INTEGRATION

To understand the promise of Europe, we must set aside some of our own prejudices about Western Europe. Granted American help which has run to over 15 billion dollars and American private investment which has been growing rapidly in the last six years, Western European achievements cannot and should not be underestimated. The people of Western Europe have made, in the last fifteen years, more rapid political and economic progress than at any other time since the Industrial Revolution:

1. They have by and large found the answer to what appears to be the most divisive issue in our own society—the relations between the state and the economy. Most West Europeans have accepted the welfare state and the imperatives of state planning and controls in investment, health, education and in the crucial economic social activities of a modern industrialized society—housing, transportation, insurance, electricity, urbanism. If we marvel at the rapid growth of the German economy under a form of economic liberalism, we cannot but admire also the relative prosperity of the British economy under moderate Socialism and the remarkable progress in France under a flexible system of economic planning. Economic planning in France, adopted under the auspices of Jean Monnet, has been largely responsible for modernization and the selective development of key industries. Nationalization of some important economic activities, implementation of broad social welfare measures, and continuing public investment in the private and social sector of the economy have all promoted an economic reconstruction whose cumulative impact was felt after 1956. Despite the vicissitudes of French political life, economic planning has continued under the Fifth Republic, and the last Four Year Plan, introduced in 1962, provides for an annual industrial growth of 5.5 per cent. Our debates about medicare, economic controls, deficit financing, and planning are more remote to most Europeans today than the debates about income tax appeared to be in this country some fifty years ago.

2. French, British, Belgians, and Dutch have disinvested themselves of their colonial Empires. It is not easy to abandon secular myths and symbolisms; yet less than 20 years after the end of World War II—whatever the frictions, the quarrels, the political crises—France, Belgium, and Holland have virtually no colonies and England is about to liquidate whatever is left of its Empire. It will be for the student of comparative

history many years from now to assess the impact of these vast changes and attempt to understand the character of the political societies that were able to accomplish them with little overt violence and with few political upheavals. What is more, colonial emancipation has been followed by strong economic and cultural links between the colonies and the metropolis. Economic aid to Africa was shouldered primarily by England and France; training of African teachers, engineers, technicians, administrators, and doctors continues to take place in France and England. Over a period of years France has shouldered the burden of economic, cultural, and technical aid in the colonies at the rate of at least a half billion dollars a year (excluding Algeria). The Common Market allocated another half billion to Africa and Malagasy for 1958-62, and a sum of some 700 million dollars has been allocated for eighteen African independent states for the period 1962-66. By the end of 1962 these African states had become Associated Members of the Common Market, a membership that entails reciprocal tariff benefits and the establishment of a trading bloc between the Six and the greater part of Africa.[1]

3. Despite the ideological and often extremist character of European politics, their performance shows a deep attachment to democratic pluralism. In England the Communist Party has literally disappeared; in Germany the Party was virtually extinct when it was outlawed. In both countries, however, strong Socialist parties have been very much in evidence. In Italy and France the strong Communist parties have lived, in one manner or another, within the body politic, and all their efforts and ambitions have been thwarted without resort to punitive or repressive measures. In France the Party has little hope of success even if it remains strong; in Italy efforts are being made to readjust the Party to the prerequisites of Italian needs, rather than to continue it as a Soviet arm. The freedom of the Party, however, has not been qualified, and its decline is associated with tolerance. Given the proximity of the Soviet Union and the recurrent imminence of a Soviet thrust, what may be to some a complacency about a serious domestic and international danger is for others the only attitude consistent with a democratic policy. This applies even to de Gaulle's France.

4. Western Europe (noticeably the Six) is in the process of crossing the Rubicon as far as national sovereign states are concerned. With the Schuman Plan, the first real step was taken by the Europeans themselves. Previously the groundwork had been laid by the OEEC to administer the Marshall funds, the European Payments Union, the GATT, the NATO, and other schemes of economic and military cooperation. But co-

---

[1] The eighteen states are the following: Senegal, Mali, Mauritania, Upper Volta, Dahomey, Ivory Coast, Niger, Gabon, Congo (Fr.), Congo (Eng.), Tchad, Central Africa, Malagasy, Togo, Cameroun, Somalia, Rwanda, Burundi.

operation remained at the governmental level and took the form of consultations between independent and sovereign states. The Schuman Plan
represents the first genuine effort to give a permanent institutional framework to European cooperation, and with it the first step was taken in
favor of qualifying the veto power of the Six states and allowing the Coal
and Steel Community to make decisions by a weighted majority vote. The
same can be said for the Common Market that came into effect in 1958.[2]

SUPRANATIONAL ASPECTS OF THE COMMON MARKET

There are at least four important institutional arrangements and developments that bring clearly into light some of the supranational aspects of
the European Common Market:

1. In the future the decisions of the Council of Ministers can be taken
increasingly by a qualified majority in which France, Germany, and Italy
have four votes each; Belgium and Holland, two; and Luxemburg, one.
By 1970 virtually all decisions will be made by a qualified majority of
12 votes.[3]

2. A greater role will devolve upon the Commission of the Common
Market as a policy-initiating and policy-executing organ. By 1970, when
the veto power of any single member will have virtually disappeared, the
Commission representing the Community will have assumed an independent powerful role.

3. It is possible, though conjectural at this stage, that the European
Assembly will represent a larger constituency and will act in terms that
transcend strict national considerations, especially if elected directly by
the peoples of the member countries and if given broader powers.

4. Decisions made by the Commission apply directly to the individual
citizens of the member states. Agricultural prices and subsidies; common
tariffs, social harmonization, wage policies—all such matters once decided
become enforceable in the individual states, and every individual will
have the right to appeal to his national jurisdictional organs and ultimately to the Community Court in order to make them enforceable.

In the light of these trends the old argument between the functionalists
and the integrationists—that divided many European political leaders

---

[2] See Jean Marie Lebretton in *Seides,* "Le Pouvoir Supranational et les Institutions
Européenes en 1971," No. 806, 1962; and Walter Hallstein, *United Europe* (Cambridge,
Mass.: Harvard University Press, 1962). See also Ernest B. Haas, "International Inte-
gration: The European and the Universal Process," *International Organization,* 15
(Summer, 1961), 366-92.

[3] Any twelve votes are sufficient on all matters presented to the Council of Ministers
by the Commission. In all other cases the twelve votes cast must include four out
of the six states. This means that when the Commission makes a proposal, no single
state can veto it. If the three large states were in agreement to initiate a policy, they
could not impose it upon the three smaller states.

and intellectuals and continues to agitate some of them—has lost its significance. The functionalists argued in favor of the establishment of organizations to decide only on specific matters delegated to them: economic, social, or military matters. They believed that political integration of a federal nature would be more likely to develop and to become more acceptable only when the social or economic institutional framework had been set in motion. The political integrationists argued for a political union first, with an executive, a legislative, and a judiciary to become a supranational political entity to tackle all economic, military, and social issues. Today both aims have been realized up to a certain point, for the Common Market has to make economic and social policies that are inextricably associated with what might be called political decisions. Both the Commission of the Common Market and the Council of Ministers perform genuine political functions in initiating policies and in deciding on them. The latter assumes a supranational political character when it makes decisions by a qualified majority, or even when it realizes that it must reach a compromise upon which decisions can be made. It is not surprising, therefore, that two European leaders who respectively expressed the point of view of the functionalists and the integrationists— de Gaulle and Hallstein—are in virtual agreement about the character of the Common Market.

De Gaulle, after insisting upon the uniqueness and durability of independent states and after rejecting a federal political union, pointed out that the economic and agricultural problems confronting the Six are ultimately political problems to which the answers given are invariably of a political nature:

> . . . *It is a political action when tariffs are dealt with in common, when coal-mining areas are converted, when wages and social welfare funds are made the same in the six states, when each state allows workers from the five other states to settle in its territory, when decrees are taken and parliament is asked to vote the necessary laws, funds and sanctions. . . . It is a political action when the association of Greece or of the African states or of Malagasy Republic is being dealt with. . . . It is still a political action when one comes to consider the request that the United States announces that it will make with regard to its economic relations with the Community. In fact the economic development of Europe cannot be assured without its political union. . . .*[4]

After discussing the Common Market provisions regarding welfare, harmonization, antitrust rules, "coordination," and collaboration on a

---

[4] President de Gaulle, Sixth Press Conference, May 15, 1962, in *Ambassade de France, Service de Presse et d'Information.*

number of social and economic matters, Hallstein, long the champion of political integration, writes:

In my view, the logic of economic integration not only leads on toward political unity by way of the fusion of interests; it also involves political action itself. What, in fact, are all matters that I have mentioned if they are not political? What issues could be more burningly political than those of agriculture? [5]

Every reliable observer seems to agree that, barring dramatic events, the course of European development toward increasingly greater political ties is irreversible. The fact that the best barometer of European trends, the Action Committee for the United States of Europe under Jean Monnet, has asked for political integration is quite conclusive. Although some marginal agricultural groups, left-wing intellectuals, and the Communist parties do not agree, the most powerful lobbies now and most of the European political leaders and parties (including even the German Socialists) concur—even if they differ about tactics and timing—that the future of the Common Market states lies in the direction of political union.

THE GROWTH OF EUROPEAN CONSENSUS

To discuss the whys and hows of this monumental evolution is to search for the factors that account for political unification: Compatibility of major values, mutual responsiveness (the "we" feeling), superior economic growth, expectation of joint economic rewards, wide range of mutual transactions, broadening of elites, mobility of persons, outside military threat, and some others all exist to solidify the growing trends.[6] The specific goals of unification must also be included in the search: ranging from a loose cooperative system to a security community in which independent states agree to exclude war as a means of solving differences; to a confederate system that involves only a qualified, conditional, and very narrow delegation of sovereignty; to a federation; and finally to political amalgamation. It requires also an understanding of the developmental stages of political integration and particularly of the two basic landmarks: (1) "irreversibility," when the drive toward cooperation has reached a stage at which it is irreversible, and (2) "snowballing," when the accom-

[5] Hallstein, *op. cit.*, pp. 65-66.

[6] Ernest Haas, *The Uniting of Europe* (Stanford, Calif.: Stanford University Press, 1958); *passim*. Karl W. Deutsch provides us with a conceptual scheme for the study of the process of political unification in Deutsch, *et al.*, *Political Community and the North Atlantic Area* (Princeton, N.J.: Princeton University Press, 1951); Amitai Etzioni, "A Paradigm for the Study of Political Unification," *World Politics*, XV (October, 1962), see also 44-75.

plishments toward cooperation create a situation that accelerates the process of political unification.

Though it may be true that for the majority of Europeans the supreme and ultimate loyalty remains still their nation-state, we also note the growth of what is often referred to as a *European consensus.* The consensus may be defined first in negative terms. There seems to be a beginning of shared attitudes not only among the Six, but also among the Seven and all of them, to consider war as virtually impossible in order to solve their problems. This contrasts sharply with any other period in the history of Western Europe. But there is also a more positive aspect, limited perhaps to the Six: a growing inclination to use the existing European organizations for the discussion and the solution of differences or of common problems. Nothing illustrates this better than the debates in December, 1961, on the passage from the first to the second stage of the Common Market and the complex adjustments made for the establishment of an agricultural market. Sacrifices were made by some countries in the context of a broader goal of shared participation and achievement.

Naturally for those who envisaged a rapid political amalgamation of the Six (and perhaps of some of the Seven and England) and who even spoke of Atlantic Union, the accomplishments fall short of the mark. But political amalgamation in which traditional national sovereignties yield to a new supranational political entity—unitary or, in this case, federal —cannot be brought about by the fiat of a legislator or even, to use General de Gaulle's term, of a federator. Easy to arrange on paper, a political union—even of a federal nature—has to meet the stubborn imperatives of secular national attachments and habits in a region and among peoples whose history in the last 150 years has been that of nationalist rivalries and conflicts. What has been accomplished thus far remains, even if it were not to move in the direction of closer political ties, one of the most singular innovations of the post-World War II period. The Europe of the Six, as the decision to increase its external tariffs or to exclude England indicates, has become a loose but nonetheless a real political entity. It still has to meet the acid test of closer military cooperation, or what ultimately may be the revival of the European Defense Community with the pooling of military resources, the formulation of common strategy, the development of a common banking system and a common currency, and the creation of federated political organs.[7] The

---

[7] The Franco-German treaty provides for closer ties in matters of defense, military training, foreign policy, and cultural affairs. Periodic meetings are institutionalized. It is presumed that in de Gaulle's eyes, in addition to consecrating in special terms the Franco-German rapprochement, the treaty may be a "pilot" scheme in which the other Six may participate. In fact the differences between the Fouchet plan that had been suggested earlier by the French to the Six and the Franco-German treaty are not great.

Common Market Commission is already working on some of these measures, and the pace of growth in the last five years, if continued, may soon
start producing snowballing effects. Consensus that will take more concrete political expression in the form of closer cooperation or integration
is in the process of being fashioned.

In my opinion, herein lies the promise of Western Europe—of the Six
and some others, including England, who are beginning to look for membership. The European political communities are beginning to overcome
the most tenacious secular internal divisions between the "haves" and the
"have nots" and between the two ideologies that split their societies into
warring classes for so long—collectivism and economic liberalism. Some
have embarked upon the road of planning, and all have accepted broad
programs that require planning. In the last ten years they have registered
spectacular economic gains. Their national income has grown fast; the
trade of the Six has virtually doubled; their per capita income has registered impressive gains; and wages have risen, except for some marginal
groups and unskilled workers. Their rate of economic growth has been
double that of the United States. Despite many crises they have maintained their attachment to the principles of democracy, notably individual
and political freedoms. With the Adenauer-de Gaulle era coming perforce
to an end, it remains to be seen whether or not the peculiar one-man
governments of France and Germany will continue and will remain
reconciled with individual and political freedoms. Finally, the Western
European countries, specifically the Six, have developed ways and means
of solving their differences, have buried for good the possibility of war,
and are on the road to the realization of a supranational community.

These conclusions naturally relate to the broad currents and to the
long-range future. They apply mainly to the Six but they do not exclude
the rest. Everything does not appear as serene and secure. The nagging
fear that de Gaulle was using the European idea and the Common Market
to his own ends in order to exclude England and undermine NATO has
now become a reality to be reckoned with.[8] German acquiescence to
French leadership, because of Berlin, doubts about American strategy,
and the remote prospect of reunification, may not survive Adenauer.
There is danger that a French atomic force will not be harnessed to a
European body—even the Six—but will become the symbol and the
reality of the secular ambitions of France to "protect" Europe, thus pro-
voking divisive nationalisms that will spill over into a proliferation of

---

[8] See Roy C. Macridis, "De Gaulle's Foreign Policy and the Fifth Republic," *Yale
Review*, 50 (Winter, 1961), 172-87; and "French Foreign Policy," in *Foreign Policy in
World Politics* (2nd ed.), ed. Roy C. Macridis (Englewood Cliffs, N.J.: Prentice-Hall,
Inc., 1962), Chap. III. A good summary account of French foreign policy is given by
Jean Baptiste Duroselle in Stanley Hoffman *et al., In Search of France* (Cambridge,
Mass.: Harvard University Press, 1963), Chap. 5.

atomic weapons. Finally, there are all the problems involved in stream-lining and strengthening of the institutions of the Six and the abortive efforts of the Seven.[9] One can't exclude the hypothesis that the Community may be unable to surmount these problems.

The coming years will determine the answers to two more formidable questions: How European will the Community be, and how Atlantic will Europe become? The answer to these questions will depend on a great number of factors, especially upon American economic, strategic, and foreign policy and upon Soviet attitudes. Paul Henri Spaak and Jean Monnet have conceived of the Six (the little Europe) as a stepping stone to the development of a larger participation of other European states, including Great Britain. Some European and American writers and statesmen have pushed this idea to larger Atlantic horizons to include the United States and Canada.[10] It must be said that neither the British statesmen, despite Churchill's lip service to it, nor the majority of the French statesmen, for whom de Gaulle is prime spokesman, have accepted the notion of Greater Europe. No British statesman has endorsed the idea of supranationality; many Europeans foresee in the addition of other European states to the Common Market countries a dilution of the common spirit and a weakening of the existing bonds and political institutions. Nor can it be argued that American statesmen have given much thought to the over-all implications of the Grand Design with regard to trade, defense, and particularly to political cooperation and to the political institutions. The "Little Europe" of the Six has at present a far greater reality and is more likely to become a genuine community than any other arrangement. The coming decade will see the realization of European political unity (with the Six alone or the Six and others); or it will bring a stalemate; or it will see the dissolution of the bonds and the weakening of the consensus that have been built in the last years.

EUROPEAN UNION OR ATLANTIC COMMUNITY?

Strangely enough, it is both the relative fragility and the apparent strength of European consensus that create serious dilemmas for the United States. To put it bluntly, we have the means to destroy it and to recreate a Balkanized Europe. We have also the means to further and strengthen it and to enhance a European bloc that will be a genuine "Third Force" with a population and an industrial complex rivaling ours. Such a force will no longer be subject to our counsels and will no

---

[9] For a summary account, see Joseph Kraft, *The Grand Design from Common Market to Atlantic Partnership* (New York: Harper & Row, Publishers, 1962). See also Michael Shanks and John Lambert, *The Common Market Today and Tomorrow* (New York: Frederick A. Praeger, Inc., 1962).

[10] Monnet's Action Committee for a United States of Europe, while envisaging a broad European Federation, has not pressed for an Atlantic Union.

longer accept our leadership. It will shape its own fortunes and destinies and will possess what Raymond Aron has called the ultimate sign of independence—the right to make peace or war. The dream of European unity is an old and noble one. A United Europe of the Six (or more) will be a democratic community second only to the United States to bring together so many millions of men and women. It may also be a new power attempting to mediate between the "two empires," as its interests demand. The demon of European power politics will have been exorcised only to hide under the altar of a United Europe. And if one were willing to play with the demon, how can one be sure that it can be trusted to take sides with the United States? Finally, we have the choice of joining Europe—in the form of a genuine Atlantic Community in which the United States will be, at least from a legal point of view, a willing partner to accept under the appropriate arrangements the logic of even a modicum of supranationality.

The basic dilemma, then, is European Union or Atlantic Community. In terms of American foreign policy, President Kennedy seemed to prefer the latter, both in his television conference late in 1962 and in his State of the Union Message of January, 1963. At the same time, General de Gaulle also considered it but rejected it in the most emphatic terms. In President Kennedy's statements there crept a wistful note. He seemed to expect a show of understanding and appreciation on the part of the Six in return for earlier American foresight and generosity. I do not think such expectation is wise. Europe's cooperation with the United States in one form or another will be based upon common perceptions of common interests. It will also depend upon relative shifts in the global distribution of power that no longer answers the neat categories of bipolarization and nuclear supremacy to which we continue to pay lip service. De Gaulle was simply answering President Kennedy accordingly. He rejected the American monopoly within NATO; he reasserted the European identity (under France's guidance); and he continued to be adamant on the simplistic but nonetheless highly persuasive correlation between national nuclear force and national independence. A small well-knit Europe of the Six appeared to de Gaulle vastly superior, as an instrument of France's independence and leadership, to a Common Market in which England was a member or to an Atlantic arrangement in which the United States played the dominant role.

Nowhere does the dilemma become more bedevilling than with military cooperation.[11] The crux of the problem has been the following: The

[11] For background material, see Henry Kissinger, *Nuclear Weapons and Foreign Policy* (New York: Doubleday & Company, Inc., 1958); Robert Osgood, *Limited War* (Chicago: University of Chicago Press, 1957); the most comprehensive and scholarly study on the NATO that has appeared thus far is Robert Osgood, *NATO—The Entangling Alliance* (Chicago: University of Chicago Press, 1962).

United States has demanded that the Europeans put as much emphasis as possible on conventional arms in the context of NATO, while maintaining, both within and outside NATO, what amounts to an exclusive freedom to use nuclear power. This puts the Europeans in a state of military inferiority to both the United States and Russia. It creates an additional problem for them—and I use a new term to add to the existing jargon of politico-military expressions—that of *credible credibility*. No matter how credible our nuclear power is to the Russians, is it credible to the Europeans that American power will be used to defend, not so much Europe, as the interests that are of paramount importance to France and to the Six and that are only of secondary importance to America? If this is not credible, not only is Europe's defense mortgaged heavily, but also their independence of action.

What then is to be done? To give atomic weapons to the European countries or to assist them with technical aid in constructing the weapons is to envenom our relations with Russia—perhaps to leave the Soviet Union with no alternative other than returning to what might be called the Chinese line; giving atomic weapons will also inject an element of intense nationalism that will destroy European unity. To allow European nations to build their own nuclear weapons is to scrap the relative division of labor between conventional and nonconventional forces written in the logic of NATO and also to provoke their resentment because we failed to give them the technical help they need. To cooperate fully with them and pool our resources, or rather put them under an Atlantic directorate on all matters of global strategy, is to deprive ourselves of the very independence we want to maintain. In fact, we are unwilling to accept de Gaulle's simple argument that national independence and power—nuclear power—go hand in hand, because we practice it every day.

The dilemma has led to the search for alternative solutions.[12] Some argue that we must face reality and give nuclear arms to the European nations; others suggest that they be given to a genuine "European body." The Kennedy administration, after scrapping Skybolt, seems willing to give to the British and the French Polaris missiles that will be used by their own submarines (constructed by them or bought in the United States) and that will be armed with their own atomic warheads. These arrangements will be integrated in the present plans of NATO; that is,

---

[12] Many semiofficial and officious arguments have appeared in *Foreign Affairs* for 1960, 1961, and 1962. See particularly Heinrich von Brentano, "Goals and Means of the Western Alliance," 39 (April, 1961), 416-29. Dean Acheson, "The Practice of Partnership," 41 (January, 1963), 247-60; Altiero Spinelli, "Atlantic Pact in European Unity," 40 (July, 1962), 542-52; Henry Kissinger, "The Unsolved Problem of Foreign Defense," 40 (July, 1962), 515-41. The author is unable to go along with Professor Kissinger's emphasis upon the military nature of the predicament of NATO or to agree that solutions should be sought exclusively in terms of military considerations.

they will remain under United States control. Few continue to put their faith in disarmament. The limited test ban treaty without disarmament has been rejected by de Gaulle.

Dean Acheson and McGeorge Bundy apparently think that the hard realities of the situation—both the supremacy of the American nuclear arsenal and the overwhelming Russian strength—make the French (and what used to be the British) efforts a sham and a pretense, since it is only United States nuclear power that, in Clausewitz terms, speaks the true language of war. Walter Lippmann has tried to convince the Europeans (in this case, the French and the British) that at their best they can never have more than two per cent of the American nuclear capabilities; but he forgets that two per cent is better than nothing and, in the age of nuclear warfare, may be all that is needed!

"But since when," de Gaulle asked, "has it been proven that a people should be deprived of the most effective weapon for the reason that its chief possible adversary and its chief friend have means superior to its own?" [13] He alluded in no uncertain terms to the particular destructive features of an atomic force—no matter how small—and concluded that even such a small force in the hands of France "cannot fail to have at least some bearing on the intentions of any possible aggressor." [14] The argument, in my opinion, is irrefutable. What the French leader did not mention, however, was that a French independent deterrent would render the present NATO arrangements obsolete, reduce the significance of American military presence, and perhaps give to France the leadership and the initiative to negotiate a European settlement according to her own interests and on the basis of her own traditional European vocation. A reunified but demilitarized Germany; a gradual withdrawal of American forces from the Continent on condition that the Soviets would withdraw from Eastern Europe; and perhaps a nonaggression pact between France and the Soviet Union—any such arrangement might restore France, now free from colonial burdens, to her European position. It would also make the American "entanglement" progressively unnecessary.

These may well be farfetched speculations. If so, France, thanks to her atomic power, might assert her own independence and presumably that of the Six to act according to their interests. NATO would then be reduced to what it originally was—an American guarantee or a simple military alliance for mutual defense against Soviet attack. *All* allies (not only the United States) might, however, assert formally their complete freedom to act as they please and where they please. Such an alliance

---

[13] President de Gaulle, Seventh Press Conference, January 14, 1963, in *Ambassade de France, Service de Presse et d'Information*.

[14] *Ibid.* Early in the Fall of 1963 atomic weapons were made available to French bombers.

would naturally follow the course of world developments and would survive only if the participating nations shared the same interests. The American guarantee to fight for Europe would be maintained as long as Europe wished to see it maintained and as long as American interests made it necessary. Such an alliance, instead of NATO, would liberate the Europeans from the present stage of tutelage[15] and make them for the first time actually responsible for the nuclear and military stance they want to assume. An alliance of this type, however, would also dissipate the hope of political integration at the Atlantic level. It would gradually separate Western Europe from the United States both politically and militarily.

The dilemma is perhaps an insoluble one, but only because we have made it appear so. NATO may no longer be a viable *military organization*. It has failed to grow according to its logic. It must either be drastically overhauled and become a truly cooperative military *and* political undertaking in which the United States is an equal (even if the strongest) partner, or it must be turned into a purely military alliance in the classic sense of the term.

THE COMMON MARKET: TRADING AREA OR ECONOMIC PARTNERSHIP?

The Western Europe we have helped to reconstruct is becoming an independent power bloc whose actions are beginning to escape from our control. To this basic dilemma of foreign policy and military strategy there is, ironically enough, a second one—one that those who listened to General Marshall's memorable speech at Harvard in the summer of 1947 never expected to face within a period of fifteen years: an economic dilemma. We have helped create a unified Western European economic bloc. It is now limited to the Six. That it may include others is both possible and extremely significant, for the Six have set a pattern of their own that will be followed by others. It is a pattern that is beginning to shake profoundly the myths of American economic supremacy and the superiority of the American economic system.

By 1970 the Six (and presumably new members) will have eliminated internal tariffs and all restrictions; they will have attained uniform social legislation; they will have reached a state where free mobility of capital and labor will be the rule; they will have adopted a common external tariff against all nonmembers; they will have gained a firm foothold among the economies of associated members like Greece, and perhaps Turkey, Austria, Denmark, Sweden, Spain, and others, as well as the greater part of Africa. In other words, they will have formed a formidable trade bloc. This may be only a minor problem for the American economy,

[15] Altiero Spinneli, *op. cit.*

since it can be argued that trade is relatively unimportant for this country in terms of gross national product and even in terms of balance of payments. The Six (or whatever the number may be) will by 1970 have a population that will be about as large as that of the United States today. If they continue to experience the same industrial growth, they will have a national income that will be about half of that of the United States; and they will begin to enjoy an average per capita income that will be second only to the United States in the world.

This may not be a serious challenge. The American predominance is so overwhelming that it will take a long time for our complacency to be shaken. Unfortunately, there is something more important and urgent: Western Europe will present the picture of an expanding economy, secure in its old trade areas and implanting itself in new ones—notably the United States itself. Higher productivity in a number of areas will make European products competitive with our own in the home market and in many other areas, Latin America for instance. It will attract American capital, as it has in the last years. Its growth and full employment will contrast sharply with the slow rate of growth and pervasive unemployment that has afflicted the American economy and that is beginning to affect England.[16]

President Kennedy himself has outlined the problem:

But the greatest challenge of all is posed by the growth of the European Market. Assuming the accession of the United Kingdom, there will arise across the Atlantic a trading partner behind a single tariff similar to ours with an economy which nearly equals our own. Will we in this country adapt our thinking to these new prospects and patterns or will we wait until events have passed us by? . . . If we move decisively, our factories and farms can increase their sales to their richest, fastest growing market. Our exports will increase. Our balance of payments position will improve. And we will have forged across the Atlantic a trading partnership with vast resources for freedom.[17]

[16] An excellent account of the Common Market and associated economic problems for Europe, England, and the United States is in Emile Benoit, *Europe at Sixes and Sevens: The Common Market, The Free Trade Association and the United States* (New York: Columbia University Press, 1962).

[17] *The New York Times*, January 12, 1962. How "decisively" we move is a matter for speculation. The Trade Expansion Bill became law in August, 1962. Some of its crucial provisions, especially those empowering the President to eliminate tariffs when trade between the United States and the Common Market amounts to 80 per cent of the world total, can be of little use, since the figure was calculated on the assumption that England would become a member. As was the case with the European Defense Community, but perhaps even more so at this time, we were caught without an alternate plan. Even as President Kennedy spoke, the Common Market had reached an agreement on agricultural policy and variable levies which were to discriminate

This was an unprecedented admission. What was less than twenty years ago the most powerful arsenal, banker, and producer of the world was in effect now asking for the tonic of European competition in order to recover its economic posture.

The second dilemma, then, is how to cope with the Common Market. The first way is a return to "protectionism," a policy of higher tariffs with controls on capital export. In a period of expansion, to which the United States is committed through its membership in the OECD, such a policy would have disastrous effects upon our present foreign and strategic arrangements. Yet under certain conditions—especially if tariffs are accompanied by a massive effort toward technological improvements that will raise the productivity of labor and by massive investments under government planning in both social and private sectors of the economy—protectionism may prove to be a tonic far stronger to our economy than competition with the Common Market countries.

The second way to cope with the Common Market is, of course, *more trade*—lowering the tariffs across the board and developing a trade policy with Western Europe on the basis of reciprocity. This seems to be the policy of the Administration, both because of economic considerations and also because of strategic and foreign policy considerations. The policy is implicit in the transformations of the OEEC into the OECD and explicit in the Trade Expansion Act; yet it begs the frightening question of whether our economy is truly competitive. Can we outsell the Six at their home market? If so, in what products and for how long? Can the Six outsell us in our home market? In what products and for how long? Can we compete in the world market? If so where and in which products? The answer to these questions is beyond the scope of this essay, but there are some interesting indications.

Professor Benoit [18] in a detailed account shows that in many areas United States products are no longer competitive, not only because of wage costs—as it is generally assumed—but also because of drastic increases in the productivity of European labor. Indeed, we held the advantage in many fields and products when wage differentials were far greater. With the rise of European wages, European production costs for many products are now at a level that is competitive with the American

---

directly against some American agricultural products. At the same time, under French leadership, the Common Market was using economic tools for the furtherance of political aims: Greece became an associate member; Denmark began to receive preferences over American agricultural goods; and it is not unlikely that Spain will enter the club in one form or another. President Kennedy urged the country to move "decisively" in forging "a trading partnership." But the Common Market is more than a trading area. As we have seen, it involves common institutions that have a degree of supranationality.

[18] Benoit, *op. cit.*, Chap. 4, 5, 6.

ones. I am not suggesting that competition should be avoided, but merely that we may not be quite prepared for it. This became abundantly clear when in 1960 the Common Market countries proposed, on the basis of reciprocity, a twenty per cent reduction of their common tariff wall for American products. We were unable to meet such a proposal, and the Trade Expansion Act empowering the President to do this and more has not as yet been implemented. Since the Act was passed, no concrete steps have been taken (partly because of the exclusion of Great Britain from the Common Market) to put into effect a policy that was of crucial nature in the Kennedy administration. Perhaps important domestic reforms have to take place: first with the Trade Unions and their defensive mentality; with the business groups and industrial firms that have grown complacent because of a large guaranteed market at home; with the role of the government in matters of investment and development; and with our military expenditures and foreign aid program. More trade through a lowering of the tariffs is not a panacea.

These, then, are the two basic dilemmas: the political integration and the economic union of Western Europe, with all the ramifications and the complexities they entail. As a direct outcome, the United States is losing military and political leadership, and our economic world supremacy is challenged. The challenge leads us inevitably to a reexamination of our own system, our own values, and our own aspirations. To those who talked about the American Century and the *pax Americana,* the challenge is painful; to those who assumed the unqualified American leadership of the non-Communist world, the challenge is bitter. It feeds the "neo-isolationist" current of American public opinion.

There is, however, another choice open to the United States. It lies in cooperation—with *all* that cooperation entails. But it must be clearly understood that cooperation does not mean trade areas, customs unions, or military arrangements in which we insist on both binding the free world to our leadership and keeping our freedom to act as we please. It means taking a definite step in the direction of everything that Burke meant by "partnership." Innumerable ties connect us with Western Europe and England, and the destinies of the free world depend upon the existence of prosperous democratic societies. The Europeans have paved the way to the creation of narrow and functional European bodies. With the shrinking of the world similar developments for a larger unit may be the only answer.

The United States, England, and the Commonwealth (especially since the latter is left out of the Common Market) may easily initiate their own Atlantic organs for a number of selected economic activities and invite and promote cooperation with the Common Market. Or, we may ourselves begin to follow what we have been preaching to others and seek wider participation in the Common Market, not by considering it a trade area or a customs union, but by taking it for what it is—a co-operative scheme in which certain functions and economic activities are so intimately integrated as to necessitate the creation of supranational political organs with supranational powers. We may have to accept the logic of supranationality and planning which will mean that for certain areas of economic and social activity our exclusive and sovereign powers will be seriously qualified.

In other words, the Grand Alliance must be either a mere alliance—which does not mean very much—or more than an alliance which calls for *the establishment of genuine international bodies binding the United States with the rest of the free world* (just as they are beginning to bind the Six of Europe and all those that might adhere to the Common Market). American isolation, then, will be broken for good in the eyes of the Europeans. European isolationism in the form of a Little Europe will not survive either. Thus the Atlantic Community will be born, not in terms of a great political federation—something which is premature—but in terms of *small functional cooperating bodies* from which a new life and a new vision will emerge in the hard processes of compromise and bargaining. This was not unknown to the framers of the Constitution of this country.

Suggestions for Further Reading

Benoit, Emile, *Europe at Sixes and Sevens: The Common Market, The Free Trade Association and the United States.* New York: Columbia University Press, 1962.

Deutsch, Karl W., *et al., Political Community and the North Atlantic.* Princeton, N.J.: Princeton University Press, 1951.

Haas, Ernest, *The Uniting of Europe.* Stanford, Calif.: Stanford University Press, 1958.

Hallstein, Walter, *United Europe.* Cambridge, Mass.: Harvard University Press, 1962.

Kraft, Joseph, *The Grand Design from Common Market to Atlantic Partnership.* New York: Harper & Row, Publishers, 1962.

Macridis, Roy, ed. *Modern Political Systems: Europe.* Englewood Cliffs, N.J.: Prentice-Hall, Inc., 1963.

Osgood, Robert, *NATO—The Entangling Alliance.* Chicago: University of Chicago Press, 1962.

Shanks, Michael and John Lambert, *The Common Market Today and Tomorrow.* New York: Frederick A. Praeger, Inc., 1962.

BRITISH POLITICS
AND AMERICAN POLICY

William S. Livingston

United States foreign policy, like that of any other nation, is conducted in an inescapable environment of forces and influences of such a character that the United States has no direct control over them. It is obvious, for example, that United States policy is influenced by the Soviet possession of nuclear weapons. It is perhaps less obvious that there are factors in our relationship with Great Britain that have a similar effect; but what Britain is, wants, and does is also part of the environing circumstances that shape American policy. The aim of this essay is to assess the character and significance of these British influences; its thesis is that their character is complex and diverse and their significance great.

THE ENVIRONMENT OF AMERICAN POLICY

From the beginning of our national life, our interests, our character, and our policy have been closely linked with those of Britain. The two countries were not consciously pursuing similar goals nor were they formally united in their pursuit, but the conduct of American affairs and the objectives of American policy were regularly shaped by conditions in, and by the policies of, Great Britain. Indeed, the basic character of our

WILLIAM S. LIVINGSTON *is Professor of Government and Graduate Adviser in Government at The University of Texas. He has recently been a Guggenheim Fellow in England. He has published numerous articles in the professional journals, is the author of* Federalism and Constitutional Change, *and is the editor of* Federalism in the Commonwealth.

society and our policy was molded by our British background and traditions, in part because we adapted and maintained them, and in part because we reacted against and rejected them.

The very position of America as an independent and viable state was determined by forces and elements within Britain and in Britain's own international environment. One of the basic reasons why America achieved and maintained her independence was that England did not exert all her strength against us in 1781 or 1814; and she did not because she could not. Her policy, too, was circumscribed by an external circumstance that required all the energies she might otherwise have directed against America: the mortal threat from France.[1]

It will be observed that this argument is not confined to the formal acknowledgment or the self-conscious articulation of interests or policy —to say nothing of formal alliances. Indeed, this first point illustrates a negative influence, by enmity, rather than influence through alliance or support. Our concern is with the *position* occupied by a nation, with the conditions of life that shape its relations, and not merely with what it wants and whom it considers to be its friends or enemies. We are concerned, that is to say, with the fundamental realities of relationships and the plain facts of international life. As for America, the plain fact is that for most of our national life our position, our security, and our very existence have been shaped not by our own aspirations and policies, and still less by our own capacities, but by the power position and external policies of other powers, principally of Great Britain. For most of our history our ambitions and expectations have exceeded our capabilities and our will to act; our successes must accordingly be attributed to something more than our own valor and virtue. In Walter Lippmann's phrase, our foreign policy has been "insolvent." [2]

BRITAIN AND AMERICA IN THE NINETEENTH CENTURY

The nineteenth century, which for our purpose is roughly the period from Waterloo to the end of the century, or perhaps to 1914, was the age of the *Pax Britannica;* it was Britain's dominant power during this long and critical era that provided America's security and gave her the oppor-

---

[1] Among the useful collections of materials illustrating British views on the Revolution and British policy toward it are Max Beloff, ed., *The Debate on the American Revolution* (London: Kaye, 1949); and Martin Kallich and Andrew MacLeish, eds., *The American Revolution Through British Eyes* (New York: Harper & Row, Publishers, 1962). Useful monographs include D. M. Clarke, *British Opinion and the American Revolution* (Cambridge, Mass.: Harvard University Press, 1930); and Charles R. Ritcheson, *British Politics and the American Revolution* (Norman, Okla.: University of Oklahoma Press, 1954).

[2] Walter Lippmann, *U.S. Foreign Policy: Shield of the Republic* (Boston: Little, Brown & Co., 1943), pp. 9-10.

tunity to expand and grow strong.[3] Britain for a hundred years was the world's most powerful nation. Her navies ruled the seas; her industries supplied the needs of the world; her peoples were settling the far continents; and with her overwhelming might she served as the world's policeman. In control both of the seas and of far-flung interests and strategic bases, she stepped in whenever necessary to keep the peace (by fighting occasional small wars)—in Africa, China, Persia, the Crimea, and the Near East. By reason of this British power, America remained safe from external threats, although, so far from recognizing or acknowledging this benefit, the Americans remained profoundly skeptical of Britain, believing that she harbored ambitions against them, that she could not be trusted, that she represented the "old" system of privilege, hierarchy, and dynastic ambition. But the truth was that American security was protected, without cost to America, by the British fleet and nation.

Ultimately, the explanation for this state of affairs lies in Britain's disinclination to interfere with America or with America's development. There was no direct clash of interest between the two. Britain did not see America as holding ambitions contrary to British interests or as seeking expansion at her expense.[4] We had no navy and no concern with European and world affairs. Even then we had learned to talk of "no entangling alliances." We placed our confidence in the expanse of oceans that separated us from European threats, taking little note that the seas were moats rather than waterways only so long as a friendly power controlled them. Indeed, the success of the Monroe Doctrine was largely assured by the British fleet rather than by anything America did or could have done.[5] Britain was even more interested than America in keeping the European powers out of Latin America, where they might jeopardize British trade routes, markets, and sea communications. The Monroe Doctrine serves as a good example of the informal and unacknowledged collaboration between the two nations during much of this whole period.[6] We declared it and Britain enforced it. There was no alli-

---

[3] See the discussion in Cecil V. Crabb, Jr., *American Foreign Policy in the Nuclear Age* (New York: Harper & Row, Publishers, 1960), pp. 224-25. See also the comment by Lord Strang, *Britain in World Affairs: The Fluctuation in Power and Influence from Henry VIII to Elizabeth II* (New York: Frederick A. Praeger, Inc., 1961), p. 292.

[4] Joseph Chamberlain, Colonial Secretary in 1896: "War between the two nations would be an absurdity as well as a crime. . . . The two nations are allied and more closely allied in sentiment and in interest than any other nations on the face of the earth. . . ." Cited in Samuel F. Bemis, *A Diplomatic History of the United States*, 3rd ed. (New York: Holt, Rinehart & Winston, Inc., 1950), p. 421.

[5] Lippmann, *op. cit.*, p. 30; Charles P. Schleicher, *International Relations: Cooperation and Conflict* (Englewood Cliffs, N.J.: Prentice-Hall, Inc., 1962), p. 621; H. C. Allen, *Great Britain and the United States: A History of Anglo-American Relations, 1783-1952* (New York: St. Martin's Press, Inc., 1955), p. 203.

[6] Bemis, *op. cit.*, p. 203.

ance but there was a meaningful, if unrecognized (in America), congruence of interests.

Toward the end of the century things began to change. First, Germany, by then united under Prussian leadership, unveiled new ambitions and rose to challenge Britain's control of the seas, a development that was heavy with meaning for America as well as for Britain. Second, Russia, Japan, and Italy all began to take an increasingly important place in world affairs. Third, America began to turn away from her inward concerns and to assume a more important interest in the world. She became a "world power," it is often said, as she emerged from the Spanish War. But this experience did more than disclose America's broadening concern and increasing power; it also demonstrated how important to America was the benevolence of the British fleet.

Most important of all—and doubtless a consequence of these other developments—Britain and America (particularly the latter) began to acknowledge their common interests and their dependence upon each other.[7] Britain seemed much less a threat to the United States, and, as the nations jostled one another in their rush toward the cataclysm, the similarity of traditions, values, and institutions took on a new importance. America was beginning to look about her and to assess her true position in the world. New threats were arising from Germany and elsewhere, and the Anglo-Saxons drew together in response. America was a trading nation and had an interest like Britain's in the availability of markets and the freedom of the seas; the interests of the two were complementary rather than competing. Moreover, Britain, by amicably settling the Oregon and Maine boundaries, by accepting the peaceful arbitration of other issues, and by turning the isthmian canal project over to the United States, convinced many Americans of her friendship and earned their confidence.[8]

All this did not happen at once and the *rapprochement* was not obvious to all Americans. Even after World War I, many of us continued to warn one another of the persistent perfidy of Albion, and Big Bill Thompson could warn King George to keep his snoot out of Chicago. Twisting the lion's tail had become a national game. But a change was taking place nonetheless, not so much in the fundamental relations be-

[7] See Lionel Gelber, *The Rise of Anglo-American Friendship: A Study in World Politics, 1898-1906* (London: Oxford University Press, 1938).

[8] The intricacies of these events and the American reaction to them may be followed in two standard histories: Bemis, *A Diplomatic History of the United States, op. cit.,* and Thomas A. Bailey, *A Diplomatic History of the American People,* 4th ed. (New York: Appleton-Century-Crofts, Inc., 1950). For the Maine Boundary, see Bemis, p. 262, and Bailey, pp. 217-22; on the Oregon dispute, see Bemis, pp. 279-81, and Bailey, Chap. 15; on the arbitrations, see Bemis, Chap. 23; on the isthmian canal question, see Bemis, pp. 509-11, and Bailey, pp. 533-35.

tween the two countries as in the attitudes and acceptances of their peoples. Their interests and policies remained the same; the change was in the recognition and acknowledgment of the similarity of their objectives and values. Indeed, the complaints and frictions, though superficial, tend to obscure a fundamental fact of Anglo-American relations, namely, that from the late nineteenth century onward there existed an informal and unstated "alliance" between Britain and America, based squarely on the similarity of their interests.[9]

This was a peculiar alliance, for it was not an "alliance" at all. There were no documents displaying it and no treaty was signed; as an alliance it was never formalized and seldom articulated. But the similarity of interests was so clear that no formalization was necessary—a similarity that rested on a common concern for the freedom of the seas and open access to markets. As the twentieth century continued, moreover, a different and more strictly political concern was added: a vital interest in the maintenance of the balance of power in Europe. This was no new matter for Britain, but it was at least newly recognized in America, for it was a consequence of the broadening interests of America in the world. Both nations found themselves opposed to the domination of Europe by any single European power, a domination that would of itself upset the balance and threaten the interests of Anglo-Saxony.[10] Britain was doubtless the senior partner in this alliance and America the junior partner; the management of its policies was largely left to Britain. America did not skillfully assess her own role in the alliance or her own advantage in its strength.[11] We were too proud to fight. We blamed the war as much on Britain as on Germany, and we refused to support Britain in 1915. We insisted afterwards on limiting her naval armaments along with those of potential enemies. We passed neutrality legislation to keep us out of future wars, regardless of our interests. But when the chips were down, America, perceiving that her vital interests lay with England's, came to her aid (in both cases belatedly) in the struggle to prevent German domination of the Continent.

There is a magnificent irony in this whole Anglo-American relationship through the period from the Civil War to the Second World War. America remained uninterested and unconcerned about the outer world, from which she was protected by the unrecognized similarity of her interests and Britain's, and by the consequent benevolence of British policy. America concerned herself instead with her own internal development, with westward expansion, with industrial investment and

[9] Allen, *op. cit.*, pp. 202-3.

[10] Hans J. Morgenthau, *Politics Among Nations,* 3rd ed. (New York: Alfred A. Knopf, Inc., 1960), pp. 182-84.

[11] The same was sometimes true of Britain. See, for example, Lippmann, *op. cit.*, p. 116.

growth, with settling her constitutional and regional problems, and with the development of her own power and capacity. America spent her time, energies, and resources in developing her own power position. and was protected in the process by Britain's tolerance. All of which led, in the phrase and theory of A. F. K. Organski, to a "power transition" by which America in time replaced Britain as the world's leading power—a transition made possible by the amiable and avuncular tolerance of that very Britain that might have prevented it.[12]

One may pause to ponder what might be the state of America today if Britain (for whatever reasons) had given her support to the Southern Confederacy? If she had not invested large sums in the economic development of America? If she had not been preoccupied elsewhere in 1898 (in Africa, India, and the Sudan) or had taken a firm stand against us? And above all, if she had not stood firm in 1916, to say nothing of 1940?

The argument, then, consists of three points: first, that American interests were safeguarded through the nineteenth century by a friendly Britain; second, that America's isolationist policy was conditioned and made possible by the factors in Britain's position and in her outlook toward the world; and, third, that there was a close identity, usually unacknowledged and seldom articulated, between the interests of Britain and America from the early nineteenth century onward. America could grow to her present position, in part at least, because of British power and British good will.

THE SHIFT OF POWER FROM BRITAIN TO AMERICA

All that is now drastically changed. British power is nowadays much reduced, to the point where her needs threaten to overbalance her capacities, and *her* foreign policy is in serious danger of insolvency. The decline in British power is not a recent development, as these things are ordinarily measured; it is not merely an event of the postwar period. Power is inevitably relative, not absolute, and the relative power of Great Britain has been declining since the late years of the nineteenth century. This decline must also be measured in terms of the rise of the United States to world influence after 1898, and in the light of the rise of modern Germany after 1871, and more especially after 1890.

Drained in resources and manpower by the First World War, Great Britain faced a changed situation in the interwar period. Like others, she was compelled to abandon the gold standard and devalue her cur-

[12] A. F. K. Organski, *World Politics* (New York: Alfred A. Knopf, Inc., 1958). For the theory of the "power transition," see Chap. 12; for the attitude of Britain toward the growth of America during the power transition, see pp. 336-37.

rency, the currency that had been the world's measure of value and medium of exchange for a century and more. London's function as the world's chief trading and financial center was shifted more and more to New York. Britain accepted naval parity with the United States, abandoning her firm and ancient two-navy policy, in accordance with which she had for generations maintained a navy equal in strength to those of the next two leading naval powers. She retained her leading role in world affairs, which America was neither interested in, nor capable of, taking over. But her leaders recognized her reduced circumstances and adapted her responsibilities to those reduced capacities.[13]

The major consequence of the Second World War was the acceleration of this decline and—of equal importance—the demonstration of it to the rest of the world. The decline took several forms. In the first place, Britain's military capacity was further reduced. In a world where the military giants measured their land forces in hundreds of divisions, Britain's armies were no longer able to match them in force or numbers. Her manpower was again reduced, and her navy was no longer the mistress of the seas. During the war, she had been unable to replace the ships that were lost, and the task of replacing and maintaining the Allied naval and merchant fleets fell to American shipyards, which were expanded to an unprecedented capacity. While American ships were devoted to the common cause, American shipyards were out of range of German bombs and, being newer, were not subject to the same wear and tear as the British yards. After the war, it was America that possessed both the ships and the shipyards.[14]

In the second place, Britain's colonial empire was no longer the great source of strength it had once been. With the end of hostilities, colonial nationalism rose at once to new heights of intensity. Britain had made promises during the war of more self-government, and indeed independence, for many colonies, which she now proceeded to redeem. In many areas the colonies had become an expense rather than an asset. Rebuilding and development were draining British resources, not only for her own sake but for that of the colonial territories. Some had become not merely competitors, but creditors of the mother country.

Third, the condition of the British economy was perilous in the extreme. Needing vast imports to live, to feed her people, and to supply her industry, Britain had lost the ability to pay for them and had no real prospect of recovering this ability. Before the war she had paid for her imports in several different ways in addition to her own exports, which were never sufficient in themselves. She had an immense volume

[13] Lord Strang, *Britain in World Affairs*, p. 328.
[14] See Crane Brinton, *The United States and Britain* (Cambridge, Mass.: Harvard University Press, 1945), p. 141.

of investments overseas, both in the Empire and elsewhere; but these had been sold off in large part (and frequently at fire-sale emergency prices) to help meet the costs of the war. She had the world's largest merchant fleet, and her shipping services earned a substantial income; but this fleet had been much reduced by the war, by ordinary attrition, by sinkings, and by the fact that the shipyards that replaced the lost ships were American, not British. She had also had a variety of other "invisible exports," such as insurance, that had been similarly reduced in significance during the war. As the world's financial center, she had benefited from the widespread practice of arranging financing, of holding deposits, of making loans, and so forth, all of which had earned foreign exchange; but still more of this had been shifted to New York during the war years.

Above all, Britain's industrial plant, which was the major source of her economic strength, had suffered the same decline. War had prevented the maintenance and replacement essential to keeping it fully productive, and bomb damage had destroyed extensive portions of it. After the war, therefore, she faced an increased demand upon her industrial capacity (to supplant the lost "invisible exports," to assist her colonies, to replace her own industrial capacity) with a much diminished ability to produce the export goods on which all this depended. It is not necessary here to recite the herculean efforts (the "austerity" programs, the husbanding of resources through careful economic planning, the Canadian and American loans, the Marshall Plan assistance) that made possible her recovery. The main point is that Britain emerged from the war much reduced in strength and stature, military, economic, and, inevitably, political.[15]

Meanwhile, America had become the "arsenal of democracy," had remained safe from war damage, had achieved a fantastic enlargement of her industrial capacity, had produced the largest fleet, merchant marine, and air force ever seen, had, in short, replaced Britain as the world's leading power. And—most significant for our present purpose—America, whether she willed it or not, had inherited the responsibilities of power

---

[15] These postwar economic difficulties have been the subject of many works, many oriented toward the Labour government's efforts to deal with them. A good brief summary oriented toward relations with America may be found in Brinton, *op. cit.,* Chap. 8, written during the war. A more detailed analysis is Andrew Shonfield, *British Economic Policy Since the War* (Harmondsworth: Penguin Books, Ltd., 1958). The decline in British power, economically and otherwise, may be followed in Alfred Havighurst, *Twentieth-Century Britain* (New York: Harper & Row, Publishers, 1962); Michael Shanks, *The Stagnant Society* (Harmondsworth: Penguin Books, Ltd., 1961); Henry Pelling, *Modern Britain, 1885-1955* (Edinburgh: Thos. Nelson, 1960); F. S. Northedge, *British Foreign Policy* (New York: Frederick A. Praeger, Inc., 1963); and especially in Drew Middleton, *The Supreme Choice: Britain and the European Community* (London: Secker & Warburg, 1963).

that she had traditionally ignored, that she had neither liking for nor experience in, and that Britain had theretofore performed.[16]

DIFFERENCES BETWEEN AMERICA'S ROLE AND BRITAIN'S

The decline in British power was not only reflected in, but also contributed to, the vast increase in the power of America and the scope of its responsibilities. Some like to describe the new relationship by saying that the United States has inherited the tasks that Britain once performed. While there is truth in such an assertion, it is not the whole truth and, stated in such simple terms, it seriously misrepresents the situation.

The role that Britain sought to play—usually with success—was that of the "balancer" in the traditional balance-of-power system. Holding herself aloof from continental politics, she was prepared to throw herself on the scale against whichever power threatened to upset the balance. More explicitly, she was prepared to oppose with force any nation that threatened to dominate the continent of Europe. While Britain can no longer play that traditional role, it is clearly not true that the United States can or should play it instead, for in these days there is no role for such a "balancer" to play. Whether it be explained in terms of a power transition or in terms of the postwar bipolarization of world politics, the European balance of power has disappeared. Thus, while we sometimes speak of America's inheriting Britain's role, that is only a partial characterization. The role as she played it no longer exists, and the nature of the world in which the inheritance must be used is entirely different.

Britain was long able to perform this role because of three conditions that no longer obtain. First, she was physically removed from the arena of the struggle (Europe) and, though occasionally threatened, she proved to be immune in her island from attack from the Continent. She is now neither removed nor immune; her island no longer makes her impregnable; her navy is no longer a sufficient guarantee of her security; indeed, her island is no longer a fortress, but a target.

Second, she was, for the most part, not concerned with the rights and wrongs of the European struggle or with the virtues of the strugglers; hence she could throw her weight either way. Today she is no longer unconcerned, but is deeply committed on one side of the bipolarized world. There is now no multiplicity of powers and hence no balance in the old sense that left room for a "balancer." If there is a balance of power today, it is a balance in the sense of a teeter-totter, not in the

---

[16] The most thorough effort to analyze this shift of power and responsibility from Britain to the United States is Lionel Gelber, *America in Britain's Place* (New York: Frederick A. Praeger, Inc., 1961).

sense of a chandelier, and Britain is firmly planted on the Western or American side of the balance. Neither she nor America could conceivably play the traditional role.[17]

Third, she did not need Europe for her own development. On the contrary, from the seventeenth to the end of the nineteenth century she could satisfy her needs and aspirations in an expanding colonial empire in an overseas emptiness. She increased her power and fulfilled the expectations of her people in colonial investment, settlement, and development. But the vacuum overseas has been filled, and the new lands are no longer available; in Walter Webb's phrase, the "Great Frontier" has been closed.[18] Empires have given way to colonial nationalism and a self-governing Commonwealth has now replaced the glories and wealth of Empire.

In consequence of these changes, Britain must now find other sources of strength. She must satisfy her aspirations, protect her security, and derive her sustenance from a world in which she has much the same needs as before but is without the means of assuring their satisfaction; in which she must assume a responsibility for, and be concerned with, Europe and the power struggle there; in which her traditional weapons of defense—insularity, navy, finance—are inadequate or irrelevant to the power alignment of the new age. It is imperative, therefore, for her to realign her own position, and this she has been struggling to do in the years since 1945.[19]

Britain must reorient her economy, her defense, and her policies in directions that have yet to be worked out. It is still an open question whether in the next fifty years she will solve her problems (1) through a restructured Commonwealth, (2) by joining a renascent and reunited Europe, (3) by some sort of Atlantic Union with Canada, America, and others, or (4) by withdrawing into herself, exporting still more of her population, contracting still further her overseas obligations, abandoning her independent defense system, and accepting a small-power status dependent upon the protection of the United States. How she works out these problems will be of prime importance to the United States, not only because our ties of kinship make her interests and security of importance to us, but also because she remains our chief ally and because her response to, and mastery of, this new situation, together with the role she finds to play in it, will profoundly affect the nature of the world arena in which the United States performs its much heightened responsibilities.

[17] See Morgenthau, *op. cit.*, pp. 352 ff.
[18] The reference is to Walter Prescott Webb, *The Great Frontier* (Boston: Houghton Mifflin Company, 1952). I counted Walter Webb a friend, as did all who knew him. Word of his death came to me at the very moment these words were being written.
[19] See Schleicher, *op. cit.*, pp. 483-85.

This brings us now to the central inquiry of this essay. Given the predominance of American power and the replacement by America of Britain in the power structure of the world, how are we to assess the extent to which, and the way in which, the position and policies of Great Britain affect United States foreign policy?

There is an extremely intimate and reciprocal relation between domestic and foreign policy, and all policy, whether foreign or domestic, must be made (or more accurately "conducted") in an environment that is shaped by other internal policies, by other countries' policies, and by previous decisions and policies. It is particularly true of foreign affairs that policy cannot be made in a vacuum. The factors that mold any country's foreign policy include a great many matters over which the country concerned has literally no control. Such limitations are rightly taken for granted by students and practitioners of foreign policy, but they are not widely understood in America. Many Americans regularly entertain the false notion that the United States has unlimited influence and control, that events throughout the world are subject to its decision, and that unsatisfactory developments (for example, the Communist seizure of China, war in the Middle East, a *rapprochement* between Tito and Khrushchev, the abortion of the Cuban revolution) are somehow America's fault and that such developments are thus manifestly to be attributed to the incompetence or worse of American policy makers.[20] Precisely the opposite is the case. American policy must operate within the limits of the possible alternatives open to it; it is shaped and frequently determined by facts and factors over which America has no control at all; it is limited to a remarkable degree by what Charles Burton Marshall calls the "externalness" of foreign policy.[21] Part of the external circumstances that circumscribe America's policy lie in the character and position of Britain and in Britain's relations with the rest of the world and with us.[22]

THE ESSENTIALS OF BRITAIN'S POSITION

The fundamental character of Britain's world position—the sharp decline in her power and her influence, and thus in her capacity to perform her responsibilities—has led to two closely related developments: The

[20] See D. W. Brogan, "The Illusion of American Omnipotence," *Harper's Magazine,* 205 (December, 1952), 21-28. There is an interesting attempt by Brogan to reassess the "omnipotence" thesis a decade later, in the *Washington Post,* March 10, 1963, p. E 1.

[21] Charles Burton Marshall, *The Limits of Foreign Policy* (New York: Holt, Rinehart & Winston, Inc., 1954), p. 15.

[22] This is an argument to which Lord Strang is most sympathetic. He pursues it both in general terms and from the point of view of the limitations on *British* foreign policy making. See his *Britain in World Affairs,* pp. 369-79.

first is Britain's own contraction of her responsibilities, the better to meet them from her own resources; the second is the shift of many of these responsibilities and functions to the United States.

Britain's relations with the rest of the world, including America, are fundamentally determined by her needs and circumstances at home. It may be useful here briefly to catalog these needs and circumstances:

1. She is a small, overcrowded island, hard by a turbulent continent.
2. She cannot feed even half her people from her own resources.
3. She must accordingly import to live.
4. Similarly, she must export to pay for her imports.
5. She can thus exist only as a highly industrialized nation.
6. Her industries require vast quantities of raw materials.
7. She possesses no raw materials of her own except coal.
8. Her isolated position is no longer safe from attack and is indeed almost indefensible in the nuclear age.

Taking all these requirements and conditions into account, it will be seen that the absolute fundamentals of British policy must be trade and defense and, most particularly, the defense of trade. On these, Britain can afford no compromise, for without them she abandons her vital interests and perhaps ceases to exist.[23]

But Britain, too, must conduct her foreign policy in a set of environing circumstances shaped by her past policies, by her relations with other parts of the world, and by her domestic political imperatives. Thus, while she seeks to protect herself and her trade, her foreign policy, too, is guided by factors that she cannot control:

1. By her obligations to and relations with the Commonwealth and Empire;
2. By her commitments in the system of alliances of which she is a part;
3. By her dependence on American strength;
4. By the need to maintain, so far as possible, full employment and a decent standard of living for her people;
5. By her membership and obligations in the United Nations and other international organizations;
6. By the standards of morality of her people, which preclude an international conduct repugnant to the inherent sense of decency of the British community.

Insofar as she can do so in her reduced circumstances of power, she

[23] Strang, *op. cit.*, p. 380; Morgenthau, *op. cit.*, p. 113; C. M. Woodhouse, *British Foreign Policy Since the Second World War* (New York: Frederick A. Praeger, Inc., 1962), pp. 7-8.

must conduct her relations with the world in the light of these objectives, commitments, criteria, and limitations.

BRITAIN'S IMPORTANCE TO AMERICA

America, no less than Britain, must take into account these factors that influence the formation and conduct of British policy. It may appear to some that there is an unexplained (or unwarranted) assumption in this line of argument, namely that what is important to Britain is *ipso facto* important to the United States. In a broad sense this is true, but the assumption deserves explication. It rests on the need of the United States for competent and reliable allies. Given the nature and scope of American responsibilities in the present world, it is no longer possible to cling to the outworn traditions of isolation and neutrality.

The United States needs allies and alliances and must accept its allies as equally interested, if not equally powerful, partners, cooperating with them in the defense of our vital interests and theirs.[24] Although such a thesis needs no elaborate defense, one may observe that America needs overseas bases, an adequate and distant early-warning system, adequate sources of intelligence, the trade that sustains its economy, and a variety of materials critical for defense which it cannot supply from its own resources. In short, America can no longer indulge its penchant for isolation; no *"festung America"* is adequate to assure our national security. That being the case, there can be no question that the United Kingdom is now, and has long been, our strongest and most dependable ally. The health and security of our primary ally is one of the prime and vital interests of the United States, and hence the security of Britain must be an objective of United States policy. While it is true that British policy and objectives help shape American policy and objectives, there is a more fundamental influence that turns merely on the fact of the Anglo-American alliance. Given her importance to us, the major fact about Britain that conditions our policy is simply *the existence of Great Britain.*

The proposition that Britain is important to America and that America must pay heed to British needs and policies actually takes two different forms. One of these rests on sentiment, the other on realism and the hardheaded assessment of self-interest. The first sort of imperative might well be challenged by those who insist that foreign policy must be shaped exclusively by consideration of power, but it is nonetheless influential in the shaping of policy. By this is meant such things as the long association of the two countries, their shared historical traditions,

---

[24] The point is argued in Charles P. Schleicher, *Introduction to International Relations* (Englewood Cliffs, N.J.: Prentice-Hall, Inc., 1954), p. 338.

their common language, their common pride in free government under law, their common customs and institutions. Also included is what can only be called America's proper sense of respect and gratitude to Britain for standing off the enemy in the years while America was hesitating and preparing. In two world wars, to say nothing of the century that preceded them, Britain protected our security and fought our battle for us. In simple human terms, it would be unthinkable for America to return these favors with ingratitude.

Beyond these matters of sentiment, affection, and gratitude, however, there are other more immediate and more "realistic" reasons for continuing our support for Britain, and other reasons for asserting that Britain is important to America. In the last analysis, the extent to which British factors shape and circumscribe American policy will be measured by the extent to which the British alliance helps America to perform her own responsibilities. To measure this we have only to ask what America's position and strength in the world would be without the British alliance; without our air force, missile, and submarine bases in Britain; without the British Army of the Rhine to support the American forces on the continent; without NATO, CENTO, SEATO, and other regional defense pacts; without the British naval bases in the United Kingdom, the Mediterranean, and elsewhere; without the British nuclear capability aligned on our side; without British assistance and support in our diplomatic dealings with others; and without our ability to rely on a nation of fifty million people committed to the same values as ours, "resolute, ingenious, and brave in war, progressive and industrious in peace." [25]

If this argument is to be accepted, there are two ways in which Britain and British policy must impinge upon and help shape American policy. First, since we need her, we must conduct our policy so as not to jeopardize her vital interests; and second, her own responsibilities and her conduct of affairs will limit and influence the way in which we can conduct our own.[26]

BRITISH POLICIES AND AMERICAN REACTIONS

We have already examined the essentials of the British position that shape her policies and in turn influence ours. Let us now examine some of the specific policies that Britain is compelled to pursue and note how

---

[25] Drew Middleton, *These Are the British* (New York: Alfred A. Knopf, Inc., 1957), p. 160.

[26] A first-rate analysis of the way the British political system has adapted itself to the American alliance is Leon D. Epstein, *Britain—Uneasy Ally* (Chicago: University of Chicago Press, 1954).

they affect American interests and sensibilities. It should be observed that these are only illustrations and by no means a catalog either of British policies or of British policies that affect America.

Trade policy. An extensive foreign trade is a fundamental necessity in Britain's relations with the rest of the world. To live, Britain must keep a healthy import and export trade flowing, in food, raw materials, and manufactures. The habit and exigence of foreign trade is deeply ingrained in the British scheme of politics, for without it she dies. Thus she is predisposed toward a liberal trading policy and toward a trading system as free of restraints as possible. Restrictions on international trade, for whatever purpose and from whatever source, are viewed as imperiling her viability. The United States is not in so exposed a position and is thus freer and more likely to consider foreign trade merely as a part of its total economy, and the regulation of it, whether for economic or political purposes, as merely a part of its total policy. We can use trade barriers, tariffs, embargos, export licensing, and the like as political weapons. We can forbid trade with nations with whom we disagree politically; but when we adopt such policies, we cannot expect Britain to conform to them or to accept them gracefully. Hence, the British resentment against our Battle Act and her refusal to restrict her trade with Russia and China, her complaints of our ban on ships in the Cuba trade, and her entirely different attitudes toward trafficking with such nations as Poland and Yugoslavia. To America trade is important; to Britain it is the whole of existence.

Colonialism. Colonialism represents a whole complex of related problems. The first is the sharply differing attitudes which the two nations bring to the question of colonial empires, "imperialism," and to colonial self-determination. America has traditionally opposed the maintenance of the European empires, doubtless because her own birth took the form of a revolution against the imperial control of Great Britain. With this background, she finds herself instinctively sympathetic to the aspirations of modern colonial peoples. Britain, on the other hand, has never conceived of her empire as a device for exploitation and quite rightly feels that her own empire, at least, has brought a great deal of good to the peoples of her far-flung dependencies. This difference of view has led to repeated disagreements between the two countries. More significantly, it has led them to open disagreements in the councils of various international organizations and in the forum of world opinion. These disagreements extend beyond the bounds of the British territories themselves, ranging across the whole attitude of the two countries toward colonies in general and toward the policies of other colonial powers. Disagreements (concededly sometimes only of degree) have developed over Katanga, Indonesia, South Africa, and Portuguese Africa. The form these questions take in the postwar world confronts America with a difficult policy problem.

America has a natural sympathy for colonial peoples seeking independence, a sympathy born of its own experience and tradition. But she has an equal sympathy for Britain and France and a competing desire to stand firm beside her allies. Thus there is a second problem that disturbs our relations, for British policy and the British position have on many occasions placed America in a dilemma from which there is no easy escape.[27] The problem is all the more acute since America's anticolonial tradition constitutes one of her strongest appeals to the underdeveloped, uncommitted parts of the world in the Cold War struggle. To remain true to this tradition strengthens her appeal to the emerging nations, but doing so risks a loosening of the bonds that tie her European allies to the Atlantic alliance.[28]

Third, despite the speed with which the British colonies have been achieving self-government and independence in the postwar world, some critical problems remain. Britain has accepted responsibilities for the governance, development, welfare, and defense of her colonies, and she cannot easily evade these responsibilities, however much she might like to do so. For some years to come she will have to continue such responsibilities in Africa, Asia, and the Indies. In many areas—Rhodesia being a good current example—the problems to be solved simply cannot be solved to the satisfaction of all the contending parties, let alone to that of the critical observers in the "outer" world. For some "colonial" problems there is simply no solution consistent with responsibilities Britain has undertaken.

Fourth, as the colonies have achieved independence, some of them have been disillusioned with its substance. Economic prosperity and national prestige do not always follow, and the needs of the new nations can sometimes be met only by assistance and support from outside, if not from Britain, then from America or perhaps from Russia. The very withdrawal of Britain from her colonial empire has itself confronted the United States with a host of new problems. However much the United States may wish to settle all these problems with justice and dispatch, she nonetheless is limited in what she can do about them. The diminishing empire, the newly independent circle of nations, and the rapidly changing Commonwealth delimit America no less than

[27] See Leon D. Epstein, "British Foreign Policy," in *Foreign Policy in World Politics* (2nd ed.), ed. Roy C. Macridis (Englewood Cliffs, N.J.: Prentice-Hall, Inc., 1962), pp. 24-25.

[28] See Philip W. Bell, "Colonialism As a Problem in American Foreign Policy," *World Politics*, 5 (1952), 86-109; also Jules Davids, *America and the World of Our Time* (New York: Random House, 1960), pp. 482 ff.

Britain in matters of policy, and constitute factors in the conduct of policy over which America, even more than Britain, has no control.

Defense policy. An area that constitutes an open invitation to misunderstanding and controversy is that of defense policy. Britain has been determined to maintain her own means of defense, including an independent nuclear deterrent, even in an age when an independent system is prohibitively expensive to all but the superpowers. One reason for this is her firm determination to contribute her fair share to the common defense; another is her conviction that only by maintaining her own system will she retain influence in the defense councils of the West and the respect of her potential enemies; still another is the lurking fear in some quarters that the United States might not move to protect Britain in some situations if America herself were not directly threatened. That these reasons are not consistent with one another is of little importance.

Britain now has her own nuclear weapons but still lacks the means of delivering them. The development of the Blue Streak missile, which was intended to be the means of delivery, had to be abandoned when its costs of development rose beyond her capacity to pay. She then made an arrangement with the United States to share the development of the air-to-ground missile, Skybolt, which was to be designed for use in her excellent V-bombers. But the United States, for reasons of its own defense costs and defense planning, decided to abandon Skybolt, which left Britain with no delivery system and no independent deterrent. A heated row ensued, which led to the Nassau agreements by which the United States offered the submarine-launched Polaris to take the place of the abandoned Skybolt. But this left Britain with still another weapon for which she had no method of delivery, for she had no appropriate submarines and would have to obtain them from America; it also left her with a great sense of unease and dissatisfaction. The political debate in Britain that followed these events threatened at one point to topple the Macmillan government.

Running through all these concerns are the chagrin and resentment of a nation that once was and is no more a first-class power. Intellectually, this diminished position has long been accepted, but psychologically the British have a profound, significant, and quite human reluctance to accept it and to face up to its consequences. They are, not surprisingly, more than a little resentful of American strength and leadership, especially when these are displayed in forms and circumstances that pointedly illustrate Britain's decline. The British press spends part of its time admiring and praising America and part of its time scorning and depreciating it. In this continuing mixture of pointing-with-pride and viewing-with-alarm, there is a running temptation to pull Uncle Sam's beard in much the same way we used to enjoy twisting the lion's tail.

When Dean Acheson suggested (as many Britishers had done before him) that Britain was uncertain of her role and was seeking a new place in a changing world, an explosive reaction came from the British press, not because it was untrue or had not been said before, but because an American had said it. When, within a few months of one another in 1962, British aircraft and a British submarine penetrated America's continental defense, the press indulged itself in an orgy of self-congratulation, ill befitting an ally whose security might one day depend on the efficacy of those very defenses.

Britain has sought a special place in the alliance based on her unique Commonwealth ties and on a "special relationship" with the United States, which she could quite legitimately claim. But the withdrawal of Skybolt without prior consultation shattered this special claim to a special relationship. The same thing is true of America's virtually unilateral decision to quarantine Cuba, a policy which Britain supported but which she resented not being consulted upon in advance. Above all, the decision to offer Polaris to France on the very same terms on which it was offered to Britain seemed to make a mockery of the "special relationship." We badly need in international politics an equivalent to the old maxim that "hell hath no fury like a woman scorned."

These attitudes are no doubt inevitable. The United States must learn to understand them and take account of them, to shoulder its own responsibilities without scorning, offending, or patronizing its friend, to make clear its confidence in, and its reliance upon, its British ally. But to do these things requires an acceptance of the limitations on its own conduct and policy that stem from the conditions of Britain's existence.

ANGLO-AMERICAN FRICTIONS

A number of factors produce friction between Britain and the United States.[29] Some have already been mentioned or are implicit in what has been said above, but several others may be identified.

First, there is a mutual skepticism of each other's social patterns and mores. We lampoon the British "accent" and they decry ours, and each tends to stereotype the other's mode of speech in a mold quite unrelated to reality. We are perplexed by their habit of understatement; they tend to accuse all Americans of noisy braggadocio. We scorn their private schools and public medicine; they do not understand why we set so high a premium on public schools and private medicine. We do not under-

---

[29] See the discussion of frictions between the two nations in H. C. Allen, *The Anglo-America Predicament* (New York: St. Martin's Press Inc., 1960), pp. 227-28; also H. L. Roberts and P. A. Wilson, *Britain and the United States: Problems in Co-operation* (London: Royal Institute of International Affairs, 1953).

stand their veneration of tradition and antiquity, and condemn it with
vigor when it extends to plumbing and personal services; they dislike
the hurried pace of our cities and our concern with modernism and
progress, especially when the results appear garish and charmless. They
enshrine tradition; we ennoble efficiency. There is little that either can
do about any of these things.

Second, the British have a difficult time understanding our system
of government, for which one can scarcely blame them. They seem to
have greater difficulty in understanding ours than we have in understanding theirs, perhaps because theirs gives the appearance of somewhat greater simplicity.[30] Their intellectuals have a fair understanding
of the American system and can explain its intricacies without hesitation; yet even the intellectuals are frequently disturbed when something
takes place that illustrates and exemplifies its complex diffusion of authority. When a general tries to frighten Congress into increasing the
military appropriation, when the chairman of an important Senate Committee decries the Russian missiles in Cuba or the advance of Communism in Ghana, when a leading public figure condemns the United
Nations, or when an obscure figure proposes the impeachment of the
Chief Justice, the Englishman doesn't merely point to the diversification
of power in America; he shakes his head and shudders. He does not
fully grasp the basic point that in our fragmented system—with its separation of powers, its constitutional limitations, its federalism, its de-
centralized political parties, its powerful interest groups—a statement
by one person or group, even one with official standing, cannot be taken
as an authoritative statement of United States policy.

Of profound significance in this connection was the checkered, though
brief, career of Senator McCarthy. The techniques he employed and
the attitude he symbolized, perhaps more than any single development
in the postwar era, shook England's confidence in America.[31] McCarthyism appeared to the British to undermine the very foundations of the
free society, the more so because of the extensive public support it
seemed to attract. McCarthy struck fear into the hearts of Britain, not

---

[30] The British system concentrates control over foreign policy no less than over domestic policy. There is a useful brief comparison of the British and American methods
in Morgenthau's chapter on "The American Tradition in Foreign Policy," in Macridis,
op. cit., pp. 216 ff. The standard work on the machinery of government is Lord Strang,
The Foreign Office, in the New Whitehall Series (London: George Allen & Unwin,
1955); but see also the more recent book by Donald G. Bishop, *The Administration of
British Foreign Relations* (Syracuse, N.Y.: Syracuse University Press, 1961), which is
considerably broader in scope.

[31] See two comments, one by an Englishman and one by an American correspondent
in Britain, written while McCarthyism was still active: Oliver S. Franks, *Britain and
the Tide of World Affairs* (London: Oxford University Press, 1955), pp. 28-29; and
Drew Middleton, *These Are the British*, pp. 163-66.

only because he was distasteful and frightening in his ruthlessness, but because he represented a shocking irresponsibility in the use of public power. The British are not quite prepared to trust United States leadership, all the more perhaps because they must. They have not accustomed themselves to the American propensity for all-or-nothing alternatives that categorize everything into win or no-win, peace or war, black or white. They have not by any means forgotten John Foster Dulles's threats of "brinkmanship," of "massive retaliation," and of "agonizing reappraisal." These things give our policy making, in British eyes, the appearance of being mercurial, volatile, unreliable, unskilled, and unsophisticated.

Beyond these concerns, though perhaps related to them, there is a profoundly important difference in the character of the two communities and in the political style and value system of the two peoples. Britain still retains much of the character of the old organic, pyramidally structured, highly integrated state of prerevolutionary days. Her society retains much of the old order, with its stable hierarchy of classes, its habitual deference to authority, its crown power and paternalism.[32] America, on the other hand, was born into the age of liberalism, individualism, and rationalism. The very founding of America, to say nothing of its revolution against the old authority, was a protest against the norms and conformity of the older system, and the values of our founding fathers were those of eighteenth-century liberalism, which have been perpetuated, not only in our constitutional system, but in our habits of thought about politics.

Thus we tend to be extremely sensitive to what people think of us. We look for quick and ready solutions—"rational" solutions—to foreign policy problems, conceiving war and stress to be unusual and temporary aberrations from the "normalcy" of peace and prosperity. We scorn a "no-win" policy and demand a total victory. When war comes, we abandon politics in the conviction that wars are military matters and are to be won, not dickered about. We yearn for the unconditional surrender of our enemies, and find it burdensome and exasperating to think in terms of long-run struggles, cold wars, and peace without victory. We tend, moreover, to think that our values are universal and that those who differ with us are either charlatans or simpletons.[33]

The American tradition is pragmatic, just as the English tradition is empirical. Thus we should both be able to accommodate to new situations, eschewing logic as an alien French invention. But the British are

---

[32] See the analysis in F. S. C. Northrop, *The Meeting of East and West* (New York: The Macmillan Company, 1946), Chap. 4.

[33] There is a lucid and vigorous argument on the effect of American liberalism on United States foreign policy in John Spanier, *American Foreign Policy Since World War II*, rev. ed. (New York: Frederick A. Praeger, Inc., 1962), Chap. 1. See also Morgenthau, *Politics Among Nations*, 3rd ed., pp. 36-37.

more consistent in their empiricism,[34] while we are more ideological about our pragmatism. There is a great deal of ideology and doctrinaire argument in the American political habit[35] which frequently leaves our British ally not a little impatient. Our attitudes toward Yugoslavia, Poland, and China may serve to illustrate the difference.

The truth is that the British are more tolerant than the Americans, however much the latter speak of freedom and the melting pot. The British toleration of diversity and eccentricity, especially political eccentricity, is a constant mystery and a frequent irritant to Americans. While our consensus is as broad as theirs, it is a more insistent consensus, and its very breadth makes us suspicious of the eccentric. As likely as not, whenever we are threatened externally, we decide that someone has broken the consensus, and we seek to explain the threat by searching out scapegoats and calling them subversives.[36]

There are elements in the domestic politics of Britain that provoke American distrust, just as there are elements in our politics that the British find distasteful. One of these is the deep strain of British pacificism that colors much of the debate on military and security matters. This harks back to the missionary zeal of the early nineteenth century and even farther to the exactions of the "nonconformist conscience." It leads in these days to the Committee of 100 and the movement for unilateral disarmament. It leads to the running fire of criticism of American "militarism" and American leadership. But Americans often forget that this does not constitute majority opinion in Britain any more than McCarthy represented majority opinion in America.

Another sore point in American eyes is the British resort to socialism in the years after the Second World War. It is no good arguing that this is quite irrelevant to the issues of Anglo-American relations (which it is), in view of the widespread American antipathy toward anything called "socialism." Americans are gradually learning that socialism is not communism, that it is not a dirty word everywhere, as it has been in America, and that British socialism is a rather pale version, after all. But it is a source of skepticism in the United States and a point of irritation between the two countries. It seems fair to say that more Americans than not are skeptical of the British left, just as it seems fair to say that more Britishers than not are apprehensive of the American right. Each nation, however, must make a point of not intruding upon the other's

---

[34] See Strang, *Britain in World Affairs*, pp. 359-60.

[35] This is a principal thesis of Louis Hartz, *The Liberal Tradition in America* (New York: Harcourt, Brace & World, Inc., 1955). On the American inexperience in world leadership and the problems this creates, see the trenchant essay by William Lee Miller, "The American Ethos and the Alliance System," in *Alliance Policy in the Cold War,* ed. Arnold Wolfers (Baltimore: The Johns Hopkins Press, 1959).

[36] Spanier, *op. cit.,* p. 3.

domestic party struggles. On the whole, the record of each is very good on this score, but it is a permanent problem and requires continuous self-restraint, for the issues between the parties in either country are frequently the issues that are critical in the relations between the two countries. Provocation is easy to incur and rifts are difficult to mend.

But when all these things have been said and when all the sources of friction have been catalogued, one must still conclude that the factors that unite the two countries are far more profoundly important than those that divide them.[37] The possession of common traditions, values, language, institutions, aspirations, and objectives will, because it must, overcome the divisive influences. Bernard Shaw once remarked that we are two people divided by a common language, a remark which, however witty, is not true. What is true is rather that we seem to be so much alike that we run the constant risk of assuming that we are more alike than we are. What is important is not the superficial similarity of speech and style, nor indeed the fleeting frictions fostered by our fears and phobias, but the profound likeness of our long-run interests and our mutual interdependence in their pursuit. American policy can only be conducted with these interests in view; which is to say that Britain will continue to influence our conduct of affairs because her existence, her prosperity and strength, and her continued support are important to us. One need not perhaps belabor the obvious point that America is even more important to Britain.

[37] For attempts to catalog these factors, see Brinton, *op. cit.*, p. 266; Allen, *Great Britain and the United States*, pp. 202-7; Allen, *The Anglo-American Predicament*, pp. 229-30; and L. M. Hacker, *England and America: The Ties That Bind* (Oxford: Clarendon Press, 1948).

Suggestions for Further Reading

Allen, H. C., *The Anglo-American Predicament*. New York: St. Martin's Press, Inc., 1960.

——, *Great Britain and the United States: A History of Anglo-American Relations, 1783-1952*. New York: St. Martin's Press, Inc., 1955.

Bishop, Donald G., *The Administration of British Foreign Relations*. Syracuse, N.Y.: Syracuse University Press, 1961.

Brogan, D. W., "The Illusion of American Omnipotence," *Harper's Magazine*, 205 (December, 1952), 21-28.

Epstein, Leon, *Britain—Uneasy Ally*. Chicago: University of Chicago Press, 1954.

Franks, Oliver S., *Britain and the Tide of World Affairs*. London: Oxford University Press, 1955.

Gelber, Lionel, *America in Britain's Place*. New York: Frederick A. Praeger, Inc., 1961.

Middleton, Drew, *The Supreme Choice: Britain and the European Community.* London: Secker & Warburg, 1963.

Northedge, F. S., *British Foreign Policy.* New York: Frederick A. Praeger, Inc., 1963.

Strang, Lord, *Britain in World Affairs: The Fluctuation in Power and Influence from Henry VIII to Elizabeth II.* New York: Frederick A. Praeger, Inc., 1961.

————, *The Foreign Office,* New Whitehall Series. London: George Allen & Unwin, 1955.

Woodhouse, C. M., *British Foreign Policy Since the Second World War.* New York: Frederick A. Praeger, Inc., 1962.

THE FUTURE OF
THE COMMUNIST BLOC
AND AMERICAN FOREIGN POLICY

Merle Fainsod

Prophecy in human affairs is a notoriously hazardous enterprise; veteran practitioners of the craft have learned through sad experience either to hedge their bets or to reserve their flat predictions for periods so distant from the present that those who read them will never have an opportunity to check them. In undertaking to discuss the future of the Communist bloc, this writer lays no claim to prescience; indeed, he is profoundly skeptical of anyone's capacity to foresee the precise shape of future events. The aim in this essay is not to predict what will happen, but to project various alternative paths of development and to examine their implications for American foreign policy, while recognizing that the actual sequence of events may not conform to any of the alternatives considered.

THE NEW PARTY PROGRAM AND THE KHRUSHCHEVIAN PROPHECY

Khrushchev's vision of the future as it was unveiled in the new Party Program approved by the Twenty-Second Party Congress serves as a

MERLE FAINSOD *is Professor of Government and Director of the Russian Research Center at Harvard University. He is author of* American People and Their Government *(with A. J. Lein),* Government and the American Economy *(with A. L. Gordon),* Smolensk Under Soviet Rule, *and* How Russia is Ruled. *An earlier version of this paper was originally prepared for a May, 1962, Conference on the Soviet Bloc, sponsored by the Public Affairs Conference Center of the University of Chicago. The Center has kindly granted permission to publish the paper in this form.*

convenient starting point for this discussion. The Program outlines a series of ambitious and grandiose goals for the next two decades. It predicts that the Soviet Union will surpass the United States in "production per head of population" within the current (1961-70) decade, and that by 1980 total industrial output will increase by not less than 500 per cent over the 1960 level. It proclaims that agricultural output will mount by 150 per cent in the next ten years and by 250 per cent in twenty years. It promises that Soviet national income will increase 400 per cent by 1980, and that real income per capita will grow by more than 250 per cent in the same period. To Soviet workers and farmers who are still plagued by an inadequate supply of consumer goods and housing, it holds out the alluring prospect of an abundance of goods; a 34-36 hour work week within the next decade; solution of the housing problem; free rent, water, gas, heating, and public transport; free midday factory and school meals; and an expansion of free medicine, vacation, education, and other social services.

But the new Party Program also makes clear that these goals cannot be attained without hard work. "To achieve [them] it is necessary to raise productivity of labor in industry by more than 100 per cent within ten years, and by 300 to 350 per cent within twenty years." Communism, the Program adds, "does not release the members of society from work. It will by no means be a society of anarchy, idleness, and inactivity." [1] The Program also warns that the promised material benefits can only be vouchsafed under conditions of peace and a substantial reduction in the armament burden. "Complications in the international situation and the resultant necessity of increasing defense expenditures may hold up the fulfillment of the plans for raising the living standards of the people." As long as imperialism survives and the threat of war persists, "the strengthening of the defense potential of the USSR" will remain "a most important function of the Socialist state." In the words of the Program, "the Soviet state will see to it that its armed forces are powerful; that they have the most up-to-date means of defending the country—atomic and thermonuclear weapons, rockets of every range—and that they keep all types of military equipment and all weapons up to standard." [2] Khrushchev's welfare blueprint is thus hedged with reservations.

The new Party Program must, of course, be read as music of the future with the notes still to be played. It incorporates the hopes, aspirations, and dreams on which Khrushchev and company subsist. The prediction that the Soviet Union will attain industrial supremacy within the next decade assumes that the American and West European economies will be stagnant or grow very slowly, an assumption that the future is very likely

[1] *Pravda*, November 2, 1961.
[2] *Ibid.*

to belie. The ambitious goals projected for the development of the Soviet economy posit an extraordinary effort on the part of the Soviet populace, which may or may not be forthcoming.

Given the history of past agricultural failures and disappointments, the likelihood of an expansion of Soviet agricultural output on the scale projected by the Party Program appears remote, unless the Party leadership pours much heavier capital inputs into agriculture than it has been prepared to do up to this time. The standard of living of the Soviet citizenry can be expected to register improvement over the next decades, but it has far to go before it can begin to catch up with the prevailing level in the advanced countries of the West. Given the Soviet commitment to continuing heavy investments in basic industries and the possibility that the arms burden will not lessen and may even increase, the vision of plenty which the Program outlines for the Soviet consumer may well prove a mirage. Should an improvement in relations with the West make a substantial reduction of armament expenditures possible, the prospect of more rapid improvement in the level of consumer welfare would brighten considerably.

The vista which Khrushchev holds out to his followers is the inevitable triumph of communism on a world scale, to be achieved without igniting a thermonuclear holocaust. In his view the Soviet Union is no longer an isolated island in the capitalist sea. It has broken out of the ring of capitalist encirclement, and it is now a system on the move, destined to sweep the world. Equipped with the most advanced military weapons and supported by powerful allies in Asia and Europe, it need fear no attack from the declining capitalist world; a world war, in Khrushchev's words, "is no longer fatalistically inevitable." As Khrushchev sees it, the magnetic attraction of the Soviet example, with its demonstration of the superior productivity of the Soviet system, will attract increasing numbers of converts throughout the world. In many countries, local Communist forces mobilizing sympathetic allies may come to power by parliamentary means; in other countries where "capitalism" is strongly entrenched and offers armed resistance, force may be necessary to dislodge oppressor regimes.

Kremlin dreams of world power are not based on military force alone. It is an article of faith among Khrushchev's ideologues that economic crises in the West, the rivalries of the so-called imperialist states, the disintegration of the colonial system, and the superior production potential of the Soviet planned economy will ultimately lead to the collapse of capitalism and the triumph of world communism. As Khrushchev said in an interview with Adlai Stevenson, "You must understand, Mr. Stevenson, that we are living in an epoch when one system is giving way to another; . . . a process is taking place in which the peoples want to live under a new system of society; and it is necessary that one agree and reconcile oneself to this fact. The process should take place without interference." [3]

But Khrushchev is also prepared to prod history along where it appears to need prodding. His strategy dictates constant probing for weak spots in the enemy armor, exploiting divisions within the camp of his opponents, and pressing forward to consolidate new positions wherever the will to resist crumbles. He sees particularly promising opportunities in the underdeveloped parts of the world. He woos the new nations of Asia and Africa and independence movements struggling to cast off the shackles of colonialism by identifying himself with their national aspirations and their historic anti-imperialist grievances, and in return he hopes for their support in his drive to undermine the position of the West. Wherever the situation is ripe and local nationalist leadership is receptive, Communist leaders are encouraged to form coalitions with friendly elements in so-called national democratic governments, to strive to attain strategic positions within them, and to press for their ultimate transformation into full-fledged Communist regimes. As Khrushchev envisages the world, communism is on the march and capitalism is in decline. By a skillful combination and application of Soviet military and economic power, diplomacy, propaganda, and infiltration, he hopes to accelerate the process, to force the so-called capitalist nations to surrender their positions without offering forceful resistance, and to win his way to victory without the destruction of his own home base.

The 1960 Moscow Declaration of the Representatives of the Eighty-One Communist Parties makes these designs clear:

The near future will bring the forces of peace and socialism new successes. The USSR will become the leading industrial power of the world. China will become a mighty industrial state. The socialist system will be turning out more than half of the world industrial output. The peace zone will expand. The working-class movement in the capitalist countries and the national-liberation movement in the colonies and dependencies will achieve new victories. The disintegration of the colonial system will become complete. The superiority of the forces of socialism and peace will be absolute. [4]

In these preconditions Khrushchev sees the possibility of achieving a Communist victory on a world scale without precipitating a nuclear war.

The doctrine of peaceful coexistence which Khrushchev preaches is not a formula for stabilizing the boundaries between the Communist and non-Communist parts of the world; it is rather a recipe for "weakening

[3] Quoted in David J. Dallin, *Soviet Policy After Stalin* (Philadelphia: J. B. Lippincott Co., 1961), p. 506.
[4] *Pravda,* December 6, 1960.

imperialism" and neutralizing and eliminating any opposition to the Communist forward march. The Declaration is explicit on this point: "Peaceful coexistence of states does not imply renunciation of the class struggle, as the revisionists claim. The coexistence of states with different social systems does not mean conciliation of the socialist and bourgeois ideologies. On the contrary, it implies intensification of the struggle of the working class, of all the Communist Parties, for the triumph of social-ist ideas. . . ." [5] While the Declaration expresses the hope that the so-called capitalist nations will retire from the world scene peacefully, it also adds the following warning: "The possibility of nonpeaceful transi-tion to socialism should be borne in mind. Leninism teaches, and experi-ence confirms, that the ruling class never relinquishes power voluntarily. In this case the degree of bitterness and the forms of class struggle will depend not so much on the proletariat as on the resistance put up by the reactionary circles to the will of the overwhelming majority of the people, on these circles using force at one or another stage of the struggle for socialism." [6] In any case, the Declaration promises: "The working class and its revolutionary vanguard [read Communist Party] will with increasing energy press forward its offensive against the domination of oppressors and exploiters in every field of political, economic, and ideo-logical activity in each country. In the process of their struggle, the masses are prepared and conditions arise for decisive battles for the overthrow of capitalism, for the victory of socialist revolution." [7]

This, then, is the Khrushchevian prophecy, the plan of action, and the path of development outlined for the next decades. Whether it will be realized depends not only on internal developments within the Soviet Union and the Communist camp, but perhaps even more on the character of the response which it elicits in the West and in the underdeveloped parts of the world. If Western military, scientific, and technical progress lags behind Soviet achievements, if the Western economies enter a phase of depression and stagnation, if the West is unable to maintain its solidarity in the face of the Soviet challenge and weakly yields to Soviet pressure, and if the non-Communist leaders of the underdeveloped na-tions encounter insurmountable obstacles in attempting to resolve their problems, then the Soviet leadership will, of course, be greatly aided in fulfilling its professed objectives. If, conversely, the West enjoys military, technical, and scientific superiority, maintains a dynamic, growing, and expanding economy, preserves its solidarity and its capacity to resist Soviet pressure, and finds ways of helping the underdeveloped nations to ease the strains of modernization and industrialization, the prospect that the Khrushchevian vision will be realized would appear to be dim.

[5] *Ibid.*
[6] *Ibid.*
[7] *Ibid.*

POLYCENTRIC TENDENCIES WITHIN THE COMMUNIST ORBIT

Meanwhile, the Soviet leadership faces problems within the Communist camp itself—problems which are likely to affect the shape of things to come. Relationships within the Communist orbit have changed considerably since Stalin's time. Under Stalin, Yugoslavia was lost to the bloc, but the remaining European satellites were tightly controlled from Moscow and subject to Stalin's every whim. Communist China constituted a special case; its economic needs and political orientation enforced a certain dependence on Moscow, but its political leadership was independently based and outside Stalin's control.

Under Khrushchev, polycentric tendencies within the orbit have become more sharply evident.[8] Efforts to woo Tito back into the fold have thus far enjoyed only partial success, though relationships have substantially improved, and on many important foreign policy issues Soviet and Yugoslav positions coincide. The Hungarian revolt and the Polish display of independence in the fall of 1956 provided dramatic evidence of the resentment which Soviet domination inspired, and though the Hungarian uprising was suppressed and terms of accommodation were worked out with the Poles which yielded them a measure of autonomy in domestic affairs, the underlying lack of support which Moscow could command in these areas was strikingly demonstrated. While Poland managed to retain a certain special position in regulating its internal life, and while Albania (most distant from the Soviet Union) placed itself under Chinese protection after breaking with Khrushchev, the rest of the European satellite regimes follow the Soviet lead and remain dependent on Moscow for their lives.

Khrushchev's formula for holding the remaining European satellites in check and welding them to the Soviet Union is a complex mixture of a number of ingredients. The overhanging threat of Soviet military intervention is designed to prevent a repetition of the Hungarian revolt. Stalin's policy of exploiting the satellite economies in the interest of the Soviet Union has been substantially abandoned, and in a number of instances Soviet aid has been extended to prop up shaky regimes. The effort to build unity on a basis more solid than brute force alone has taken the form of seeking to integrate the economies of the satellites with each other and with the Soviet Union, establishing a joint military command, stressing common interests in foreign policy, cultivating ideological and cultural ties, and permitting the satellite parties to accommodate their patterns of rule to the diversities of the local scene.

Despite these efforts, it appears extremely doubtful that the deeply

[8] See Zbigniew Brzezinski, *The Soviet Bloc: Unity and Conflict* (Cambridge, Mass.: Harvard University Press, 1960).

rooted national loyalties of the people in the European satellite nations can readily be transferred to the Soviet cause. Where fairly strong indigenous Communist parties existed prior to the Soviet take-over, as in Czechoslovakia and Bulgaria, the task may be somewhat less difficult; but even in these countries national feelings run strong, and they will not easily be obliterated. The combination of Soviet military power and the controls exercised by local Communist cadres appear sufficiently formidable now to prevent the secession of the remaining European satellites from the Communist camp. Underlying yearnings for freedom and independence persist, however, and they may yet rise to plague the Soviet leadership if circumstances develop which permit their effective expression. Any long-term developments which serve to weaken the Soviet control system and to discourage direct Soviet military intervention in the satellite areas should operate to give these forces freer play. In preparing for such a contingency, Western policy makers would probably be well-advised to keep their channels of communication with the satellite peoples open, and to exert such leverage as they possess to reinforce and strengthen the remaining aspirations for independence.

RELATIONS WITH COMMUNIST CHINA

Relations with Communist China present the Soviet Union with a different array of problems.[9] At the present time, the Soviet Union and Communist China are both increasingly uneasy partners and bitter competitors —partners in the sense that they both share a common interest in weakening and eliminating their "imperialist" antagonists, and competitors in that they find themselves divided by profound conflicts on appropriate strategy and tactics and by rival ambitions to assert authority and establish spheres of influence in the Communist camp. At the root of these disagreements are very great discrepancies in the developmental levels of the two nations and very different conceptions of the priorities which the needs of development and revolutionary advance impose.

The Soviet Union has reached a relatively high stage of industrialization; it believes that its experience has universal validity for the entire Communist movement, and it is not ready to sacrifice its own further development to the task of bringing the Chinese economy up to the level of its own. The Soviet leadership, moreover, has a vested interest in preserving its own hard-won gains, and it sees the future triumph of communism as evolving out of the power which it is building and the magnetic attraction of the example which it represents. While the Soviet leadership is prepared to take risks to speed victory, it seeks to avoid a

---

[9] See Donald S. Zagoria, *The Sino-Soviet Conflict, 1956-1961* (Princeton, N.J.: Princeton University Press, 1962).

thermonuclear Armageddon which would destroy everything that it has so painfully achieved since 1917.

Communist China, on the other hand, is still an industrially backward country with acute economic problems. Its ambitious industrialization program has been slowed down by severe internal strains and the relatively limited economic aid which has been forthcoming from the other members of the Communist camp. Its efforts to raise the output of its primitive agricultural sector by imposing the discipline of the communes on the countryside have largely been nullified by a combination of natural disasters, the pressures of a burgeoning population, and the passive resistance of the peasantry. While modifications have been made in the commune system to placate discontent, and while industrialization goals have been trimmed to take account of realities, the frustration which this has engendered has only served to accentuate the sense of urgency which impels the Chinese Party leadership to press for a speedy Communist victory on a world scale.

Deeply resentful that more generous aid from the Soviet Union has not been forthcoming, and breathing the evangelical messianism so characteristic of the first phase of the revolutionary cycle, the dominant Chinese leadership has been severely critical of Khrushchev and his cohorts for their lack of revolutionary ardor and their unwillingness to take risks to advance the Communist cause. As the Chinese see it, the balance of military power now lies with the Communist camp, and they would like to see it brought to bear to achieve quick political gains. In their eyes, the task of revolutionaries is to make revolutions, and they criticize the Russians for their failure to pursue more aggressive tactics. They profoundly distrust the Khrushchevian view that the road to communism lies through propaganda for peace and disarmament, or through interim cooperation with bourgeois nationalist regimes, or through any other tactics which run the danger of diverting revolutionary energies from the direct realization of revolutionary aims.

From Peiping's point of view, the most important arena of struggle is Asia, since this is the area where Communist China's vital interests come to a focus. Of these interests, none is more immediately important than a Communist take-over in Taiwan, though Chinese expansionist ambitions are by no means limited to Taiwan. Soviet support for an all-out assault on Taiwan has been inhibited by the fear of igniting a nuclear war. The Chinese Communist leaders find this fear hard to understand or forgive since in their eyes the Americans are a "paper tiger" doomed to collapse in the face of Soviet military superiority. As Peiping sees it, the highest priority should be given to strengthening the military and industrial might of Communist China itself; again, they find it hard to comprehend why the Soviet Union should be squandering large resources to bulwark non-Communist states such as Egypt and India, when such resources might better be used to strengthen China and other members of the Communist camp, or be made available to support the revolutionary activities of Communist parties in non-Communist lands. While the Chinese Communists themselves pursue the contradictory line of wooing neutral support through aid programs in their own immediate interest, they view Soviet efforts in the same direction as strengthening the very forces which will oppose communism in the long run. They see the danger dramatically illustrated in the Soviet posture of neutrality on the Sino-Indian border dispute; the facts that the Soviet Union has done much to ingratiate itself with India and that the leadership of India's Communist Party, under Soviet tutelage, has supported the position of the Indian government only add fuel to the flames.

Nor do these exhaust the issues in dispute. The Chinese have looked to the Soviet Union to provide them with a nuclear capability and missile strength; so far, Moscow has withheld them, though it has made an experimental nuclear reactor available and has trained Chinese physicists and engineers. The dimensions of economic and technical aid and the terms of trade between the two countries have provided still another fertile source of friction. From the Soviet point of view, the help granted after the Chinese Communist victory appeared generous; the Chinese, on the other hand, saw Soviet assistance as meager and niggardly, all the more so because of the large Soviet commitments to such non-Communist countries as Egypt, India, Indonesia, and Iraq. By 1956 Chinese exports to the Soviet Union slightly exceeded imports. As relations between China and the Soviet Union continued to deteriorate during the next years, the Soviet Union applied economic sanctions. Soviet technicians in China were ordered home; trade between the two countries contracted sharply; and by 1961 Chinese exports to the Soviet Union (in repayment of earlier debts) were substantially in excess of imports.[10] As the Chinese later revealed, "After the Bucharest meeting [June, 1960] some comrades who had attacked the Chinese Communist Party lost no time in taking a series of grave steps applying economic and political pressure against China. Disregarding international practice, they perfidiously and unilaterally tore up agreements and contracts they had concluded with a fraternal country. These agreements and contracts are to be counted, not in twos or in threes, but in hundreds." [11]

There are also border problems. Since the Communist victory in China, the Russians have withdrawn from Manchuria and Sinkiang, both regions of traditional Russian interest, and the Chinese have consolidated their control in these areas. Soviet influence is paramount in Outer Mongolia,

---

[10] For trade data, see William E. Griffith, *Albania and the Sino-Soviet Rift* (Cambridge, Mass.: The M.I.T. Press, 1963), p. 154.

[11] *The People's Daily*, February 27, 1963.

while North Korea has increasingly been drawn into the Chinese camp. China's teeming population generates pressure for expansion, and the common border between China and the Soviet Union is a long one. Responding to taunts from Khrushchev that the Chinese Communists have yet to reclaim Hong Kong and Macao from the "imperialist" powers, a Peiping *People's Daily* editorial on March 8, 1963, reminded him that the Soviet Union still occupied territories north of the Amur River and in Turkestan which China had been forced to cede to Tsarist Russia under pressure. Peking thus implicitly raised the question of a redrawing of the Sino-Soviet frontier. While there is no present indication of any Chinese disposition to do more than stake out legal claims, over the long run the possibility of a Chinese advance into the relatively open spaces of the Soviet Far East cannot be foreclosed.

RIFTS IN THE WORLD COMMUNIST MOVEMENT

Sino-Soviet rivalries have also manifested themselves in a struggle for power and influence within the world Communist movement. The latest phase of the conflict has been building up since 1957. Central to it are two very different conceptions of Communist global strategy as well as important differences on the question of how communism is to be built once a Communist Party achieves power. As D. S. Zagoria recently put it:

Not only does Peking reject the "general line" of the USSR both in foreign and domestic policy for itself, but, in many areas of the world, particularly in the underdeveloped countries, it seeks to impose its own line. It seeks to change the revolutionary strategy of many of the Communist parties in the underdeveloped countries in a left-wing direction, and in those underdeveloped countries ruled by Communist parties, it seeks to export some of its own experience in building Communism at a headlong pace. . . . The Russians, for their part, although aware that they cannot impose their will on the Chinese, will not allow the Chinese to set themselves up as leaders of Communism's Eastern empire. The result is fierce competition and conflict in many areas throughout the world, competition which has already produced profound changes in the relations between Moscow and Peking; in the relations within the Communist world, and, not least important, in the relations between the Communist Bloc and the Western World.[12]

In recent years, evidences of the struggle have become openly visible and are reflected in the marked cooling of relations between the two

[12] D. S. Zagoria, *The Sino-Soviet Conflict Over the Transition to Communism*, RAND Corporation Study P-2397 (August 7, 1961), pp. 1-2.

Communist giant powers. The available reports on the Bucharest Conference of Communist Parties in Moscow in November-December, 1960, indicate that they were characterized by the sharpest kind of disagreement between the Russian and Chinese delegations.[13] The Declaration which emerged from the Moscow meeting, although intended as a demonstration of unity, actually represented a patched-up compromise which could not obscure the fact of fundamental differences. During the next year, the leaders of the Albanian Party, Hoxha and Shehu, who had been disaffected in the first instance by Khrushchev's efforts to woo their enemy Tito back into the bloc, who were critical of the consequences of the 1956 de-Stalinization campaign, and who resented Soviet intervention on behalf of their intra-Party opponents, moved toward open defiance of Khrushchev and found protectors and patrons in the Chinese Party.

The widening rift found dramatic expression at the Twenty-Second Congress of the Soviet Party in October, 1961. Fearing that the Albanian heresy would infect other parties unless it was quickly checked, Khrushchev used the platform of the Congress to launch a wholesale condemnation of the Albanian Party leaders, charged them with all the sins of Stalinism, and identified them with the splitting tactics of the anti-Party group. While Khrushchev's attack was directed against the Albanians, its application to the Chinese Communists was unmistakable. Chou En-lai, the leader of the Communist delegation at the Congress, rose to the challenge and replied in kind. Without directly attacking the Soviet Party leadership, he nevertheless made his displeasure clear and, by the sharpness of his denunciation of American imperialism and Yugoslav revisionism, he implied that Khrushchev was "soft" on both. His departure for China shortly after concluding his speech, the full-dress welcome which he was accorded in Peiping, and the subsequent support given to the Albanians, indicated the Chinese determination to stand firm.

Khrushchev's campaign against the Albanians at the Party Congress was far from being an undiluted success. Of the sixty-eight foreign delegates whose speeches were published in *Pravda,* forty-four denounced the Albanians and twenty-four refrained.[14] With the lone exception of the Ceylonese, all the delegates of the Asian parties abstained from the attack. While these abstentions did not necessarily imply support of the Chinese or Albanian position, they did point to a desire not to offend the Chinese. The striking concentration of a neutral stance among the Asian parties could only have given Khrushchev pause.

In the aftermath of the Party Congress, relations between Khrushchev and the Chinese Communists continued to deteriorate. At the Fifth

---

[13] See especially, William E. Griffith, "The November 1960 Moscow Meeting: A Preliminary Reconstruction," *China Quarterly* (July-September, 1962), 38-57.

[14] D. S. Zagoria, *The Sino-Soviet Conflict, 1956-1961,* p. 451.

World Federation of Trade Unions Congress at Moscow (December 4-15, 1961), at the Stockholm session of the World Peace Council (December 16-19, 1961), and in meetings of the Afro-Asian Solidarity Committee (December, 1961) and the Afro-Asian Writers Conference in Cairo (February, 1962), differences between the Soviet and Chinese delegations were openly and sharply ventilated, and polemics between Soviet and Sino-Albanian ideological spokesmen became increasingly bitter in tone. After a brief lull in April-June, 1962, when an effort was made on both sides to limit public airing of the dispute, by midsummer the conflict resumed in intensified form as Khrushchev pursued his *rapprochement* with Tito and moved to complete the isolation of Albania from the Soviet European bloc.

The Sino-Indian border conflict and the Cuban crisis in October, 1962, contributed to deepening the cleavages between Moscow and Peiping. From the Chinese point of view, Soviet neutrality on the Sino-Indian border dispute and the continuation of Soviet military and economic aid to India constituted a clear betrayal of the demands of international Communist solidarity. In the eyes of Khrushchev, on the other hand, the Chinese invasion of India constituted a deliberate attempt to sabotage Soviet policy toward the neutral world, with the possibly disastrous consequence of pushing one of its leaders, Nehru, into the arms of the West. Soviet behavior during the Cuban crisis also became a bitter focal point of dispute. While Khrushchev sought to justify his actions on the ground that he had obtained an American guarantee that Cuba would not be invaded, the Chinese charged him with the double crime of "adventurism" and "capitulationism," of first taking excessive risks and then retreating in the face of American pressure.

These events were succeeded by a renewed outburst of polemics and maneuverings for support in the international Communist movement. During the winter of 1962-1963, five Communist Party congresses took place: the Bulgarian (November 5-14), the Hungarian (November 20-24), the Italian (December 2-8), the Czecho-Slovak (December 4-8), and the East German (January 15-21). Khrushchev used them not only to rally his followers, but also to condemn the Chinese position and to obtain a formal ratification of his policies in what Soviet commentators sought to present as a series of international Communist forums. The Chinese, as might be expected, refused to recognize the proceedings as in any way binding and continued firmly to press their views. Each succeeding Congress added to the discord and contributed to highlight the substantive differences on policy and organizational questions. In the aftermath of the Congresses, the feuding intensified, with both sides restating their basic positions and refusing to give ground.

Both the Chinese and the Soviets thus far appear reluctant to press their differences to the point of a complete organizational break. Neither, however, has yet evidenced any readiness to make significant concessions on the basic issues involved in the dispute.[15] Whether the momentum of the dispute will carry forward to a complete break depends on how both parties strike a balance between mutual need and an intransigent determination not to compromise their views. If the Chinese leadership continues vigorously to press its drive to gain hegemony within the international Communist movement, Khrushchev may be left with no alternative except to move toward a split. Yet if one takes into account Communist China's present economic difficulties, her need for economic, military, and political assistance, and the palpable short-run advantages which would accrue to both Moscow and Peiping in coordinating their efforts, reason would appear to dictate an effort on both sides to impose limits on the dispute. That reason will prevail is no more certain in the Communist world than anywhere else.

Over the long run, the prospect that the Soviet Union and Communist China can compose their differences does not appear bright. Should China succeed in its drive to industrialize and build economic and military strength, its capacity to pursue an independent policy and challenge Soviet leadership of the bloc will be sharply reinforced. In their present relatively weak position, the Chinese Communists have already thrown down the gauntlet to Moscow; as their power grows, they can be expected to intensify the challenge. Over time, the relations between Communist China and the Soviet Union are likely to become increasingly troublesome; should China spurt ahead to become a leading military and industrial power, it is not inconceivable that the day may yet come when the Soviet Union will help forge a Grand Alliance to contain China's outward thrust.

Meanwhile, the effect of the Sino-Soviet dispute is to undermine the political and ideological unity of the Communist world. The world Communist movement can no longer be viewed as a monolith subject to Soviet direction and control. The emergence of two centers of power in Moscow and Peiping, with Tito representing still another magnetic pole of attraction on the fringes, makes for a much more complex equation in which the loyalties of Communist believers are exposed to great strain. Carried to an extreme, the struggle between the Chinese and the Russians could lead to a split in the international Communist movement, with

[15] See the recent exchanges of letters between the Chinese and Soviet Communist Parties: the Russian letter of February 21, 1963, the Chinese reply of March 9, 1963, the Russian response of March 30, 1963, the Chinese answer of June 14, 1963, and the Open Letter of July 14, 1963, from the Central Committee of the Communist Party of the Soviet Union to Party Organizations . . . of the Soviet Union. (All these documents are available in English translation in Volume XV of the *Current Digest of the Soviet Press*.) A meeting of delegates from the Chinese and Soviet parties held in Moscow July 5-July 20, 1963, ended on a note of sharp disagreement and mutual recriminations.

separately organized Chinese-oriented and Soviet-affiliated Communist parties waging bitter battle around the world. Even if an organizational schism be avoided, the rival efforts of the two parties to rally followers are likely to intensify the intra-party factionalism which is already apparent. At the same time, the absence of agreement on basic strategy and tactics poses a fundamental challenge to the universal pretensions of Communist ideology. If other Communist parties choose to regard the Soviet position as a rationalization of Russian interests and the Chinese credo as reflecting its specific interests, they may well be tempted to adjust their own ideological perspectives to their particular local needs. As long as Moscow and Peiping maintain their formal alliance while continuing their efforts to mobilize support in each other's camp, the very existence of Sino-Soviet rivalry is likely to increase the maneuverability and bargaining power of other bloc members and Communist Party leaders who are being wooed. The reverberations are likely to be reflected in a reinforcement of polycentric tendencies and a diffusion of authority within the Communist camp.

The impact of the Sino-Soviet conflict on Soviet foreign policy offers still another tempting subject for speculation. While the Soviet Union under Khrushchev remains committed to revolutionary advance, it recognizes that thermonuclear confrontation with the United States imposes limits on the risks which it can assume. As the Cuban crisis vividly demonstrated, the Soviet Union is not prepared to increase the hazards of conflict to the point of igniting a nuclear war. At the same time, Soviet policy makers find themselves in a position where the existence of a challenger on the Left cannot be ignored. An intransigent China forces the Soviet hand, as it criticizes the Soviet Union for its excessive caution and mobilizes increasing support among impatient revolutionaries anxious to come to power.

The pressure is likely to be most acute in the underdeveloped areas. Moscow's efforts to woo the support of such nationalist leaders as Nehru, Nasser, and Sukarno have involved corollary restraints on the revolutionary *élan* of the Communist parties in their dominions. While the Soviet leadership warns against the danger of premature outbreaks and counsels delay and patient preparation, the Chinese urge action. Indefinite postponement of bids for power, and fears that the national regimes which are the recipients of Soviet aid may consolidate their strength, are likely to persuade impatient local Communist leaders that Peiping's policies are closer to their own interests. Moscow may soon confront the unpalatable choice of either giving a more militant lead to Communist leaders in the underdeveloped countries or resigning itself to the prospect that their loyalties will turn in a direction where revolutionary enthusiasm is more highly valued.

IMPLICATIONS FOR AMERICAN FOREIGN POLICY

What implications do these developments have for American policy? What can the United States do to influence change in directions most favorable to Western interests? It is sometimes argued, with the Sino-Soviet dispute in mind, that since Khrushchev's attitude toward the West is less militant and aggressive than Mao's, the West ought to do what it can to strengthen Khrushchev's hand, that concessions should be made to him on such issues as Berlin in order not to discredit his strategy and weaken his position. Implicit in this line of argument is the notion that a *modus vivendi* with Khrushchev is now possible, and that such an accommodation would be placed in extreme jeopardy if our failure to appreciate the pressures under which he operates resulted in pushing him toward a more adventurous course. What advocates of this strategy tend to forget or ignore is that Khrushchev, for all of his differences with Mao, remains a Communist, and that, like Mao, he is committed to a view of the world in which "capitalist" weakness in the face of Communist pressure represents an opportunity to be exploited, rather than an invitation to strike a bargain once and for all.

Retreats in the face of Communist pressure can only speed up the processes of Western disintegration; firmness backed by strength, combined with a constant willingness to seek common ground in negotiating differences, offers the primary hope of keeping the peace and checkmating Communist expansionism. Whether Western determination not to yield to Soviet or Chinese demands will contribute to healing or widening the Sino-Soviet breach is by no means easy to determine. The effect may be to cause Moscow and Peiping to subordinate their differences in the interests of presenting a more powerful common front to the West. But if Moscow maintains its reluctance to run the risk of a nuclear war, its decision may well be received in Peiping as further confirmation of Soviet opportunism. In either case, it is difficult to avoid the conclusion that only Western strength will serve to dampen Communist messianism.

It is sometimes suggested that American policy makers should seek out opportunities to widen the rift between the Chinese and Russians, on the assumption that anything which contributes to weakening the unity of the Communist bloc is certain to redound to Western advantage. While the suggestion has its obvious attractions, it also raises problems. There is, first of all, the question of precisely what the West can do to deepen the cleavage. It has already been suggested that unilateral concessions to the Russians on such issues as Berlin are hardly likely to serve Western interests. Trade with the Russians could be broadened, but it would still have to be carefully regulated with an eye to its impact on the strategic power balance. Measures such as Soviet-American cultural exchanges, the recently concluded limited test ban pact, the broadening of arms control agreements, collaboration in outer space exploration, and striving with the Russians to limit local wars in areas such as Laos may have the incidental result of deepening Sino-Soviet differences, but any too obvious effort to exploit them for these purposes may well have a boomerang effect.

On the Chinese side, the possibilities, for the moment at least, appear less promising. The American presence in Taiwan, South Korea, and South Vietnam stands as a formidable barrier to the realization of Chinese Communist ambitions. The American policy of nonrecognition and opposition to the admission of Communist China to the United Nations is not likely to be reversed soon, and it is difficult to see how it can be reversed, as long as the United States continues its special relationship to Taiwan. In theory, at least, the United States could supply Communist China with food and aid in its industrialization drive, thus lessening its need to look to the Soviet bloc for support, but given the present relationship between Washington and Peiping, the likelihood that such aid would either be offered or accepted appears very dim indeed. Communist China has turned to Canada, Australia, France, and Burma for emergency food purchases, and, to some extent at least, industrial goods from Japan, Western Europe and Britain are flowing to China and could help to fill the gap if trade with the Soviet European bloc is substantially diminished or altogether cut off. Conceivably, over a period of time, increasing dependence on the West might operate to deepen the gulf with the Soviet Union, but, since such a policy would also contribute to China's growing economic potential and thus run the serious risk that such strength would eventually be turned against the West, it is not a program calculated to have much appeal in China's present intransigent mood.

For the moment at least, any flagrant American attempt to exploit the Sino-Soviet rift is likely to bring Communist China and the Soviet Union together, rather than to drive them apart. The Sino-Soviet conflict, like the Soviet-Yugoslav dispute before it, has its own internal logic, and an American hands-off policy at this stage perhaps represents the most effective contribution the United States can make to assure that the strains of the alliance will increase.

Nor can we be sure that an open and complete break between the Soviet Union and Communist China will necessarily promote the cause of peace. If the effect of a powerful Chinese bid for leadership of the Communist movement in Asia, Africa, and Latin America is to lead the Russians to embark on more aggressive tactics there and elsewhere, there is the danger that Soviet challenges to Western positions may move out of control and escalate local conflicts into a nuclear war. If, on the other hand, the Russians prudently limit their risks and leave the revolutionary initiative to the Chinese, there is the danger that the West may soon be faced with a whole series of Chinese-inspired guerrilla wars and revolutionary outbreaks spreading from Asia to other parts of the underdeveloped world.

It is, of course, also possible that an isolated Communist China will for a number of years be so embroiled in its own domestic problems that its capacity to make mischief will be largely neutralized. China today, for all of its vast territory and teeming population, is still a second-class economic power. It has, however, made significant strides in industrialization over the last decade, and despite its present economic difficulties, its military and economic power can be expected to mount over the years. If aid is denied it by both the Soviet Union and the West, the processes of industrialization will be slowed down, but, given the commitment to industrialize and the totalitarian discipline which the Communist leadership has at its disposal, industrialization appears to be primarily a matter of time. Communist China, experts agree, will shortly be conducting nuclear tests, and a delivery capability will eventually be attained. At that point China will be able to intensify its military pressure on neighboring areas; a China driven by great population pressures and motivated by a powerful combination of nationalist and Communist messianism appears destined to present a grave problem for the world.

ALTERNATIVES FOR AMERICAN AND WESTERN POLICY MAKERS

The West faces two very different polar alternatives in shaping its long-run China policy. One alternative would involve vigorous efforts to bring Communist China into the comity of nations, to seek to resume full-scale diplomatic and cultural ties with it, to discontinue the boycott on trade, and to offer it substantial assistance in meeting its food deficiencies and helping it to industrialize. Policies directed to these ends would gamble on the possibility that a China strengthened with the help of the West would not turn its strength against the West. Implicit in this perspective is the hope that Chinese nationalist and revolutionary fervor will decline over time, that as China becomes a developed country, growing affluence will serve to moderate its militancy and contain its outward thrust.

The other polar alternative, which in its essentials is epitomized in present American policy, proceeds from the assumptions that a Communist China, whether affluent or not, will remain dedicated to the destruction of the West and that the most effective way to temper Communist militancy is to continue to demonstrate that the risks of adventuring outweigh the possible gains. In short, this policy line coun-

sels the strengthening of barricades against possible Chinese expansionism, the use of every means available to weaken the mainland economy,
and the continuation of present efforts to isolate Communist China in
the international community. Those who share this view hope that the
Communist regime in China will eventually be overthrown from within,
but even if they believe it unlikely, they see no alternative except to
resist all efforts to expand Communist China's domain. They recognize
that the policies which they espouse run the risk of forcing Communist
China back into the Soviet embrace, but since they see both Soviet and
Chinese ambitions as adverse to Western interests, they are equally determined to oppose both.

It is also possible to envisage an intermediate course of action which
would retain flexibility in the face of events. While this policy line
would make no concessions to Chinese expansionism, it would be prepared, in the event of a complete Sino-Soviet break, to offer modest and
even large-scale assistance to Communist China, provided there was
evidence that China was prepared to relax its demands on its neighbors
and abandon its bellicose stance. While such a development may appear
now to border on the fantastic, it is perhaps relevant to recall that Tito
at one time was on the left of the international Communist movement
and that his evolution in a neutralist direction was eased by the availability of Western aid. Should the possibility of a similar evolution ever
loom on the horizon in China, the line here indicated would dictate
exploiting such a contingency, however remote it now appears to be.

The loosening of the bonds in the Communist empire may also create
some opportunities for American policy makers in dealing with the East
European members of the bloc. The deterioration of relations between
Albania and the Soviet-led Communist states raises the question as to
where Albania will turn for future support. Up to this point, Communist
China has come to the rescue, but the perilous state of the Chinese
economy may well impose limits on its capacity to render continuing
aid. There have already been indications that Albania is seeking to
revive its traditional trade links with Italy, and it is not foreclosed that
it will find itself forced to appeal to the West for help. Should this happen, Western policy makers will have to decide whether they wish to
strengthen a regime which is in most respects obnoxious and oppressive
or whether they prefer to stand aside and leave the field free for the
Soviet Union, China, and Albania's neighbors, Yugoslavia and Greece,
to carry on the struggle to determine Albania's fate.

So far as the rest of the East European bloc is concerned, the opportunities and choices open to American policy makers appear more limited.
Should future revolts erupt on the order of the 1953 East German rising
or the Hungarian revolution of 1956, direct military intervention by the

West would seem to be ruled out by the high likelihood that such action would ignite a nuclear war. American policy makers must thus content themselves with the more modest objective of doing what they can to promote the forces of independence and autonomy within the bloc by peaceful means.

Measures which may serve to advance these purposes include the development of trade in nonstrategic goods, the use of Public Law 480 allowing food shipments to relieve distress, the maintenance of cultural ties with the West through the exchange of teachers and students, and similar actions designed to keep the channels of communication open. In the special case of Poland, a Western guaranty of the Oder-Neisse boundary would undoubtedly win widespread Polish acclaim, but it is difficult to see how such a guaranty could be made meaningful without Bonn's approval or consent. For the rest, the West must stake its hopes on the persistent strength of the forces of nationalism within the bloc, on the expectation that national distinctiveness and indigenous interests will express themselves even within a Communist framework and operate over time to create centrifugal pressures which Moscow will find difficult to control.

For the period immediately ahead, the principal problem which American foreign policy faces is that of countering, and, if possible, reversing the expansion of Soviet power and influence in the world. There are those who place their hopes on rising Soviet affluence, the spread of education, and a decline in ideological militancy to impose an internal brake on the Soviet regime's revolutionary *élan*. While such a development is to be welcomed should it occur, there is as yet little hard evidence to indicate that the Soviet leadership is prepared to reconcile itself to the status quo. Whether Moscow can maintain its dynamic momentum will depend in no small part on its record of achievements at home and abroad. Communism on the move vitalizes ideology and validates doctrine; it is loss of dynamism that puts the attractive power of communism in peril.

If this analysis is valid, it points to the direction which long-term American and Western policy must take. The first duty of responsible Western statesmanship is to ensure that the balance of power and the dynamics of growth remain favorable to the West. In a world where a thermonuclear holocaust is an ever-present danger, every effort should, of course, be exerted to bring the arms race under control and to reduce the possibility of war. For that reason the recent test ban pact is to be warmly welcomed. But unless further agreements can be reached which safeguard both Western and Soviet interests, there would appear to be no real alternative except to continue to maintain a capacity for instant and full retaliation against thermonuclear attack, to rely on a policy of balanced deterrence to prevent a nuclear war from breaking out, and to develop subnuclear capacities and paramilitary capabilities to deal with the contingencies and actualities of local and guerrilla wars.

Safety, however, does not lie in military potential alone. Whatever attraction the West will have for the peoples in the world in the years to come will depend on much else. Its capacity to generate rates of growth which outdistance the Soviet bloc will go far to determine its dynamic appeal. Its willingness to make large-scale support available for educational and research purposes will be crucial in deciding the outcome of the scientific and technological race in which both sides are engaged. The interest of the West in providing an expanding vista of welfare and social justice, not only for its own citizens, but also for the less privileged peoples in the underdeveloped areas, can contribute significantly toward tilting the balance of advantage away from the Communist cause. The ability of the West to preserve its unity in the face of Communist disruptive efforts, its ingenuity in overcoming historic rivalries of the kind which stand in the way of the expansion of the Common Market, and the persistence which it demonstrates in widening the area of community and raising levels of income and opportunity throughout the non-Communist world may well be decisive in ensuring a Communist defeat.

Suggestions for Further Reading

Brzezinski, Zbigniew K., *The Soviet Bloc; Unity and Conflict,* 2nd ed. New York: Frederick A. Praeger, Inc., 1961.

Dallin, Alexander, ed., *Diversity in International Communism.* New York: Columbia University Press, 1963.

Fainsod, Merle, *How Russia is Ruled,* rev. ed. Cambridge, Mass.: Harvard University Press, 1963.

Griffith, William E., *Albania and the Sino-Soviet Conflict.* Cambridge, Mass.: The M.I.T. Press, 1963.

Hudson, G. F., Richard Lowenthal, and Roderick MacFarquhar, *The Sino-Soviet Dispute.* New York: Frederick A. Praeger, Inc., 1961.

Jacobs, Don N., ed., *The New Communist Manifesto and Related Documents.* New York: Harper & Row, Publishers, 1961.

Kennan, George F., *Russia and the West under Lenin and Stalin.* Boston: Little, Brown & Co., 1960.

Mackintosh, J. M., *Strategy and Tactics of Soviet Foreign Policy.* London: Oxford University Press, 1962.

Pentony, Devere E., ed., *Red World in Tumult: Communist Foreign Policies.* San Francisco: Chandler Publishing Company, 1962.

Zagoria, Donald S., *The Sino-Soviet Conflict, 1956-1961.* Princeton, N.J.: Princeton University Press, 1962.

COLONIALISM, DICTATORSHIP, AND THE AMERICAN POLITICAL TRADITION

Frederick M. Watkins

One of the most difficult things in life is facing up to facts. Peoples, no less than individuals, are subject to this problem. Each nation, viewing the world in the light of its own particular experiences and traditions, tends to live in a private universe of its own creation, a familiar universe in which it feels at home. If this universe is sufficiently close to the real world, it provides a reasonable basis for action, and all is well; if not, there is bound to be trouble. But no expectations, however well based in terms of past experience, are proof against the challenge of new developments. This is particularly true in times of rapid change. Each private universe should therefore be subject to constant revision. And yet, it is no easy thing to abandon old certainties; most of us would rather cling to familiar fallacies than face new truths. In nations, as in individuals, the ability to make such readjustments is the mark of true maturity.

The twentieth century, with its rapid changes, has been uncommonly rich in occasions for the testing and reappraisal of traditional ways of thought. For members of the Western world, some of the more taxing of these occasions have arisen in connection with the problem of colonialism. From the days of the fifteenth century explorers down to the First

FREDERICK M. WATKINS *is Professor of Political Science at Yale University. He has also been a member of the faculties at Harvard, Cornell, and McGill Universities. He is author of* Political Tradition of the West, *and editor of Hume's* Theory of Politics *and Rousseau's* Political Writings.

World War, imperial expansion was the order of the day in Western Europe. By the end of the nineteenth century, most of the inhabitable surface of the globe had been occupied by European settlers, reduced to the status of colonial dependencies, or at least incorporated as "spheres of influence" within one or another of the Western imperial systems. This ultimately led Westerners to think of themselves as the natural rulers of mankind. Non-Westerners were nothing more than "natives," a term which in the language of the day was synonymous with "inferiors." All this has changed in the course of the present century.

The turning of the tide was marked, perhaps, by the Russo-Japanese War of 1905, which led for the first time to the acceptance of a strictly non-Western people as a modern world power. Since then the decline of Western imperialism has continued apace. Although some fragments of the older colonial empires still remain, their days are strictly numbered. Each year newly liberated colonies come to swell the ranks of the United Nations. To find timely and effective ways of adjusting to these changes is one of the most urgent problems of contemporary politics.

NATIONAL SELF-DETERMINATION AND CONSTITUTIONAL DEMOCRACY

Because of the nature of its own traditions, the United States has found it easier than many other Western powers to view the aspirations of colonial peoples in a sympathetic light. For a country that dates its own national existence from a Declaration of Independence, any claim to independence is bound to strike a familiar and favorable note. When President Wilson, in the course of the First World War, offered the principle of national self-determination as one of his celebrated Fourteen Points for the solution of the conflict, he was speaking as the representative of a typically American point of view. The appeal to American fellow-feeling is especially clear when the people in question are striving, like the Founding Fathers of America itself, to break the shackles of a colonial system. Although it is true that the United States did, in the aftermath of the Spanish-American War, acquire a modest colonial empire of its own, it was never really happy in the role, and laid little store by its new possessions. Hostility to colonialism is deeply engrained in the American political tradition. At the risk even of impairing its relations with other members of the all-important North Atlantic Treaty Organization, the United States has tended to be true to that tradition.

But if America is relatively hospitable to the idea of national self-determination, it is very far from willing to let new nations go their own way in choosing a form of government: No nation, new or old, can be thoroughly respectable in American eyes unless it adopts the ideas and institutions of constitutional democracy. This is a reflection of the ideological, almost Messianic, element which has always been a distinguishing feature of the American political consciousness. Ever since the foundation of the republic, the citizens of the United States have been accustomed to think of their own experiment in free government not as a matter of just local significance, but as a guidepost to all mankind.[1] As the Great Seal of the United States so clearly proclaims, the advent of America marks the beginning of a new era in world history, a *novus ordo seclorum*.

The idea that America is a particularly favored Land of Liberty, and that Americans are a people especially chosen to introduce less favored ones to the ways and blessings of freedom, has played from the beginning an important part in the development of a peculiarly American sense of national mission. The American belief in national self-determination goes hand in hand, therefore, with an inherited conviction that the proper end of independence is democratic freedom. Even though the difficulties of achieving constitutional government may be recognized in theory, most Americans find it hard to justify supporting any movement that does not promise to achieve, or at least to move in the direction of, liberal democracy. When Americans support the liquidation of colonial empires, it is in the expectation that the successor states will establish constitutional governments—just as the American colonies did when they gained their independence.

Such expectations do not seem to be unreasonable. Most of the colonial empires now in process of dissolution were formerly the possessions of countries which themselves have long been constitutional democracies and which share the American preference for that form of government. For generations, the standard liberal justification for imperialism has been that it is essentially self-liquidating. John Stuart Mill, in *Representative Government*,[2] pointed out that colonies are territories inhabited by backward peoples not yet capable of self-government, and that the primary responsibility of colonial administrations is to educate them in the ways of constitutional democracy. Although the various Western powers differed considerably in the seriousness of their commitment to this theory of colonialism, most of them made some efforts (and some worked long and seriously) toward the realization of this goal.[3] The result is that

---

[1] In Thomas Paine's *Rights of Man*, Part I (1791), the dedication to George Washington ends with the hope that "you may enjoy the happiness of seeing the New World regenerate the Old." Alexis de Tocqueville's *Democracy in America* (1835) bears witness to the continuation of similar ideas in the nineteenth century. George F. Kennan, *American Diplomacy, 1900-1950* (Chicago: University of Chicago Press, 1951), traces some of the consequences from the standpoint of twentieth-century foreign policy.

[2] John Stuart Mill, *Representative Government*, Chap. XVII.

[3] This tradition has been especially powerful in Great Britain. For a characteristic statement see Leonard Woolf, "The Political Advance of Backward Peoples," and D. S. Shiels, "Self-Government for Advanced Colonies," in *Fabian Colonial Essays*, ed. Rita Hinden (London: George Allen and Unwin, Ltd., 1945).

most of the colonial territories now facing or approaching the responsibilities of independence have already been subjected to a considerable
amount of liberal indoctrination and have acquired, under the guidance
of experienced Western administrators, some practical experience in the
techniques of free government. To expect them to evolve in the direction
of constitutional democracy does not seem, under these circumstances,
to be wholly unrealistic.

Unfortunately, the results to date have been quite disappointing. It
is true that there are some areas in which the development of the newly
liberated nations seems, from a liberal standpoint, to be working out
rather well. This is especially true of certain former possessions of the
United States and of Great Britain, which happen, of all the Western
powers, to have been the two which probably went farthest in their attempts to implement the theory of liberal tutelage. The relative success
of India and the Philippines[4] in their new role as independent constitutional governments is a tribute to the possible, though still somewhat
precarious, success of such efforts. But the rapid breakdown of free government in Pakistan and Burma, and the ominous development toward
a repressive one-party dictatorship in some of the former colonies of
British Africa, most notably Ghana, are an indication that even the
British were not uniformly successful in their efforts to prepare people
for the assumption of constitutional responsibilities.

When we turn to the record of other colonial empires, the picture is
still less satisfactory. Although France was probably second only to
England and the United States in its tutelary efforts, the prospects of
constitutionalism in many of its former colonies are dubious. The colonial
empire of the Dutch, who did much less to prepare their charges for
self-government, has been replaced by a regime which shows no signs
of moving in the direction of liberal democracy. The Belgians, whose
sense of tutelary responsibility was almost nil, left the pieces of a chaotic
Congo to be picked up after them by a distraught United Nations, and
the prospective liberation of Portuguese Africa is an international night-
mare. Taken as a whole, therefore, the record of colonial tutelage is at
best a spotty one. After decades—and, in some cases, more than a century
—of imperial rule, the net result is a congeries of newly liberated nations
whose prospects of becoming effective constitutional democracies are far
from certain.

In the light of the traditional assumptions of American political life,
this is a most disquieting situation, one to which it is hard, in good
conscience, to make an effective adjustment. A large and increasing body

---

[4] The standard work on this experiment in colonial tutelage is Joseph Ralston
Hayden, *The Philippines* (New York: The Macmillan Company, 1942). A new study
by Carl Lande will appear shortly.

of evidence seems to show that colonial tutelage has not yet succeeded in preparing all, or even most, colonial peoples for democratic self-government. Should the United States then try to turn back the clock, and insist on more of the same? Should it oppose all claims to national independence which, from a liberal standpoint, would seem to be premature, and should it endeavor to preserve, perhaps even to re-establish, the authority of colonial regimes whose tutelary work has yet to be accomplished? This would run counter to the traditional American belief in the right to national self-determination and would hardly be practical politics. Or should the United States quite indiscriminately support all independence movements, even though the result in many cases would be to ensure the establishments of illiberal regimes? This would be incompatible with the American national mission to spread the blessings of liberty throughout the world. To create a satisfying and self-consistent foreign policy in the face of such a dilemma can be no easy task.

The only way to escape from this difficulty, in my opinion, is to re-examine the assumptions on which it is based. Though modified by much subsequent experience, the American attitude toward colonialism is still largely and subconsciously shaped by the memory of America's own colonial experience. If the American colonies were able to proceed directly from a war of independence to the establishment of an effective constitutional order, why should not other colonies do likewise? But the fact is that the situation of the American colonists of the eighteenth century was radically different from that of the colonial peoples of our own day. To spell out the nature of that difference and to show why dictatorship, rather than democracy, is the normal aftermath of twentieth century colonialism is the purpose of this essay.

DICTATORSHIP: THE AFTERMATH OF
TWENTIETH CENTURY COLONIALISM

The essential difference is that the colonials of today are backward peoples, while the American colonists were not. The problem facing most contemporary Asian and African nations is that they are the product of traditional cultures which have proved to be hopelessly incapable of meeting the competitive pressures of twentieth century life. Rich as those cultures may be in their own right, and desirable as it may be to preserve as many as possible of the values they represent, no nation can hope to survive in the modern world, much less to maintain its independence, unless it succeeds in assimilating, at least in part, the scientific and technological accomplishments of the more highly developed industrial nations. For the present and for much of the foreseeable future, therefore, the most difficult problem for all such nations will be to find ways of adjusting traditional ways to the requirements of an alien culture.

The American colonists, on the other hand, had no such problem to face. Although their way of life was in some respects quite different from that of the mother country, they shared a common culture. Their level of accomplishment, if somewhat provincial, was essentially the same as that of the British, and their general standard of living, even at that early date, was already considerably higher. For them, the winning of independence involved no essential change in their traditional way of life. Their problems had little or nothing in common with the problems of twentieth century colonialism.

For Americans the natural, almost inevitable consequence of independence was constitutional democracy. The British tradition of local self-government was their native tradition, transplanted as a matter of course to their new homes. Far from needing any sort of special tutelage at the hands of an alien colonial administration, they were fully capable from the very beginning of managing their own affairs. In later years, as the occasion arose, they put up spirited resistance to the pretensions of royal governors who tried to interfere with what they had always regarded as their rights as freeborn Englishmen. This resistance culminated in the American Revolution. Once they had attained their independence, it called for some inventiveness on their part to create the institutions they needed for the maintenance of an effective federal union. Their long political experience stood them in good stead, however, and the constitution they created soon won them a proud and unchallenged position as the world's leading exponents of democratic government.

The twentieth century, like the eighteenth, has been an age of revolution. Revolutionary leadership has now shifted, however, to the non-Western nations, and the political consequences have been quite different from anything that the American Founding Fathers could possibly have envisioned.[5] Of all the revolutions that have taken place so far in the course of the twentieth century, the Bolshevik seizure of Tsarist Russia was without doubt the most strikingly successful. Within a single generation the new regime succeeded in transforming a traditional agrarian society into one of the two greatest industrial and military powers of the modern world. This striking development has inevitably attracted the attention, and excited the emulation, of other backward nations. A number of them, most notably Communist China, are currently engaged in a strenuous effort to match and, if possible, to surpass the Russian achievement. But constitutional democracy was not, of course, the political

---

[5] The uniqueness of the American Revolution, and its inability to provide guidance for revolutionary developments elsewhere, is one of the themes of Hannah Arendt, *On Revolution* (New York: The Viking Press, Inc., 1963).

means used by the masters of Soviet Russia; totalitarian dictatorship was the system of government that they invented and used for the accomplishment of their purposes. On the face of things it would seem, therefore, that dictatorship, rather than democracy, is the method best suited to meet the needs of backward nations under the conditions of twentieth century politics. To understand why this may well prove to be true for backward peoples in general, and for colonial peoples in particular, is an indispensable prerequisite to any realistic consideration of the problems of the modern world.

Before proceeding further, it would perhaps be well to say a few words about the nature of totalitarian dictatorship.[6] *Elitist* and *statist* are the terms in which its essential features can best be understood. The core of any totalitarian regime is a totalitarian party, an organized political elite inspired by a Messianic ideology. Convinced that they alone are the possessors of a true political doctrine, and that their doctrine is indispensable to the salvation of mankind, the members of such a party believe they have a natural right and duty to direct the lives of all those whose insight is inferior to their own. Any form of opposition to this ruling elite, or of indiscipline within it, is by definition a betrayal of the interests of mankind and ought to be suppressed by every available means. The mission of the totalitarian party is to gain complete control over the powers of the state and to convert it into the strongest possible agency for the transformation of society. Any constitutional restraints which might serve to limit the powers of the state, and thus of the ruling party, are wholly unacceptable. To achieve its reforms and to raise the rest of the population to the party's own level of enlightenment, nothing less than total and unchallengeable control suffices. Although so complete a concentration of power is hardly attainable as a matter of fact, this ideal objective guides the activities of a typical totalitarian party.

Why is it that totalitarianism, rather than democracy, has provided the model for so many of the more successful revolutionary regimes of the twentieth century? The answer should be sought in connection with the problem of consensus. Constitutional democracy rests on the assumption that it is possible, on the basis of free negotiation between competing parties and interest groups, to unite at least a majority of the voting population in support of a viable political program. Even in the comparatively experienced constitutional democracies of the Western world, this indispensable condition cannot always be realized, as France, for example, can surely bear witness. To achieve so high a degree of consensus in more backward areas, especially at a time when those areas are being faced with the novel stresses and bewilderments of modernization, is

---

[6] See C. J. Friedrich and Z. K. Brzezinski, *Totalitarian Dictatorship and Autocracy* (Cambridge, Mass.: Harvard University Press, 1956).

even more difficult. It is not surprising that reformist minorities in many such countries despair of securing, within the limitations of constitutional democracy, majority support for necessary but painful changes. Thus they are attracted by the prospect of some less taxing way to accomplish their purposes.

The essential difficulty is that when a traditional society is in the throes of rapid modernization, the channels of communication which normally lead to the formation of a political consensus are seriously strained. Although few societies of any size are strictly homogeneous, the common acceptance of well-established ideas and institutions normally suffices, in traditional and slow-moving societies, to constitute an effective bond uniting the whole community. In times of rapid cultural change, however, those bonds are in danger of being broken, because the impact of novel influences is seldom felt simultaneously and with equal weight throughout the whole society. In general, the more highly educated and the more fully urbanized are most susceptible to such influences and first become convinced of the necessity or desirability of making an adjustment to them. But in proportion as these people are modernized, they are likely to become estranged from their more traditional brethren. Attempts to explain the need for change are apt to be received with incomprehension and hostility. In extreme cases the result may very well be a complete breakdown of social communications and the loss of even the most elementary forms of consensus.

This failure of social communication was a striking feature of Tsarist Russia, the country where totalitarian dictatorship first arose and where it was destined to register its most spectacular successes. Although the beginnings of the attempt to Westernize Russia date back to the reign of Peter the Great, it was only partly successful then. At the time of the Bolshevik Revolution, the Russian Empire remained in the typical posture of a traditional society in the throes of modernization. At one end of the cultural scale was a small class of well-educated aristocrats, industrialists, and intellectuals who were fully conversant with, and often brilliant contributors to, the most advanced achievements of Western civilization. The process of industrialization had already begun, a good deal of it still controlled by Western capitalists and under the management of Western technicians, and an ever larger army of factory workers was being drawn from the countryside to man the new machines. The vast majority of the population was made up, however, of peasants whose traditional way of life was still essentially unchanged. As a result of their acquaintance with Western conditions, many upper-class reformers were shocked by the misery and ignorance of the Russian peasantry, and tried to do something about it. At great personal sacrifice they tried to educate the rural masses, thus enabling them to participate more fully in the benefits of modern civilization. These efforts at best were generally ineffective and were often met with active hostility.[7] The backward-looking and the forward-looking elements of the Russian people had drawn so far apart that it was nearly impossible to re-establish communication between them. These frustrating experiences did much to determine the course of the subsequent revolution.

ROLE OF THE NATIVE ELITE IN UNDERDEVELOPED COUNTRIES

Lenin,[8] the founder of the first totalitarian government, was a thoroughly Westernized Russian who devoted his life to the task of overcoming the backwardness of his native country and raising it to the most advanced levels of Western civilization. According to him, the peasantry were little more than an inert and potentially antagonistic mass which would have to be led or driven into the ways of the future by the more enlightened classes. As an ardent Marxist, he believed that the good society could come about only in a highly industrialized society, where the factory workers, or proletariat, had expropriated the capitalists and assumed control over the instruments of production. The difficulty from his standpoint was that the Russia of his own day was very far from being highly industrialized. His final answer to the problem was to organize a small but highly trained party of professional revolutionaries to overthrow the existing order and establish a dictatorship. Though described as a dictatorship of the proletariat, it was destined in fact to become a means whereby the party would be enabled to exercise unchallenged rule over the rest of the population. On this basis the enlightened elite would proceed to industrialize Russia as rapidly as possible, until it had finally equalled or surpassed the accomplishments of the West. The end result would be a society so completely homogeneous that there would no longer be any class barriers to stand in the way of perfect communication. At this point the dictatorship of the proletariat would no longer be necessary, and the state would wither away.

Although totalitarian dictatorship first arose in a country which had never undergone the experience of being incorporated in a Western colonial empire, the Russian case throws significant light on some of the forces at work today in the world of colonial and ex-colonial nations. Since the dictatorial system of government was specifically designed to meet the needs of a backward region, it can hardly fail to attract the attention of men trying to cope with similar problems elsewhere. This is true even of those who, through long and conscientious colonial tutelage, have been exposed to the counter-attractions of constitutional democracy. Every colonial administration, no matter how liberal in intent, is bound

[7] See Franco Venturi, *Roots of Revolution* (New York: Alfred A. Knopf, 1960).
[8] See A. G. Meyer, *Leninism* (Cambridge, Mass.: Harvard University Press, 1957).

to be somewhat dictatorial in character. While preaching the virtues of constitutional democracy, the colonial officer is exercising a form of authority which, for the time being at least, is not in itself democratic. Thus the lessons that men learn from their colonial masters are, to say the least, ambivalent. If they follow the preachments of liberal colonialism, they will try to become good democrats; but if they choose, instead, to follow its practice, they may well find dictatorship the form of government with which they are already most familiar and which corresponds most completely with their needs.

In the first stages of any colonial regime, the political model presented to the natives is uncompromisingly elitist in character. The situation is rather more reminiscent of Plato's *Republic* than of any known constitutional democracy. At the top of the political and social hierarchy stand the colonial officials. They are a small body of unusually able and well-trained Westerners selected by a rigorous process of competitive examination. Upon them rests the final responsibility, within the framework of policy set by the home government, of bringing the weight of a superior civilization to bear upon the local population. Waited upon by a small army of native servants, they are conspicuously set apart from lesser men by their high and alien standard of living and by their membership in prestigious social clubs from which natives are regularly excluded. Associated with them, as auxiliaries, are a considerable number of more or less Westernized natives who, having achieved literacy or other useful skills, have qualified for inferior positions in the civil and military services. The orders of colonial officials are normally enforced, for example, by native soldiers and policemen acting under the orders of Western officers. At the bottom of the heap is the great mass of mere natives, whose sole duty is to obey the orders handed down from on high. The whole system is based, therefore, on the assumption that the right to rule is the prerogative of a highly qualified and exclusive Western elite, and that the only way for a native to acquire any sort of authority is to become Westernized as rapidly as possible.

Of the three basic classes created within such a system, the Westernized native subelite (or auxiliaries) most concern us here, since, with the decline of Western imperialism, they are the ruling class of the future. The shape of that future largely depends, therefore, on the way in which this particular group is shaped by, and reacts to, its colonial experience. This differs from place to place. In the case of countries like England and France, which have been relatively serious in their commitment to the theory of colonial tutelage, the policy of the imperial government has been to make the more advanced forms of Western education available to a considerable number of promising natives, and to admit the more successful into the upper ranks of the colonial administration. This leads to the creation of a large and relatively well-trained native elite, experienced in the more advanced techniques of Western civilization. Other countries, such as Holland and Belgium, have preferred to rely more heavily on the manipulation of traditional institutions, and to do correspondingly little in the way of preparing natives for the assumption of administrative responsibilities. Even in these cases, however, the inordinate costliness of European officials, with their high standards of living, has made it necessary to recruit the lower ranks of the colonial services from the local population and to give them a corresponding measure of special training. Here, too, the effect of colonialism is to create a native subelite which is at least partially Westernized, and on whom the responsibilities of national independence will ultimately devolve.

The most important consequence of this situation is to create, in an especially heightened form, that breakdown of social communications which is characteristic of backward areas in general. Because of their need for a Westernized subelite, the tendency of all colonial administrations, including even the less progressive, is to speed up and intensify the normal process of alienation between the modernizing and the tradition-oriented sectors of society. This process is apt to be particularly abrupt and drastic in those areas where the liberal theory of colonialism is most vigorously applied. Although the final object may be to make the advantages of modern education available to all, a program of intensive mass education would be so hopelessly expensive that it is necessary to start by concentrating most of the available resources on a small minority of especially promising candidates. Under forced draft, these selected natives are brought to a high level of Westernization and are rewarded by admission to responsible positions in the colonial administration. The result is to raise up a native elite which, as it becomes more thoroughly convinced of the need for modernization, becomes yet more alienated from, and less capable of communicating its insights to, the general population. In the case of the more illiberal colonial regimes, the situation is less acute in degree, but similar in kind. Although the native elite in these regions is less numerous, less fully Westernized, and entrusted with fewer responsibilities, it too becomes aware of progressive possibilities which can hardly be realized within the framework of that traditional society which the colonial authorities have been so careful to preserve. Here, too, alienation and frustration are the normal consequences of living under a colonial regime.

The current erosion of Western imperialism is an expression of this fact. Wittingly or unwittingly, colonial administrations everywhere have given rise to unhappy native elites who perceive the necessity of imposing modern ways upon their more backward fellows and who find it impossible to work their will within the established imperial framework. In liberal empires, well-educated and self-confident minorities feel that they have long outgrown the need for Western tutelage. They resent the restrictions that this threatens to impose upon them in their attempts to complete the modernization of their own countries. In illiberal empires, less Westernized but increasingly ambitious minorities have grown discontented with regimes which have tried to insulate them from the modern world, and want to take matters into their own hands. In either case, alienation from their more tradition-bound fellow citizens has given the elite a sense of urgency in the pursuit of modernization; it has also given them a corresponding unwillingness to tolerate interference with any future attempts, however drastic, to force others to fall in line with their own vision of the future. From their contact with Western ideas they have learned, moreover, that national self-determination has long been accepted as a basic right of man. By claiming this right for themselves they have tried, with ever greater success, to undermine the foundations of Western colonialism and to assume the powers and responsibilities of sovereignty.

Under these circumstances, is it likely that the newly liberated nations will move in the direction of constitutional democracy? If the country in question has had no experience of preliminary liberal tutelage, the prospects are far from promising. Dictation by an autocratic colonial administration is the only form of modern government with which the inhabitants of such a country have had any sort of direct experience. When the native elite succeed, therefore, in getting rid of its foreign masters, the natural thing for them to do is to try to step into their predecessors' shoes, imposing themselves as a new ruling class upon the rest of the population. There can, of course, be no assurance that they will succeed. Having been denied, under the earlier regime, any substantial training in even the most elementary skills of modern administration, they may well prove incapable of maintaining effective control over the country they have inherited. As the tragedy of the Congo shows, however, anarchy rather than democracy is the probable consequence of such a failure. Powerful and continuing intervention by the United Nations, or by some other external force, may indeed suffice to keep the situation under control. But this is simply a return to colonial tutelage, albeit in a somewhat different and possibly more acceptable form. It is hard to see how the experience of any such people could lead to the establishment of any immediately viable form of constitutional democracy.

THE FAILURE OF LIBERAL COLONIALISM TO ACHIEVE DEMOCRACY

In countries which have undergone a considerable period of liberal tutelage, the situation is more complex. There the Platonic model is not the only one to which the native elites have been exposed; they have also had some experience of constitutional government. In an attempt to prepare their charges for future independence, liberal regimes regularly try to arrange an orderly and gradual retreat from dictatorship to democracy.[9] Legislative councils, at first purely appointive and consultative, are made more democratic through the addition of an increasing proportion of elective members. The scope of their authority is also progressively enlarged. By such devices the colonial administration voluntarily surrenders its original powers of uncontrolled dictation and approaches the Western model of responsible government. Success in freely competitive elections becomes the normal road to political power for members of the native elite. This encourages them to make a genuine effort to overcome the barriers of communication that separate them from the masses. Political parties arise to give leadership to the electorate and to give it some familiarity with the ways of constitutional government. When the time for independence comes, therefore, democracy should be the model with which the natives as a whole are most familiar and which they are prepared to support. This is the ideal objective and hope of liberal colonialism.

The essential difficulty is that liberal colonialism, especially in its later phases, is apt to generate political tensions so severe that they cannot be resolved within the framework of constitutional democracy. Ideally, of course, the transition to independence should proceed in a smoothly evolutionary fashion, allowing the natives to assume at every stage of their development a measure of responsibility commensurate with their attainments. Unfortunately, this assumes, on the part of natives and Westerners alike, a degree of wisdom and patience rarely found. Native elites, overconfident of their political maturity and resentful of the restraints to which they are still subject, usually try to cut off the period of tutelage prematurely. Colonial authorities, conversely, often find it hard to adjust to the new situation and are reluctant to surrender genuine powers to natives whose political capacities they continuously underestimate. Even with the best will in the world, moreover, it is hard to avoid bruising conflicts of jurisdiction in any situation such as that envisaged in the period of transition, when responsibilities are divided between Western and native authorities. The result is that, in most cases, the later years of liberal colonialism are marked by disturbances of greater or lesser severity, disturbances which, as in the case of Algeria, may even lead to a considerable period of open civil war. Native elites exert forcible pressures against the colonial administration and are met with corresponding measures of forcible repression. This is the background against which colonial independence has been won.

From a democratic standpoint all these pressures are quite unfortunate. The theory of liberal colonialism is based on the assumption that con-

[9] See Martin Wright, *The Development of the Legislative Council, 1606-1945* (London, 1956).

stitutional government will already be a going concern at the time of
independence and will continue uninterrupted. But constitutional governments do not function normally in crisis situations. Even in the most
mature and effective of the Western democracies, dictatorial measures,
such as the suspension of civil liberties and the deliberate curtailment of
party competition, are often taken at such times.[10] It follows, then, that
if colonial independence comes as the aftermath of a more or less pro-
tracted period of violence and disorder, dictatorship will be the form of
government most familiar to the natives, and the one most likely to
provide a model for their own political actions.

Perhaps the most important consequence is to encourage the formation
of political parties which are more totalitarian than democratic in character. If liberal colonialism worked according to plan, the natives by the
time of liberation would already be well acquainted with the operation
of two or more rival parties, freely competing with one another for the
approval of the electorate. They would also be ready to accept the verdict
of that electorate as the basis of responsible government. In the earlier
phases of colonial tutelage, the beginnings of a development in this
direction are often discernible. As relations with the colonial authorities
become more strained, however, the process is inhibited. The elimination
of colonial control looms ever larger as the central issue of politics.
Differences of opinion on other points tend to seem trivial and unworthy
in comparison with the overwhelming need for national liberation. This
often leads to the emergence of a single, militantly nationalist party
which succeeds in winning the allegiance of the great mass of the native
population. Adherence to such a party soon becomes the hallmark of
true patriotism; opposition to it, treason. This is the normal outcome of
any "we-they" situation, a situation regularly encountered in times of
international warfare, when political differences are subordinated to the
desire for unity in the face of a common foe. In colonies embarked on
a struggle for national liberation, the unifying enemy is the colonial
authority. Thus liberal colonialism usually fosters not freely competitive
parties, but a single monolithic party devoted to the single issue of nationalism, and prone to regard any opposition to itself as a threat to the interests of the nation.

When such a party succeeds in leading its country to independence, it
is hard for it thereafter to accept the risks and frustrations of democratic
competition. Although the Congress Party in India was a typical example
of this particular kind of organization, and although it still enjoys a lop-
sided advantage in competition with rival parties, the democratic con-

---

[10] On the problem of constitutional emergency powers, see F. M. Watkins, "Constitutional Dictatorship," *Public Policy*, Vol. I (1940); and Clinton L. Rossiter, *Constitutional Dictatorship* (Princeton, N.J.: Princeton University Press, 1948).

victions of Nehru and other Western-educated leaders have proved strong enough to prevent it, at least for the time being, from assuming a monopoly and suppressing all competition. This is a remarkable and hopeful fact. There are other ex-colonial territories, however, in which things have turned out quite differently. A number of the new African nations, including Ghana, have become openly and explicitly one-party states, with the right to organized political action reserved to the nationalist organization which took the lead in achieving independence. In view of its obvious attractiveness under the conditions which prevail in most underdeveloped areas, it is easy to believe that the one-party state will ultimately prove to be the standard pattern of political development in most newly liberated nations.

The transition from a colonial to an independent status has generally served not to reduce, but rather to increase, those difficulties of social communication which have already been emphasized as a characteristic feature of all underdeveloped countries. As long as native elites are able to concentrate their attention on the elimination of an alien administration, it is comparatively easy for them to achieve effective leadership over the masses. Although their more backward followers have little understanding of or sympathy for the ultimate goals of the nationalist movement, common hostility to the representatives of a foreign culture provides them both with an immediate basis for common action. This is a reliable source of strength in the course of the fight for national liberation. Once freedom has been attained, however, the problem of national leadership takes on a wholly new dimension. At this point the native elite have to face up to the necessity of launching a positive program of national development and modernization. Nationalism provides them with a sense of the need for action, but that sense is no longer easy to communicate to the rest of the population.

Adherence to traditional ways makes for widespread resistance to innovations, and the appeal of genuinely national sentiments is often very weak. This is especially true of Africa, whose present national boundaries are a result of the accidents of Western colonial expansion, and have little or nothing to do with historic traditions indigenous to the area itself. In these regions, the sense of common nationality is a very recent growth and is confined for the most part to that small minority of natives who have been most thoroughly exposed to Western cultural influences. The nationalism of these native elites does nothing to provide them with a common ground for appealing to the rest of the population; instead, it is one of the many barriers that stand in the way of communication between them and their more backward brethren, whose traditional loyalties are still essentially tribal. Under these circumstances it would be little short of suicidal for nationalist leaders to subject themselves to any serious party competition. If genuine alternatives were offered to the masses, the chances are that nationally divisive and antiprogressive forces would quickly carry the day. The obvious answer, from the standpoint of the established national leaders, is to monopolize the right to political action, doing everything in their power to prevent rival leaders from emerging to challenge their position.

As things now stand, the prospects of constitutional democracy in ex-colonial areas seem rather slim. Dictatorship, with rare exceptions, seems to be the natural outcome of the colonial experiences to which so large a part of the world has been subjected for so long. But dictatorship itself is capable of taking different forms. It would be interesting to know what shape it is likely to assume in these newly liberated nations.

A TENDENCY TOWARD FASCISM AMONG THE
NEWLY LIBERATED PEOPLES

The most frightening possibility, from an American standpoint, is that all or most of these regions may move toward Russian totalitarianism. For people now faced with similar tasks of modernization, the attractions of the Russian model are bound to be considerable. If the Russian party elite, inspired by the ideology of Marxism, was able to develop effective means of asserting control over the rest of the population, and thus to speed them along the road to modernization, would it not be wise for the modernizing elites of other countries to follow in their footsteps? This question has been asked by many, and many have answered it affirmatively. Converts to communism, often considerable in number, are to be found in most of the ex-colonial nations. The possibility of their seizing power, and thus converting their respective countries to the cause of world communism, is one of the many worries that Western statesmen have had to face in recent years, and no doubt will have to go on facing for a considerable time to come.

At present, however, the newly liberated nations seem relatively impervious to the appeals of communism. With the exception of a few Asian ex-colonies which have been open to direct intervention because of their propinquity to Communist China, none have been persuaded to adopt the Communist pattern; and even the few which, like Mali, seemed for a while to welcome Communist ties have been showing signs of disillusionment. Apparently the difficulty is that the ruling elites in these countries are too nationalist in feeling to take kindly to Marxism, which is explicitly antinationalist in its ultimate aspirations. The imperialist character of the U.S.S.R., most crassly revealed in the repression of Hungary, is also unlikely to appeal to men whose lives have been devoted to the principle of national self-determination. It would be rash, on the basis of the limited evidence now available, to write off the possibility of future Communist successes in the ex-colonial world. Communist totalitarianism does not appear, however, to be the form of dictatorship that these countries are most likely to adopt in the foreseeable future.

Much more probable, in my opinion, is the emergence of less doctrinaire and less rigidly disciplined one-party regimes, formed on the lines of Italian fascism. Devoted to a policy of national unity and aggressive self-assertion, these dictatorships would be intolerant of opposition and disrespectful of civil liberties. They would not, on the other hand, go so far as the Communists in insisting on rigid discipline within the official party, nor would they attempt to maintain an absolutely totalitarian control over the rest of society. Economically they would tend toward state socialism, without precluding some room for private enterprise. A number of the newly liberated nations have already gone quite far in the fascist direction, and more are likely to follow.

There is also the uglier possibility that some of these dictatorships may become associated with a curiously inverted form of neo-Nazi racism. Stirrings of this sort can already be detected, especially in the Negro world. In the United States a small but growing movement, the Black Muslims,[11] asserts that the black race is superior to the white, and should be recognized accordingly. In Africa systematic hostility to the white man is also a factor to be reckoned with. None of the newly liberated nations has gone so far as to adopt racism as a part of its official ideology, and hopefully they may never do so. There can be no doubt, however, that the arrogance so often characteristic of Western colonialism has left a considerable legacy of racial hatred. Informal pressures and discriminations are already making it difficult for white settlers to continue living in many parts of Africa. One of the charges recently leveled by the Russians against the Chinese Communists is that they have been trying to exploit this situation by giving a distinctly racist twist to their anticolonialist agitation. Although the charge may be unfounded in the present case, it may prove a portent of things to come.

ALTERNATIVES IN AMERICAN FOREIGN POLICY

What, then, in the light of these various developments and possibilities, should be the American attitude toward the problems raised by the disappearance of Western colonialism? Ought we, in the light of our traditional belief in constitutional democracy as a way of life for all men, give up our equally traditional belief in national self-determination? This is tempting in a situation like the present, where dictatorship, rather than democracy, is the probable outcome of national independence. Or ought we to stick by the principle of national self-determination, and

---

[11] See Charles Eric Lincoln, *The Black Muslims in America* (Boston: Beacon Press, 1961).

thus knowingly abandon a large part of the world to a dictatorial future? The alternatives seem equally unattractive.

Luckily for our peace of mind, the choice is no longer open. By adopting the policy it has actually followed in the postwar years, America has firmly and irrevocably committed itself to national self-determination, regardless of consequences. At first this was a serious source of friction with some of our more important allies. Feeling that many of their charges were not yet ripe for self-government, they often resented American pressures exerted on behalf of colonial independence. On this point, however, I believe that the American position was essentially correct, and it has gained ever wider acceptance. Although the theory of liberal colonialism is plausible, and may have done good in its day, that day is clearly over. Experience shows that foreign tutelage, if continued to the point at which it arouses serious opposition on the part of the native population, is likely to lead to dictatorship. By now, however, the demand for national self-determination has become nearly universal, and it arouses bitter hostility toward any obstructive force. Under these circumstances it makes no sense to go on defending colonialism as a means of preparing people for a democratic future. The position is no longer tenable, and has rightly been abandoned.

But even though the official policy has been essentially correct, Americans have been slow to accept its logical consequences. If colonies must be liberated, although they may clearly be unprepared for constitutional democracy, it seems to follow that a considerable number of nondemocratic governments will have to be accepted. This is something that Americans still find hard to do. The vision of Liberty Enlightening the World is still a potent one. Although we have learned to get along, more or less, with Tito, Franco, and other serviceable dictators, it goes against the grain. Whenever an ex-colonial country shows signs of becoming dictatorial, our immediate impulse is to be dismayed and to consider using economic pressures to bring it back in line. But the nature of the postcolonial world is such that dictatorships will probably be no rarity there in the immediate future. Among them will be many potentially valuable allies and associates, who will be repelled by any attempt of outsiders, and especially of Western outsiders, to interfere with their affairs. This is one of the many unwelcome but important facts that Americans will have to learn to live with in the contemporary world. The sooner they start doing so, the better it will be for all concerned.

Suggestions for Further Reading

Almond, Gabriel A., and J. S. Coleman, *The Politics of Developing Areas.* Princeton, N.J.: Princeton University Press, 1960.

Attlee, Clement R., *Twilight of Empire*. New York: Barnes & Noble, Inc., 1961.
Carter, Gwendolen M., *The Politics of Inequality: South Africa Since 1948*. New York: Frederick A. Praeger, Inc., 1958, 1959.
Emerson, Rupert, *From Empire to Nation*. Cambridge, Mass.: Harvard University Press, 1960.
Plamenatz, John P., *On Alien Rule and Self-Government*. London: Longmans, Green, & Co., 1960.
Strausz-Hupé, Robert and H. W. Hazard, *The Idea of Colonialism*. New York: Frederick A. Praeger, Inc., 1958.

Autobiographical and other writings by the leaders of newly liberated nations are also well worth reading for the light they throw on the ideological commitments of the new elites and on the circumstances which shaped them. Particularly recommended are:

Duffy, James, ed., *Africa Speaks*. Princeton, N.J.: Princeton University Press, 1961.
Nasser, Gamal Abdel, *Egypt's Liberation*. Washington, D.C.: Public Affairs Press, 1956.
Nehru, Jawaharlal, *Toward Freedom*. New York: The John Day Company, Inc., 1941.
Nkrumah, Kwame, *Ghana: the Autobiography of Kwame Nkrumah*. New York: Thomas Nelson & Sons, 1957.

UNITED STATES FOREIGN POLICY
TOWARD SOUTH AFRICA

Gwendolen M. Carter

Africa has become the latest, and in some ways most complex, field for American foreign policy. As long as it remained largely under colonial control, Africa could be looked on as an extension of Europe, and issues affecting Africa could be viewed as aspects of American relations with the metropolitan countries: the United Kingdom, France, Belgium, Portugal, and Spain. But with the startlingly rapid drive to independence of African countries from 1957 to 1962, the continent became an area of direct concern to the United States because of its size, its strategic position, its obvious need and desire for outside aid, and the increasing pressures its countries are exerting within the United Nations.

In the history of international organization, no bloc of states has so successfully dramatized and organized support for its objectives as have the newly independent African states with their vehement attacks on racial discrimination within the continent of Africa. Since the Afro-Asian

GWENDOLEN M. CARTER *is Sophia Smith Professor at Smith College and in September 1964 becomes the Melville J. Herskovits Professor of African Studies and Director of the African Studies Center at Northwestern University. She has also been on the faculties of McMaster University, Wellesley College, and Tufts College. She was a researcher in the Office of Strategic Services during World War II. She is author, co-author, and editor of numerous books in comparative government, including* The Politics of Inequality: South Africa since 1948, Independence for Africa, Major Foreign Powers *(with John H. Herz),* Government and Politics in the Twentieth Century *(with John H. Herz),* Transition in Africa *(with William O. Brown), and* African One-Party States.

group now includes more than half the members of the United Nations, its voting strength can decide any procedural question in the General Assembly and can powerfully influence decisions on important questions of substance.[1] But beyond this fact lies the emotional appeal of the African demands for majority rule based on "one man, one vote" and for the right to determine conditions within the whole of Africa.

The basic aspirations of the independent African states coincide at most points with the objectives of the United States.[2] Their desire to evolve into well-knit entities with maturing and balanced economies is exactly in the American interest which, negatively, is to prevent East-West rivalries from using Africa as a battleground and, positively, is to encourage the economic growth and rising standards of living which, hopefully, will result in the new nations' stability and increased participation in world trade. Their objective of racial equality is one which the American nation has accepted for itself and toward which it is moving, however haltingly. The United States stands publicly for the same objective of racial equality in the international community.

DIVERGENCE BETWEEN AFRICAN DESIRES AND AMERICAN AIMS

African desires and American aims have threatened to conflict, however, over the kind of policies which should be adopted toward the Republic of South Africa, the one independent state in Africa dominated by a white minority. Its rich mineral resources and capitalist initiative have given it by far the most advanced and integrated economic structure on that continent, but its policies of racial discrimination against nonwhites in the name of *apartheid* (apartness) make it the chief target for African attacks.

Throughout the long course of the United Nations' efforts to persuade South Africa to change its policies of racial discrimination, the United States has persistently, and with increasing emphasis, made clear its basic opposition to apartheid. Acknowledging their country's own inadequacies, and also the existence of discrimination in most parts of the world, American representatives have placed the situation in South Africa in a special category because its "violation of human rights is buttressed and

---

[1] See Vernon McKay, *Africa in World Politics* (New York: Harper & Row, Publishers, 1963), for a broad consideration of the actions of the African states in the United Nations and of United Nations activities in Africa; and see also "Africa and International Organization," *International Organization*, 17 (Spring, 1962).

[2] For a useful analysis of the American interest in Africa, see *United States Foreign Policy: Africa*, a Study prepared at the request of the Committee on Foreign Relations of the United States Senate by the Program of African Studies, Northwestern University, October 23, 1959, 86th Cong., 1st sess. (Washington, D.C.: Government Printing Office, 1959). For another view, see the pamphlet by the Africa League, *A New American Policy towards Africa*, 360 Riverside Drive, New York City, 1960.

sanctified by statute." [3] Thus, as the United States representative pointed out on November 2, 1959, this "violation is crystallized into a principle that stops the clock, silences wisdom, and prevents the educational process towards respect for human rights from functioning at all." [4]

In response to the South African argument that its racial policy is an internal matter and therefore not a subject for international discussion or action, the United States has upheld the view that issues concerning human rights are "universal in that their continued existence is properly of increasing interest to us all." [5] Following this line, the United States has associated itself with condemnations of South Africa's apartheid policies imposed both within South West Africa, technically still held under a League of Nations mandate, and within the Republic's own borders. Moreover, through private diplomatic approaches, the American government has reiterated its view that a change in policy is called for.[6] To underline its distaste for South African racial policies, the American government has also adopted a "definite policy" of not selling any arms or armaments to the South African government which could be used "to enforce its policies of apartheid." [7]

Where the United States has placed itself in opposition to the African states, however, is in regard to the imposition of specific sanctions against South Africa. Thus it has been unwilling to support their resolutions calling for the expulsion of South Africa from the United Nations and for punitive measures that are designed to force South Africa through economic pressures to modify or give up its apartheid policies.

Many reasons have been put forward to justify the American refusal to support punitive action against South Africa. The United States has opposed the expulsion of South Africa from the United Nations in part because it would relieve South Africa of its obligations under the Charter of the United Nations. More particularly, it has felt that expulsion would only isolate that country still further from the pressures of world opinion. The United States has maintained that, on the contrary, what is needed is to expand South Africa's contacts with the rest of the world so that its dominant group shall feel more keenly "the impact of universal conscience."

The American government has opposed sanctions because it believed that they would harden the attitude of white South Africans and rally

[3] United Nations, Special Political Committee, 14th Session, 141st Meeting, November 2, 1959.

[4] *Ibid.*

[5] *Ibid.*

[6] United Nations, Special Political Committee, 16th Session, 268th Meeting, October 24, 1961.

[7] Department of State, Press Release 4062, October 11, 1962. A complete American arms embargo beginning January 1964 was announced by Ambassador Stevenson on August 2, 1963.

them to the government. Moreover, it has recognized that sanctions would impose particular hardships on nonwhites, especially in the towns (a fact of which Africans are aware and from which they do not flinch), and it has long maintained the position that "our paramount consideration should be, not punitive action against a recalcitrant government, but the welfare of apartheid's unfortunate victims themselves." [8] Beyond this factor, the United States has feared that sanctions would provoke an explosion within South Africa that might plunge that country into chaos, and that such developments would jeopardize peace in the African continent "and even in the whole world." [9]

There are further reasons why the United States has opposed sanctions against South Africa. One reason is that it might be difficult, if not impossible, to provide such sanctions under the present laws of the United States.[10] But far more important has been the fear that a program of sanctions which is not adequately implemented would have less impact on the South African government than on the United Nations itself, which might become only "an instrument of empty threats." [11] Moreover, although this position has not been officially stated, there is little doubt that the United States, like most of the other Western powers, has felt that extreme measures such as sanctions should be restricted to situations in which there is a flagrant breach of international peace. Recognizing that apartheid policies may in the long run lead to international disorder, these policies have not yet had such an effect.

Thus the United States confronts a double dilemma in its foreign policy toward South Africa. It has been unwilling to endorse the extreme measures called for by many members of the United Nations for fear these measures might create chaos in South Africa, rather than a healthy reversal of apartheid policies. But the fact that the United States does not endorse these measures weakens the faith of African states in its uncompromising opposition to racial discrimination. At the same time, the United States feels frustrated over the long and apparently fruitless efforts to bring moral pressure to bear upon South Africa.

UNIQUENESS OF THE SOUTH AFRICAN SITUATION

What is it in the South African situation that creates such difficulties? The uniqueness of the South African situation is constantly affirmed, with considerable justification, by its representatives. South Africa, as

[8] United Nations, Special Political Committee, 15th Session, 236th Meeting, March 30, 1961.

[9] *Ibid.*, 243rd Meeting, April 5, 1961, p. 81.

[10] Department of State, Press Release 3833, November 10, 1961.

[11] United Nations, Special Political Committee, 15th Session, 243rd Meeting, April 5, 1961, p. 81.

already noted, is the only independent state in Africa controlled by a white minority. It lies outside tropical Africa at the southern end of the continent in a predominantly temperate area. It was settled by the majority group within its white population more than three centuries ago. That group, the Afrikaners, and the English-speaking who came from 1820 on, regard South Africa as their home quite as strongly and with as much justification as do the majority Africans in that country who outnumber the whites three to one. (There are also Colored [mixed blood] and Asians who bring the nonwhite-white ratio to four to one.) Moreover, Afrikaner nationalism in defense of Afrikanerdom is as strong as, and may be stronger than, the nationalism of any other group in Africa.[12]

When South Africa became independent in 1910 under the control of its white minority,[13] its achievement of full self-government within the British Commonwealth of Nations was hailed as a mark of British liberalism, since, for the first time, the majority of those to whom power was transferred was not British, as it had been in Canada, Australia, and New Zealand. Nicholas Mansergh has suggested in *South Africa, 1906-1961: The Price of Magnanimity*[14] that this transfer of power may have provided a precedent for the subsequent transfers of power to other non-British groups, to Asians, Africans, and West Indians—the development that has characterized the expansion of the postwar Commonwealth of Nations. But however magnanimous South African independence might have seemed to many contemporaries in 1910, others saw even then that to place ultimate and exclusive political power in the hands of a white minority was to deny the basic liberal emphasis on individual rights.

The time, the place, and the circumstances combined, however, to launch South Africa as an independent country under white control, a situation which has persisted for more than fifty years. Favored by nature with a strategic position, a wide range of temperate climate, magnificent scenery and vast subsoil resources, South Africa has advanced far faster and farther than any other part of Africa. Since gold was discovered on the Witwatersrand in 1886, South Africa has become (and remains) the world's greatest producer of that mineral. South Africa's gem diamonds have been legendary in size and beauty and remain an important source of wealth. Many other minerals, such as uranium and titanium, swell its resources. No less significant is South Africa's possession of the continent's

[12] See Sheila Patterson, *The Last Trek: A Study of the Boer People and the Afrikaner Nation* (London: Routledge & Kegan Paul, Ltd., 1957), for a useful study of the historical evolution of Afrikaner nationalism.

[13] See the thorough and able study by L. M. Thompson, *The Unification of South Africa, 1902-1910* (New York: Oxford University Press, 1960).

[14] Nicholas Mansergh, *South Africa, 1906-1961: The Price of Magnanimity* (New York: Frederick A. Praeger, Inc., 1962).

best resources of coal and iron, from which it developed in the 1920's an efficient steel industry now yielding exports as well as meeting most of its own needs. Moreover these needs are steadily increasing, for since World War I, and still more since World War II, South Africa has developed a superstructure of manufacturing, through which many of its own products are processed, as in canning, or by which imports are mixed with its own materials, as in the production of automobiles and tires. Not only does South Africa possess the richest and most diversified resources on the continent, but it also has had the only industrial revolution. As a result, South Africa possesses by far the most mature economy in Africa, very close to, if not already at, the "take off" point of self-activating, continued growth.

The diversifying of the economic process, coupled with the inability of the land to support many of the whites and Africans formerly dependent on it, has brought large numbers of all South Africa's people into the urban conglomerations in or near its cities.[15] The Africans have always provided the great unskilled labor force of the country. Today they also occupy some two-thirds of all the semiskilled jobs in industry and commerce. Less well known, however, is the fact that in the 1920's, Afrikaners (or Boers, meaning farmers, as they were then called) flooded into the urban areas to seek the livelihood their land could no longer afford them—and found that industry and commerce were in the hands of the English-speaking minority, whose allies had defeated the Afrikaners in the Anglo-Boer war. They found also that the unskilled jobs, the only ones for which they were equipped, were being done by Africans. In that decade South Africa suffered the world's worst poor white problem with some 60 per cent of all the Afrikaner people either in, or close to, poor white status.

Today there are few poor whites in South Africa. The government and the trade unions have successfully elevated the white Afrikaner to a privileged place in the economy and the administration, a place that is safeguarded by South Africa's racial policy. Thus apartheid, or racial separation, which reinforces both this privileged position and a long-standing sense of racial distinctiveness, if not superiority, looks very different to the white South African worker or farmer than it does to the nonwhite South African and to most people outside that country. Where the latter see these policies as flagrant discrimination, the lower middle-class whites, the basic strength of the Nationalist Party, look on apartheid as their shield and protection against the pressures of the majority nonwhites inside the country. The manufacturers and more

---

[15] The best short description of South Africa's peoples and policies is in Leo Marquard, *The Peoples and Policies of South Africa*, 3rd ed. (New York: Oxford University Press, 1962).

privileged white groups commonly welcome, or at least accede to, a pattern of life which assures them a controlled labor force and continued economic growth.

In this perspective, the constant attacks on apartheid in the United Nations appear to most white South Africans as threats to the distinctive position and even the livelihood of the three and a quarter million white people who make up one-fifth of the population of that country. Moreover, most white South Africans believe that the attacks are not motivated by humanitarian sentiments or by a desire for justice, but by political considerations, particularly the solidarity of the people of color throughout the world against entrenched white groups which maintain a privileged position for themselves by political, economic, or social techniques. As evidence, they point to the fact that when there was sharp criticism of the joint Pretoria communique of 1962 that had stated that the two visiting United Nations representatives had found no evidence of genocide in South West Africa and that its administration by South Africa offered no threat to international peace, Mr. Carpio of the Philippines, Chairman of the United Nations South West Africa Commission, denied that he had signed the statement, despite the insistence of the Committee's vice chairman, Mr. de Alva of Mexico, that he had done so.

Nonetheless, and despite their counter criticisms of authoritarianism, discrimination, and disorder in African and other countries, South Africans have not been untouched by pressures in the United Nations and, perhaps particularly, by the position taken by the United States. On the one hand is a growing solidarity among the white people of South Africa as the older tensions between English-speaking and Afrikaans-speaking people are overlaid by the more urgent problems of how to react to the southward thrust of African nationalism and to the increasing intensity of United Nations criticism. On the other hand is the speeding up of what the ruling Nationalist group calls South Africa's own solution to the racial problem—that is, separate development, or positive apartheid, through the establishment of African-controlled Bantustans.

POSITIVE APARTHEID: THE BANTUSTAN PROGRAM

Negative apartheid, which provides the framework of restrictions on non-whites in the so-called white areas of South Africa (the areas outside the African reserves), has always dominated race relations in that country. But the complementary aspect of this policy, positive apartheid or separate development, has also been a part of Afrikaner Nationalist ideology. In essence, positive apartheid means to establish institutions and, ultimately, communities (called Bantustans) for Africans in which they can have the authority and distinctive ways of life now denied them in the so-called white areas. The first of these Bantustans was announced in January 1962, and the legislative provisions enacted early in 1963 for the Transkei, the largest and linguistically most unified of the African reserve territories. The Transkei has possessed certain local representative institutions since 1894. Though the grant of authority to this area falls far short of full internal self-government, Nationalist leaders maintain that the territory will be led in this direction.

The Bantustan program, that the government plans ultimately to extend to eight African areas within South Africa, presents the outside world with something of a dilemma. On the one hand, all nationalist-minded Africans throughout South Africa condemn the program as a fraudulent attempt to provide an illusion of self-government, and, moreover, as promoting a harmful fragmentation of South African territory, one that divides Africans, rather than unites them, and thereby aids their control by white authorities.[16] Liberal white South Africans endorse this opposition to the Bantustans and emphasize the incompatibility of the program with the highly integrated South African economy. African leaders outside South Africa react as vigorously against the Bantustan concept as they did to Tshombe's Katanga separatism. On the other hand, in the face of the difficulties of forcing racial integration on the white-controlled government of an independent state, a nagging question persists: Could the dynamic of separate development lead not only to African self-government in part of South Africa but also to a situation in which a white majority in its own territory would feel sufficiently secure to extend rights to nonwhites? If so would it not provide an alternative both to the blatant racial discrimination of the present situation and to the use of force, economic or even military, to overthrow the present regime in South Africa, with all the violence and dislocation such action might entail?

On one occasion only has an American representative hinted at the acceptability of the Bantustan concept if it were realized to the full. In the course of the sharpest criticism of South Africa ever made by an American delegate, Mr. Plimpton declared on October 24, 1961, that "carried to its logical conclusion, the result of apartheid would be real partition, with the Negro and other non-white inhabitants in possession of their own territory and independent government and with the white South Africans gathered into their own independent enclave." Although he noted that such a partition did not appear to be the objective of the South African government, he asked: Will South Africa "ever grant full independence to those so-called Bantu states," or will it keep them forever as subordinate states and still utilize African labor? This latter alternative

---

[16] A poignant firsthand account of African resistance to the attempted enforcement in Zeerust of the Bantu Authorities Act, a preliminary step to the Bantustan program, is provided by Father Charles Hooper, *Brief Authority* (Toronto: Collins, 1960).

he stigmatized as "a tragic alternative";[17] the former possibility—if, indeed, it is a possibility—he left without further comment.

Should the South African government move purposefully to implement the full potentialities of the Bantustan program, the United States will be confronted with the necessity of deciding whether this program offers an acceptable alternative to what has been its primary objective: to secure the reduction and ultimate abolition of those features of South African law which not only permit, but in practice also enforce, racial discrimination.

No one can doubt that the *de facto* and perhaps ultimately *de jure* partition of South Africa with its highly integrated economy would inevitably entail great dislocations and sufferings on the part of substantial groups of all races. Most outside observers are likely to feel that such a radical change involves still more drastic developments and changes of attitude than would accompany the gradual dismantling of the framework of apartheid laws. Left to its own determination of policy, there seems little doubt, however, that if forced to so unwelcome a choice, the South African government would prefer to transfer part of the country to African control, rather than to admit Africans and other nonwhites to a share in the political and economic control of an undivided country. At this point the vital issues would arise of where the line of partition would be drawn, and what rights would be extended to all groups within each area.

Were the South African situation to remain as tightly controlled and as relatively peaceful as in the past, the United States might continue to enjoy the luxury of condemning apartheid but of taking no overt steps to modify or to end apartheid practices. But sporadic violence in South Africa against white-owned property, and even against whites themselves, coupled with increasingly unified pressures against South Africa by the independent African States, have confronted the American government with more urgent and difficult decisions.[18] The use of violence against Africans and other nonwhites has long taken place in South Africa, but terrorist wounding and killing of whites is new. Such terrorist activity against whites may eventually increase, particularly if Southern Rhodesia and Mozambique come under African control. The moderate leaders of the Africans within South Africa are either in jail or under bans of silence, while those outside have strong enducements to adopt more radical tactics. In any case, the Africans suffer an almost uncontrollable frustration at the tightness of the controls under which they live. But

---

[17] United Nations, Special Political Committee, 16th Session, 260th Meeting, October 24, 1961.

[18] Earlier African efforts to lessen restrictions are described by Leo Kuper, *Passive Resistance in South Africa* (New Haven, Conn.: Yale University Press, 1957). Issued in paper cover, 1960.

violence from nonwhites can be expected to meet equal or greater violence from the government or, still more dangerous, from white vigilantes who seek to impose a counter terror of their own.

When the United Nations Security Council considered the 1960 Sharpeville shootings, in which some South African police panicked and killed 67 Africans engaged in a peaceful protest against the pass laws which limit so greatly, and often arbitrarily, their freedom of movement, the American representative declared that racial discrimination as a matter of governmental policy "may be even more destructive to the peace of mankind" than some of the political disputes which had been brought before that body.[19] Since that time, the South African police has been a great deal more careful and controlled in its measures for African restraint. Should there be a repetition, however, of the Sharpeville shootings, or large scale violence against nonwhites, this could hardly fail to bring another international reaction like that of 1960. Indeed, a further event of this kind would lead to major pressures for some type of active intervention.

APARTHEID POLICIES AND THEIR IMPLICATIONS
FOR THE WESTERN DEMOCRACIES

The American government and public would obviously prefer to have a judicial decision on South Africa's apartheid policies, rather than a political one. Thus the United States has endorsed wholeheartedly the reference to the International Court of Justice by Liberia and Ethiopia of the question of whether South Africa is fit to act as a mandatory power for South West Africa.[20] The Court's decision in December, 1962, by eight votes to seven, that it has competence in this case opens the way to the long process of argument on the issue, in which South Africa is prepared to participate. A judicial decision warranting United Nations action could hardly be disregarded by the United States, and in this sense South West Africa might prove to be South Africa's Achilles heel. The length of time it takes for judicial processes to run their course, however, may well force a political decision on the United States before the Court hands down its judgment.

What could the United States do to exert pressure on South Africa? In fact, a good deal. Despite the degree of development of the South African economy and accelerated efforts to make it more self-sufficient,

---

[19] United Nations, Security Council, 14th Session, 855th Meeting, April 1, 1960.
[20] International Court of Justice, South West Africa Case (Liberia versus the Union of South Africa). Memorial submitted by the Government of Liberia, April, 1961; Preliminary Objections filed by the Government of the Republic of South Africa, November, 1961; Observations of the Governments of Ethiopia and Liberia, March, 1962 (New York: The United Nations, 1961, 1962).

South African prosperity and growth still depend largely upon its external trading and financial relations.

South Africa's relations with Great Britain are by far the most important—totaling about one-third of all South African exports and imports —and have been virtually unaffected by South Africa's withdrawal from the Commonwealth. Great Britain has also been supplying South Africa with the arms it wants in a heavily accelerated program of defense. In comparison to Great Britain's share of South African trade, that of the United States is not high, but in 1962 it took about 12 per cent of all South Africa's exports (excluding gold). These exports mainly included uranium oxide (bought jointly with Great Britain under an agreement terminating in 1970) and, on a lesser scale, wool, diamonds, copper, and lobster tails. Moreover, the United States ranks after Great Britain as South Africa's major supplier. In 1961 the United States provided about 16 per cent of the Republic's total imports, including machinery, metal parts, chemicals, and automobiles. As for foreign investment in South Africa, the British share was 58.5 per cent by the end of 1960, a slight decline from 62 per cent in 1956. In the same period, the American share of foreign investment in South Africa rose from 12.3 per cent to 13.7 per cent. Over the period 1950-61, American investment rose from about 140 million dollars to 700 million dollars. A substantial part of this investment is in South African gold and diamond mining. It represents about three-fifths of all American capital investment on the African continent.

If the United States were to join in an economic boycott of South Africa while Great Britain continued to trade with that country, the result might be a still greater tension between the two key nations of the free world than that developed over Katanga. But should the two countries concert a common program against South Africa (a greater possibility if a Labor government comes into office in Great Britain), its devastating effect cannot be in doubt. Particularly if the United States and Great Britain cut off South Africa's supply of oil by boycott and blockade, the impact would be great. A further unique feature of the South African scene—the division of economic and political power between its English-speaking and Afrikaans-speaking people—might then have the effect that Afrikaners have always dreaded: the use of internal economic power to change policies and political leaders, rather than the present quiescent acceptance, if not wholehearted enthusiasm for both by industrial and commercial leaders.

Such a rousing of local economic interests against the government might be more likely, because the occupations most vulnerable to sanctions are those that employ the largest percentage of nonwhites: mining, 7.5 non-whites to every white; agriculture, 6 to one; and manufacturing, 2.5 to one. Thus sanctions would aggravate racial tension among the nonwhites, thereby almost inevitably adding to the violence which can be expected to dictate the outside intervention.

Should violence against both whites and nonwhites be successfully contained by the South African government and should the Transkei be given in practice a wide measure of control over its own affairs, the pressures for outside intervention may diminish. Under those circumstances, the decisions on South Africa's future may rest in the hands of its own people. It will then be for them to decide whether they are going to move toward one or the other of the acceptable solutions to their racial problem: the removal of discrimination and the extension of rights in a common community, or within a country that has been formally divided on a more or less equalitarian basis between predominantly white and predominantly African areas. In the eyes of the world, the former solution would be a far more desirable approach and would be no more difficult to achieve, it would seem, than the drastic dislocation of total separation.

Until South Africa moves in one or the other of these two directions, however, there will be no relaxation of formal and informal efforts to modify, and ultimately destroy, its legally enforced pattern of racial discrimination. Along with its rich potentialities, South Africa embodies in its most acute form the most sensitive problem of the twentieth century: the relation between a dominant white minority and an increasingly assertive nonwhite majority claiming the human rights to which the Western world has committed itself. There can be no genuine stability in southern Africa, or perhaps even in the relations between the Western democracies and the peoples of color, until South Africa's racial policies come far closer into line with increasingly widespread demands for human dignity and mutual respect.

Suggestions for Further Reading

Benson, Mary, *The African Patriots*. London: Faber and Faber, 1963.

Brookes, Edgar H. and J. B. Macauley, *Civil Liberty in South Africa*. New York: Oxford University Press, 1958.

Carter, Gwendolen M., *The Politics of Inequality: South Africa since 1948*. New York: Frederick A. Praeger, Inc., 1958, 1959.

De Beer, Zacharius Johannes, *Multi-Racial South Africa; The Reconciliation of Forces*. New York: Oxford University Press, 1961.

De Kiewiet, C. W., *The Anatomy of South African Misery*. New York: Oxford University Press, 1956.

First, Ruth, *South West Africa*. Baltimore, Maryland: Penguin Books, 1963.

Karis, Thomas, "The Republic of South Africa," in *Five African States: Responses to Diversity*, ed. Gwendolen M. Carter. Ithaca, N.Y.: Cornell University Press, 1963.

Luthuli, Albert, *Let My People Go.* New York: McGraw-Hill Book Company, Inc., 1962.

Pienaar, A. and A. Sampson, *South Africa, Two Views of Separate Development.* New York: Oxford University Press, 1960.

Rhoodie, N. J. and H. J. Venter, *Apartheid: A Socio-Historical Exposition of the Origin and Development of the Apartheid Idea.* Amsterdam: De Bussy, 1960.

Roux, E., *Time Longer Than Rope: A History of the Black Man's Struggle for Freedom in South Africa.* London: *Victor Gollancz,* Ltd., 1948.

Tomlinson Report, Socio-Economic Development of the Bantu Areas, *Summary of the Report.* Pretoria, South Africa: South African Government Printer, 1955.

United Nations, *Commission on the Racial Situation in the Union of South Africa.* New York: The United Nations, 1953, 1954, 1955.

LATIN AMERICA:

SOCIAL REVOLUTION AND

UNITED STATES FOREIGN POLICY

Federico G. Gil

It is likely that the twentieth century will be recorded in history not so much as the century of great world wars as the century of world revolution. If revolution is the central theme of our time, it follows logically that, in the present worldwide contest, victory may go to those who understand revolution, while (as Hannah Arendt has warned) those who put their faith in power politics and in war as effective instruments of foreign policy may in the end discover that they excel in a rather useless and obsolete trade. Miss Arendt sees the interest of freedom as having been impaired by our failure in the past to incorporate the "American Revolution into the revolutionary tradition." Considering that the inclination to lose sight of the origins of the United States "is largely

FEDERICO G. GIL *is Professor of Political Science and Director of the Institute of Latin American Studies at the University of North Carolina. As a specialist in Latin American politics, Dr. Gil has lectured and travelled extensively throughout Latin America and the United States. Among his most recent activities has been participation in the drafting of the Alliance for Progress. His honors include membership in the National Academy of Law and Social Sciences in Argentina and an Honorary Professorship at the University of Chile. With W. W. Pierson he is the author of* Governments of Latin America, *a widely used textbook and reference work. He has also written many articles on inter-American relations. His latest publications include* Genesis and Modernization of Chilean Political Parties *and "Chile: Society in Transition," a chapter in* Political Systems of Latin America.

responsible for the intense fear of revolution in this country," she maintains that "fear of revolution has been the hidden *leitmotif* of postwar American foreign policy in its desperate attempts at stabilization of the *status quo,* with the result that American power and prestige were used to support obsolete political regimes that long since had become objects of contempt among their citizens." [1]

Perhaps no other area of the world better illustrates this peril than Latin America, and in perhaps no other area is the alteration that has occurred in the foundations of our foreign policy clearer. For it is unquestionable that a wide and basic change, whose deeper implications it would be premature to assess today, is taking place in United States policy and attitude toward this region. The Alliance for Progress constitutes a major turning point in the history of the hemisphere. After over a century of giving blind support to the *status quo* in order to achieve its policy goals of peace and stability in Latin America, the United States, heeding the cries of the great masses of Latin America for radical and speedy solutions to social and economic inequities, has become the ardent, if inexperienced, advocate of social revolution. In the transition to that drastic reorientation, the United States has had no jurisdiction over many of the persons and events that, nevertheless, have been influential in the conception and birth of a new American foreign policy. It is my intent in this essay to analyze, if only briefly, some of these external forces that have shaped American policy and to identify some of the difficulties encountered by this nation in its novel role as a champion of social revolution.

Assumption of this role has forced the United States to develop a new kind of diplomacy, the diplomacy of social revolution. Events in Cuba, whose alliance with and economic subordination to the United States had been taken for granted, have broken the traditional framework in which United States and Latin American foreign policies were formulated and shaped. These events have given rise to two experiments in the grand strategy of development in the Western Hemisphere. In one, the United States itself, embarking in partnership upon social revolution, attempts "to demonstrate to the world that modernization, economic development and social revolution can be achieved through peaceful and democratic means." In the other experiment, "Cuba, following the lead of the Communist bloc, is attempting to achieve the same ends by using the formulae, the plans, and the grand strategy of development employed in the Communist world. Thus, the cold war has been linked to the problem of underdevelopment." [2]

---

[1] Hannah Arendt, *On Revolution* (New York: The Viking Press, Inc., 1963), p. 47.

[2] Gustavo Lagos, *International Stratification and Underdeveloped Countries* (Chapel Hill, N.C.: The University of North Carolina Press, 1963), p. 120. This book offers a provocative new analytical framework for the study of international relations as a stratified system in terms of economics, prestige, and power variables.

THE UNITED STATES AND LATIN AMERICAN REVOLUTIONS

With the emergence of the United States as a great world power at the turn of the century, there was need of redefining the role which this nation should play in the world. The policy which emerged "was a pragmatic attempt to define the interrelated strategic economic interests of the United States in a world of competing empires and power blocs." [3] Basic to this approach was the belief that the national interests could be best protected in a stable, peaceful world in which no one nation exercised absolute empire over extensive areas of the world. The Latin American policy of the United States was formulated in the light of the conflict between the Latin American peoples and the existing imperial systems. The orthodox implementation of this policy was rendered difficult by rising economic and strategic American interests in the Caribbean area. Thus, the expanded version of the Monroe Doctrine, embodied in the Roosevelt Corollary (which was opposed by Latin Americans), and the idea of Pan Americanism, both manifestations of the attempt to preserve the *status quo,* inevitably involved a contradiction for the United States for many years to come. The doctrine of intervention, based on the "duty" of the United States to uphold European proprietary rights as well as on the need to safeguard the growing economic and strategic stakes of the United States in this area, could not be reconciled with the ideals of Pan Americanism. Intervention provided the stability so anxiously sought but carried with it the potential destruction of Pan Americanism.

Taft's "dollar diplomacy," which in his words "substituted dollars for bullets," was designed to insure stability through the use of economic devices. The hope was that by eliminating the causes of revolution European meddling could also be eliminated. Dollar diplomacy was reshaped over the years in answer to changing conditions in Latin America and to the need for developing a Pan American system more palatable to our southern neighbors.

The first social revolution of the twentieth century began in Mexico and presented American statesmen with a new version of the old dilemma. While proclaiming a policy of noninterference, President Wilson upheld traditional economic concepts and demanded immediate and complete compensation for expropriated American property. Armed intervention, however, was not employed. There was only the insistence that Mexico moderate her revolution.

[3] Robert Freeman Smith, "The Role Played by the United States in Latin American Social and Economic Revolutions of the Last Half Century" (a paper presented at the Eighth Southeastern Conference on Latin American Studies, Miami Beach, Florida, April 29, 1961).

The next threat of social revolution, which occurred in Cuba in 1933, revealed some changes in the policy of the United States. Again, there was no military intervention, and President Roosevelt's Cuban policy at the outset of the Era of the Good Neighbor was based on the belief that restoration of Cuba's economy would put an end to unrest and instability.[4] Three programs, all applications of New Deal ideas to foreign policy, were the key instruments in implementing this policy: the sugar-marketing allotment plan, the reciprocal trade agreement, and the Second Export-Import Bank. Such a policy, although showing little understanding toward the need for basic reforms in Cuba's socio-economic structure, achieved its end of preventing undue changes in the *status quo* of the island republic.

The Bolivian social revolution in 1952 marked a decided change of attitude on the part of the United States. The Bolivian revolutionary regime expropriated the tin mines and instituted sweeping agrarian reforms. After a period of hesitation, the United States began to extend economic aid to Bolivia. United States aid, so significant a factor in the survival of the Bolivian Revolution, seemed to indicate that "this country does not necessarily support the *status quo* in semifeudal under-developed nations."[5] Nevertheless, the attitude of the United States toward Bolivia was one of caution. The United States did not extend economic aid until Bolivia had made a preliminary settlement with the mining companies, a year and a half after the revolutionary government had come to power. Just the same, it could justly be said that the United States had come a long way since 1900.

From 1953 until the advent of the Cuban Revolution, the United States lost the time needed for a policy of watchful waiting. Events outside United States control were responsible for the Cuban Revolution, and the United States no longer had the time to wait on the sidelines

[4] Concerned with the dangers inherent in social revolution and its impact on United States vested interests in the island, American policy was aimed at preservation of the *status quo*. Sumner Welles and, later, Jefferson Caffery, as personal representatives of President Roosevelt, played a major role in bringing the revolution to a halt. From then on, the revolution became chiefly political, not social and economic. One cannot help but wonder whether or not events in Cuba would have taken a different course if the United States at that time had favored needed social and economic changes in Latin America. "It is valid to pose such a question, for in some respects the Cuban phenomenon of the 1950's was simply the reincarnation of the revolutionary process interrupted in the 1930's. Set in motion again, this process was to lead, in our time, to disastrous consequences in Cuban-American relations. Also, this time the Cuban revolution was to become chiefly social and economic, not political." Federico G. Gil, "Antecedents of the Cuban Revolution," *The Centennial Review*, VI (Summer, 1962), 377.

[5] Robert J. Alexander, *The Bolivian National Revolution* (New Brunswick, N.J.: Rutgers University Press, 1958), pp. xvii-xviii.

for the revolution to moderate its pace before extending economic, political, and moral aid to the country experiencing the ordeal of revolutionary change.

THE SOVIET CHALLENGE

The new division of the world between developed and underdeveloped nations was now made very clear with the appearance in the United Nations of a group of fifty-seven underdeveloped countries of Asia, Africa, Latin America, and Eastern Europe, all sharing common hopes and interests.[6] Coincidentally, a shift of vast implications took place in Soviet foreign policy after 1955. Premier Khrushchev, reviving Lenin's ideas on the struggle of the colonial peoples against imperialistic oppression and identifying colonialism by the new trait of underdevelopment, made the Soviet Union appear not so much the leader of world communism as the champion of the cause of underdeveloped countries. Concomitantly, the Soviet Union proposed a policy of extending aid to revolutions even when not of Communist origin. The rigidity of Soviet strategy during the Stalin era was replaced by a new flexibility. Lenin's prophecy that the poor and colonial countries would become fertile ground for Communist penetration as real and potential allies is essential to Khrushchev's conception. To implement this conception, the Soviet bloc embarked upon a large-scale offensive of economic and technical aid to the underdeveloped world, an offensive against which Latin America was not immune.[7]

The response of the United States to the Soviet challenge in Latin America is embodied in the Alliance for Progress, which was launched dramatically by President Kennedy in his speech of March 13, 1961, and in a special message to Congress on the following day. Like most deep changes in foreign policy, however, there were many important proposals, debates, and decisions that took place in the course of several years and contributed to the Alliance, both in the United States and in Latin America, but mostly in the latter. The years which preceded the Alliance had convinced Latin Americans "that the United States was indifferent to the problems of economic development, of tyranny, and of social injustice." [8] Latin Americans developed two closely related and essential desires: (1) to break the chains of obsolete and unjust social

[6] For an excellent view of postwar changes in American foreign policy, see William G. Carleton, *The Revolution in American Foreign Policy, 1945-1954* (Garden City, N.Y.: Doubleday & Company, Inc., 1955).

[7] Lagos, *International Stratification*, p. 114.

[8] C. Neale Ronning, *Punta del Este: The Limits of Collective Security in a Troubled Hemisphere* (New York: The Carnegie Endowment for International Peace, 1962), p. 6.

systems perpetuated by oligarchies and military dictatorships; and (2) to attain economic development in order to put an end to widespread poverty and human misery.

During the Inter-American Conference on Problems of War and Peace held in Mexico in 1945, the Latin American countries brought to world attention two interrelated problems which affected them vitally and which became crucial in the postwar era: price fluctuations of basic export commodities and economic underdevelopment. Commodity stabilization seemed essential if the Latin American economies were to have a base stable enough to permit development of coherent policy. A drop in the price of one of the Latin American basic commodities could more than counterbalance any sums received by the way of aid. The financing of economic development in the region at a pace which would insure as rapidly as possible a minimal standard of living for all was also considered indispensable. The United States position with respect to the problem of price fluctuation was characterized, with few exceptions, by strong reluctance to enter "stabilization" agreements. As for financing economic development, the United States maintained that private investment should carry the greater burden of development for Latin America, and that governmental, international, or institutional aid should be limited to specific cases.

At the time of the general reorganization of the inter-American system in 1948, the Charter of Bogotá that was then adopted created the Organization of American States and set forth economic and social principles and objectives. The underlying philosophy of the Charter included the premises that "social justice and social security are bases of lasting peace" and that "economic cooperation is essential to the common welfare and prosperity of the peoples of the Continent." However, "after the historical 1948 date, eight years followed, characterized by hesitation, vacillation, and failure to recognize the magnitude of the problems of poverty and the urgency of its demand for a courageous and creative attack on its solution." [9] These years were not altogether fruitless, for during this time the United Nations Commission for Latin America—under the leadership of Raúl Prebisch, a Latin American economist of vision and ability—devoted itself to a keen and thorough study of Latin America's economic development problems.

The Tenth Inter-American Conference, held in Caracas in 1954, on the initiative of the United States postponed the examination of economic issues by referring them to a special conference of ministers to

[9] William Sanders, "The OAS and the Alliance for Progress" (an address delivered before the Sixteenth Annual Conference of the Oregon High School International Relations League, Eugene, Oregon, February 7-9, 1963).

take place later that year. When this conference met in Petropolis, there was available (thanks to the efforts of the Prebisch group) a body of ideas, principles, and recommendations upon which a new concept of hemispheric cooperation could be founded and applied to the tasks of economic development. The only positive result of the Petropolis Conference was a resolution, significantly adopted without United States approval, to establish a commission of experts to draft plans for the creation of an Inter-American Development Bank.[10] Thus, curiously enough, it was an organization created outside the inter-American system, the United Nations Economic Commission for Latin America, that began to vitalize the regional system.

The growing deterioration in the relations of the United States with Latin America was abruptly and sharply brought into focus in the spring of 1958 as a result of the violence attending Vice-President Nixon's visit to Lima and Caracas. Deep concern began to grow in Washington. Coincidentally, the Committee on Foreign Relations of the United States Senate took initial steps toward a broad and long-range review of the foreign policy of the United States. Hearings were held with regard to policies toward specific areas, among them Latin America. Subsequently, the Senate Committee instructed its Subcommittee on American Republics Affairs to engage in a thoroughgoing and constructive inquiry into United States relations with the other republics of the hemisphere.[11]

President Kubitschek of Brazil and President Eisenhower exchanged notes concerning the critical situation, and after a trip to Rio de Janeiro by Secretary of State Dulles, there emerged the idea of "Operation Pan America," a plan for large-scale joint hemispheric action to promote Latin American economic development for the period 1960-80.[12] While the official version of Kubitschek's "Operation Pan America" contained no figures, it was estimated that approximately 40 billion dollars would be required to attain its goals during that period.[13] To implement the

---

[10] See *Reunión de Ministros de Hacienda o Economía en IV Sesión Extraordinaria del Consejo Interamericano Económico y Social, celebrada en Petrópolis, Brasil, del 22 de noviembre al 2 de diciembre de 1954* (Mexico City: Secretaría de Hacienda y Crédito Público, Dirección General de Prensa, n.d.), pp. 147-49.

[11] Senate Subcommittee on American Republics Affairs, *United States-Latin American Relations: Compilation of Studies*, Sen. Doc. No. 125, 86th Cong., 2d sess., 1960 (Washington, D.C.: Government Printing Office, 1960).

[12] See *Operación Panamericana. Compilación de documentos* (Río de Janeiro: Presidencia de la República, Servicio de Documentación, 1958).

[13] It is interesting to note that during the Second Meeting of the Committee of 21, held in Buenos Aires in 1959, Fidel Castro stated that Latin America's development could only be accomplished through global aid on the part of the United States to the tune of 30 billion dollars, spread over a period of 10 years. This figure is close to the one proposed by President Kubitschek and his economic advisers.

proposal, a special group—the so-called Committee of 21—was appointed by the Council of the OAS. Composed of representatives from all the member nations, the Committee met over a period of three years.

As the result of its final sessions, the Committee presented a series of recommendations known as the Act of Bogotá of 1960. This document distinguished between social and economic development by recognizing that "the effects of the economic development program, while requiring urgent strengthening and enlargement, may be too slow in producing the social benefits necessary and that therefore immediate measures should be taken to meet social needs." There was also clear recognition of the relation between the preservation and strengthening of the free and democratic institutions of the American Republics and an acceleration of social and economic progress in Latin America. A complete program of social development, containing provisions on land tenure, housing, education, public health, and taxation, was set forth.[14]

Two factors of great significance characterized the Bogotá meeting. One was the injection of social development programs as the high-priority ingredient of balanced economic development; the other was a major change of attitude on the part of the United States. Until the meeting, the United States had maintained that sufficient resources for Latin American development were available in normal trade intercourse, in technical assistance programs, and in private investments, supplemented by some funds from international financial institutions. Only when these sources were exhausted should governments attempt to tap public funds, and even then only after each country had set its own economic house in order. Latin America, for its part, had been insisting that these sources were inadequate and that international financial institutions, by maintaining inflexible criteria, made no allowance for social infrastructure development projects.[15] At Bogotá, the United States showed a new readiness to discard her traditional policy that private capital should achieve Latin American economic development and to recognize the need for development by means of over-all national plans.[16]

For the financing of the program outlined in the Act of Bogotá, two chief sources were proposed. The first was the internal resources in each nation, as mobilized by the accumulation of capital through many kinds of savings and by improved fiscal procedures. The second was a Special Inter-American Fund for Social Development—to which the United States pledged 500 million dollars—to be administered by the

---

[14] Víctor L. Urquidi, *Viabilidad económica de América Latina* (Mexico: Fondo de Cultura Económica, 1962), pp. 137-54.

[15] William Sanders, "Pan Americanism—Ideal into Reality" (an address delivered before the Latin American Graduate Students Association, University of Pennsylvania, Philadelphia, Pa., October 25, 1962), p. 27.

[16] Lagos, *International Stratification*, p. 82.

Inter-American Development Bank. That institution, symbol of a long-cherished desire of the Latin Americans for a regional financing agency, had finally become a reality, although at that time it had hardly begun its operations. The first indication of the shift that was taking place in the American attitude was the abandonment by the United States of its opposition to the creation of the Bank.

The work of the United Nations Economic Commission for Latin America, Brazil's formulation of Operation Pan America, the establishment of the Inter-American Development Bank, and, finally, the adoption of the Bogotá Act laid the bases for a revitalized regional system. The revitalization would expand the activities of that system, chiefly political to that time, and convert it into an instrument capable of performing the task of promoting economic and social development. The shift in policies and the enormous increase in the scope and tempo of activity were laborious but marked in the years that preceded the official enunciation of the Alliance for Progress, which swept up these developments in the great and comprehensive current of its revolutionary approach to economic and social development in Latin America.[17]

THE ALLIANCE FOR PROGRESS

In March, 1961, six months after the Bogotá meeting, the President of the United States, speaking at the White House to representatives of the Latin American nations, solemnly pledged the cooperation of this country in a vast effort "to satisfy the basic needs of the American people for homes, work and land, health and schools." Candidly, he also stated that the proposed aid would be of limited value unless the Latin American nations themselves vigorously fostered programs of social reform. "Unless the great mass of Americans shared in increasing prosperity," the President said, "our Alliance, our revolution, and our dream will have failed." [18] The Alliance for Progress was officially launched.[19]

The program was unprecedented in the experience of the Western Hemisphere, for, in essence, the United States was offering to underwrite a social revolution for Latin America. The great plan was expected, as Adlai Stevenson said, "to take the bold, brave, difficult steps" to

---

[17] Sanders, "Pan Americansm—Ideal into Reality," pp. 27-28.

[18] Milton S. Eisenhower, "The Alliance for Progress: Historic Roots," in *The Alliance For Progress—Problems and Perspectives*, ed. John C. Dreier (Baltimore: The Johns Hopkins Press, 1962), p. 15.

[19] This now-famous slogan was first minted at Harvard University at a meeting of distinguished representatives of the international business and academic communities in the United States. See "Alliance for Progress, A Program of Inter-American Partnership," a statement developed at a Conference at the Faculty Club of Harvard University, Cambridge, Mass., December 19, 1960.

achieve peaceably and democratically reforms which in the past history of the world had been accomplished only through revolutions of blood and violence.[20]

In August, 1961, ministerial representatives of the American Republics, convened by the Inter-American Economic and Social Council of the OAS, met at Punta del Este for the purpose of formulating a concrete plan of action along the lines proposed by President Kennedy, to establish the total amount of foreign aid required, and to prescribe the necessary operational details. A declaration signed August 17, 1961, set forth the following goals:

1. the development and strengthening of democratic institutions;
2. the acceleration of economic and social development;
3. the abolition of illiteracy and the improvement of educational standards;
4. the insurance of fair wages and working conditions;
5. the promotion of health programs and the combating of contagious diseases;
6. the reform of tax laws and the encouragement of agrarian reform;
7. the curbing of inflation and the introduction of fiscal stability;
8. the stimulation of "private enterprise in order to encourage the development of Latin American countries at a rate which would help them to provide jobs for their growing populations, to eliminate unemployment, and to take their place among the modern industrialized nations of the world."

The declaration also suggested that economic, social, and cultural changes "can come about only through the self-help efforts of each country" and that "in order to achieve these goals with necessary speed, domestic effort must be reinforced by essential contribution of external assistance." The United States pledged its efforts to supply financial and technical cooperation in order to achieve the aims of the Alliance. To this end, the United States was to provide a major part of the minimum of 20 billion dollars, principally in public funds, which Latin America would require over the next ten years from all external sources in order to supplement its own efforts.

The United States also agreed to provide from public funds, as an immediate contribution to the economic and social progress of Latin America, more than one billion dollars during the twelve months which began on March 13, 1961, when the Alliance was announced. The declaration also stated that "the United States intends to furnish development

---

[20] Peter R. Nehemkis, Jr., "Some Reflections on the Alliance for Progress" (an address delivered before the Phi Beta Kappa Association, Washington, D.C., February 21, 1963).

loans on a long-term basis, where appropriate running up to fifty years and at very low or zero rates of interest."

The Latin American countries, in turn, agreed "to devote a steadily increasing share of their own resources to economic and social development, and to make the reforms necessary to assure that all share fully in the fruits of the Alliance for Progress." Further, the countries of Latin America each pledged to "formulate comprehensive and well-conceived national programs for the development of their own economies." [21]

A lengthier document, the Charter of Punta del Este, formulated the operational scheme to carry forward the plan of the Alliance. The significance of this document lies in the frank identification of issues. Starting with the recognition that Latin America is demanding profound social, economic, and political changes, and that this demand can no longer remain unheard, the Charter dealt chiefly with the indispensable requirements for economic growth and social reform. It recognized that a constructive force for the Latin American social revolution was feasible only through an infusion of outside capital of major proportions, both public and private, and that this capital must be extended under a long-run commitment to accelerate Latin America's growth and to support its reforms. Further, it recognized that external capital is needed for the development of social goals as well as for manufacturing enterprises and other elements of economic foundations. The objective was the development of self-sustaining economies, and the general assumption was that in many Latin American countries this goal might be attained within a decade. Explicit in the Charter was the notion that, while economic growth is essential to the creation of tolerable conditions of living, social reform is no less essential in giving the majority of the people a greater participation in the benefits of growth. In other words, the determined goal for economic growth should be accompanied by a social development that satisfies the aspirations of the common man. The growth of industry, then, should be matched by greater attention to the urgent requirements of the people for education, health, housing, and programs of comprehensive tax and agrarian reform.

In addition to the formulation of national development programs, which were a basic requirement of all programs under the Alliance, there was an equally important element in the Charter: the principle of self-help. The Charter implicitly recognized the serious defects and dangers which have existed in the basic structure of Latin American reforms in the past, as well as the fact that the United States cannot

[21] The text of the "Declaration to the Peoples of America," as well as of the "Charter of Punta del Este," is reprinted in *Special Report on Latin America*, Sen. Doc. No. 80, 87th Congress, 2d sess., 1962 (Washington, D.C.: Government Printing Office, 1962), pp. 33-43.

undertake these reforms herself but can only help to create favorable conditions for them by giving encouragement and support to democratic groups who have the will to institute them. By virtue of the "self-help" principle, national development plans must be based on "own effort," with the principal source of finance coming from domestic resources and with foreign aid supplying only the technical and capital resources that countries cannot themselves provide.

The Punta del Este Charter also included a commitment on the part of the American Republics to develop cooperative programs designed to avoid the damaging effects of excessive fluctuations of foreign exchange derived from basic export commodities and to adopt measures which would facilitate access of Latin American exports to world markets. The Charter itself actually failed to suggest concrete action by limiting itself to a general endorsement of all international efforts to reduce market instability. It did instruct the Secretary General of the OAS to convene a group of experts to study measures to provide adequate and effective means of offsetting the effects of fluctuations in the volume and prices of exports of basic products.

Reflecting the Latin American inclination toward regional integration, the Charter also expressed the need for fostering agreements of economic integration aimed at the creation of a Latin American Common Market. Such a Market would contribute to the economic growth of the region by broadening and diversifying trade among the Latin American nations.[22]

Another important step in the complex and arduous task of organizing a social and economic revolution was taken at Punta del Este by determining the role to be played by existing international structures: the OAS, the Inter-American Development Bank, and the UN Economic Commission for Latin America. These three organizations, having signed a cooperative agreement in 1961, will coordinate their efforts in the implementation of the Alliance. These efforts will chiefly be aimed at making available programming experts to facilitate achievement of goals. Since a basic principle was the provision that aid would be granted only to countries which propose national development plans, assistance is indispensable to insure technically acceptable programs. National economic planning, involving among other things the creation of national institutions staffed with adequately trained personnel, is an area of extreme weakness in Latin America. Consequently, among the procedural innovations required by the Charter are coordination and cooperation between inter-American organizations and between these and other international agencies; elevation of the level at which decisions are made, thereby placing them in a political context; and provision

[22] Lagos, *International Stratification*, p. 85.

for adequate preparatory work for such decisions by a qualified professional staff, with subsequent review by technical governmental representatives for submission to the high-level governmental body.[23]

To insure that programs are well conceived, the Inter-American Economic and Social Council—as instructed by the Charter of Punta del Este and on the joint proposal of the Secretary General of the OAS, the President of the Inter-American Development Bank, and the Executive Secretary of the United Nations Economic Commission for Latin America—appointed a panel of nine high-level experts, who became known as the "nine wise men." These experts are attached to the Inter-American Economic Council, but they enjoy complete autonomy in the exercise of their functions. According to the procedures prescribed, a government seeking aid will present its development program for consideration by an *ad hoc* committee. After studying the program and exchanging opinions with the interested government, the committee will report its conclusions to the Inter-American Development Bank and to other governments and institutions that may be prepared to extend financial and technical assistance for the program's implementation.

In a final step, the Inter-American Development Bank undertakes the negotiations required to obtain financing for the program, including the organization of a consortium of credit institutions and governments disposed to contribute on a continuing and systematic basis to the particular development program. This procedure, however, does not in any way restrict the freedom of each government to obtain financing in full or in part through other channels. Naturally, the recommendations of the *ad hoc* committee are given great weight in determining the distribution of public funds under the Alliance for Progress, which contributes to the external financing of such programs. These recommendations should reflect special emphasis on the objective of achieving self-sustaining development and on the Alliance's basic goal of reaching not less than a 2.5 per cent annual per-capita rate of growth within the decade of the 1960's.[24] Provision for review and consideration at a high level has been made by means of a reorganized Inter-American Economic and Social Council. This body will review every year the progress achieved in the formulation, national implementation, and international financing of development programs. It will submit to the Council of the Organization of American States such recommendations as it deems pertinent.[25]

It was fortunate that a thorough reorganization of the Economic and Social Council was undertaken in 1961, for the role assigned to

[23] Sanders, "Pan Americanism—Ideal into Reality," pp. 31-32.
[24] Charter of Punta del Este, Title II, Chapter V, Articles 1-7.
[25] *Ibid.*, Article 8.

this body in the general scheme of the Alliance is very important. The Council now meets annually, at the ministerial or cabinet level; that is, the participants are the highest officials dealing with economic affairs in their own countries. Thus, the same individuals who arrive at conclusions within the Council are responsible for putting them into effect in their respective nations. The Council has the function of serving as a forum for "confrontation" at the highest level—for evaluation and comparison of advances made in socio-economic development programs of the Alliance. *The Council operates primarily on the basis of policy determinations already made at Punta del Este.* Emphasis at these ministerial meetings is, therefore, on execution of policy rather than on its formulation.

This fact is reflected in preparations for the ministerial "confrontation." Immediately in advance of it, the Council meets at a high technical level to lay the groundwork for the ministerial consultations and to review the documents and proposals to be submitted to the ministers. Among these materials are reports from each country on problems encountered and the progress made. In addition, there is available an over-all report from the General Secretariat covering Latin America as a whole. All this documentation gives the Council a complete view of the actions to be taken individually and collectively by the member states and by international agencies.[26]

The first annual "confrontation" of the Alliance members took place at Mexico City in October, 1962. Two significant innovations were introduced in the system as a result of this meeting. First, a number of "action groups" composed of national representatives were created to deal with the problems surrounding certain of Latin America's basic export products that are affected by world market fluctuations as well as by actions of such groups as the European Common Market. These were not to be merely "study groups," for the real innovation in this case lay in the fact that these groups were sometimes actually to engage in negotiations with consuming countries or groups of such countries in order to resolve problems arising from restrictions of free entry into consuming markets. Second, the Mexico City meeting created six special committees to work in such areas as planning and project formulation, agricultural development and reform, fiscal policy and administration, industrial development and financing for the private sector, education and training, and various aspects of social, health, housing, and community development. These special committees were designed to pro-

---

[26] William Sanders, "Trends and Developments in the OAS" (an address delivered before the District of Columbia Political Science Association meeting, November 14, 1962).

vide an additional mechanism for the evaluation and "confrontation" process during the intervals when the Economic and Social Council is not in session.

One thing stands out from these descriptions: the extraordinary complexity of the multilateral mechanisms required for continuing policy formulation, programming, planning, testing, and review under the ambitious and massive program agreed upon in the Alliance for Progress. Obviously, this complexity is the result of the fact that this program was injected into an existing multilateral administrative structure basically composed of three international organizations: the OAS, the Inter-American Development Bank, and the United Nations Economic Commission for Latin America. Although greater simplicity may be desirable, it should be remembered that it was precisely the existence of such international institutions that made possible the acceptance in an international forum of the crucial commitments to undertake reforms in areas traditionally and intimately related to the domestic jurisdiction of states. The decisions at Punta del Este were made by the participating countries "in the exercise of their sovereignty," that is, by free consent and choice. "These decisions have the hallmark of their origin in these cooperative and collective deliberations; they possess an essential unity and interrelationship." [27]

Despite the great significance of multilateral cooperation, the Alliance has two other basic aspects, unilateral and bilateral. The first, represented by the principle of self-help, reflects the fact that social and institutional reforms can be brought about only by action of the respective countries—even in financing. Of the huge amount of capital needed for new investment in the next ten years, perhaps some 20 per cent will come from external assistance, but the remaining 80 per cent of the annual 10 billion dollars will have to be mobilized by the peoples of the countries of Latin America. In this light, the United States is in a real sense the junior partner in the Alliance for Progress, "junior because the effort which we can commit will be considerably less than the efforts which will be committed by all the other participating countries." [28]

The bilateral aspect of the Alliance lies largely in the areas of financing and technical assistance, and involve many official agencies. Among those of the United States government are the Agency for International Development (AID), the Export-Import Bank, the United States Food for Peace Program, and the Peace Corps. Europe, as she flexes her economic muscles again, will also begin to participate actively in Latin American

[27] Sanders, "The OAS and the Alliance for Progress."
[28] Dean Rusk, "The Alliance in the Context of World Affairs," in *The Alliance for Progress*, p. 115.

economic development. The private sector—individual banks and industrial concerns—likewise will be channeling funds toward the type of enterprises that produce relatively early returns.

IS THE ALLIANCE IN CRISIS?

Much is being said these days about a "crisis" in the Alliance for Progress. Disillusionment, cynicism, frustration, and even resentment have been frequently expressed by Latin Americans and North Americans alike. There are some who say that, organizationally speaking, the United States is "simply lacking in the requisite skill for managing a social revolution of the magnitude to which it [has] committed itself." [29] There are many serious problems impeding the progress of the Alliance. One is the widespread belief among average Latin Americans that the Alliance is another conventional foreign aid program of the United States. The program has been presented to the people, not in its true perspective as a multilateral cooperative effort, but as a vast plan for aid by the United States. They fail to realize that the underlying philosophy of the Alliance, its purposes and goals, as well as the methods and instruments it brings into play, have been advocated for many years by the countries of Latin America.

The Alliance, far from being a program imposed by the United States upon Latin America, is a body of Latin American ideas and proposals that has finally been accepted by the United States. In a very real sense, President Kennedy adapted the idea of the "Operation Pan America" advanced earlier by President Kubitschek of Brazil and later expressed in the Charters of Bogotá and Punta del Este. These documents sum up aspirations that have been voiced in Latin America almost since the end of World War II.

A recent report of the Committee of Nine notes that, to develop a sense of Latin American identification with the Alliance, steps must be taken to publicize widely the new concept of social democracy and the multilateral principle that are both basic to the program.[30] The "panel of nine," while pointing out the defects and difficulties of the Alliance, suggests also that there may be an element of artificial and calculated exaggeration in this "crisis":

The Alliance for Progress hurts powerful political and economic interests. These interests defend themselves by attacking the Alliance. Some of these attacks come from the ultranationalistic and extreme leftist groups that

---

[29] Nehemkis, "Some Reflections on the Alliance for Progress."

[30] *Report of the Panel of Experts to the Inter-American Economic and Social Council* (Washington, D.C.: Pan American Union, 1962), pp. 38-39.

are opposed to participation by the United States in the development of the hemisphere, because they attribute to it aims of economic imperialism or political pressure. Other attacks originate in conservative groups that, in addition to seeing in the program a threat to their privileged positions, feel that a policy of structural reforms brings with it disturbances seriously affecting economic development, and that the mere announcement of the policy will provoke withdrawal of national and foreign private investments in the area.[31]

A second source of difficulties is the popular lack of awareness of the revolutionary import of the Alliance. This revolutionary quality was recognized by President Kennedy when he declared: "For too long, my country, the wealthiest nation on a poor continent, failed to carry out its full responsibilities to its sister republics. We have now accepted that responsibility. In the same way, those who possess wealth and power in poor nations must accept their own responsibilities. They must lead the fight for those basic reforms which alone can preserve the fabric of their own societies. Those who make peaceful revolution impossible make violent revolution inevitable." [32]

In Latin America, while there is little understanding of the revolutionary significance of the Alliance on the part of the peoples, the forces opposed to reform have begun a campaign of implacable resistance. With few exceptions, the upper classes have not shown a willingness to accept public responsibilities or to furnish progressive leadership—perhaps because they honestly do not believe social reforms to be necessary or because they fear an economic upheaval or because they feel that their interests are being affected. A considerable segment of the upper stratum of society reacts to the Alliance with almost pathological fear. Remembering nostalgically the United States diplomacy of the past, they feel somehow betrayed by the revolutionary thrust of the Alliance and particularly by its emphasis upon tax and land reforms. This resistance to change is not only internal, but it has come in some cases from external sources, such as certain types of foreign enterprises.

A third criticism concerns the need for the Alliance to develop an ideological content. A specific accommodation to the mentality of the Latin American peoples is essential. As a businessman-scholar has put it, "Because Latin Americans are not Anglo-Americans, they can be expected to subscribe with enthusiasm to a structure which embodies both poetry and power, which dramatizes their own high destiny and has the bold sweep of Bolivarian prophecy." [33]

[31] *Ibid.*, p. 31.

[32] President John F. Kennedy's address on the first anniversary of the Alliance for Progress, Washington, D.C., March 13, 1962.

[33] Nehemkis, "Some Reflections on the Alliance for Progress."

The political meaning of the Alliance has vast and far reaching consequences. It is an instrument through which the acceleration of economic and social development can be made compatible with the improvement of the democratic process in Latin America.[34] This does not mean that the Alliance must necessarily have just one mode of political expression in Latin America. It must have an appropriate interpretation in each country in order to reach the people effectively.[35] The governments and political leaders are essentially responsible for creating the public support required to gain the people's participation in the collective effort invoked by the Alliance.

The organizational efficiency of the Alliance has also been questioned. In the opinion of many, the Alliance is in danger of rapidly becoming another isolated piece in the jigsaw puzzle of foreign aid administration —another United States assistance agency spending much of its resources on emergency measures to solve balance of payments crises. The report of the "nine wise men" dealt in some detail with the need for a complete review of the operational tools that were already in existence or that have been especially created to carry forward the purposes of the Alliance. The Committee was convinced that a review should be made of the inter-American agencies responsible for the success of the Alliance. In their view, since these agencies were created under other conditions and for different purposes, it is urgent to adapt that system to the new tasks and responsibilities that are being imposed upon it. This recommendation of the panel of experts led to the appointment of former Presidents Lleras Camargo of Colombia and Juscelino Kubitschek of Brazil as a committee which, with the aid of highest-level experts, would within a maximum of six months recommend advisable changes in all the existing machinery to fit it to the new tasks. This Committee has recently submitted its report. It should be noted that, owing to the essential role of the United States in the Alliance and its direct responsibility for the credits so far granted for projects, much of the criticism directed at this country is derived from the slowness with which loans are made and also from the administrative and operational obstacles that prevent timely use of credits.

PROBLEMS OF THE NEW DIPLOMACY

Although some of the vital changes in the attitudes and policies of the United States—economic integration, commodity stabilization, large-scale aid, and a new inter-American bank—occurred before Castro took

---

[34] Raúl Prebisch, "Economic Aspects of the Alliance," in *The Alliance for Progress,* pp. 51-52.
[35] *Report of the Panel of Experts,* p. 44.

power in Cuba, there can be no doubt that the great social upheaval sweeping that island had much to do in converting Latin America into, to use President Kennedy's phrase, "the most critical area in the world today." The Cuban Revolution served as a catalyst in inducing the United States to formulate, in response to the Soviet challenge, a diplomacy of the social revolution. The Alliance for Progress, the most revolutionary foreign policy pronouncement affecting Latin America, was envisaged as the keystone in the arch of this new diplomacy. The real significance of the change was that the Soviet camp could no longer claim monopoly of concern for social change.

As far as international politics is concerned, the impact of the Cuban Revolution was twofold. First, Cuba's incorporation into the Soviet bloc shattered the traditional pattern of power relationships and introduced the balance-of-power system into the Western Hemisphere. The latter had been traditionally excluded from the continent by three factors: (1) the Monroe Doctrine that prevented the intervention of non-American powers in hemispheric affairs; (2) the development of inter-American regional systems based on a rule of international law and on the principle of the juridical equality of nations; and (3) the great disparity in terms of power of the United States on one hand and her weak Latin American neighbors on the other. That traditional pattern of relationships was broken when Cuba sought help from the Soviet Union, the only power of sufficient strength to oppose the United States.

A second source of influence resulting from the Cuban Revolution was the fact that a small country, traditionally dependent on its northern neighbor, had challenged—in advance of any other Latin American nation—the influence, the might, and the prestige of the preponderant power of the Western Hemisphere. The Cuban experiment not only affected the foreign policy of the United States by unfurling the banner of Marxist-Leninist social revolution before the astonished eyes of the great masses of Latin America, but it also broke the centuries-old traditions which had shaped the foreign policies of the Latin American countries. Through the Cuban Revolution, the countries of Latin America became really involved in world politics, and the inter-American system ceased to be a "closed system" and became open to all types of interaction with the rest of the world. "Even if the Alliance for Progress strengthens the inter-American system, the trend of Latin American foreign policy is no longer confined to the Western Hemisphere but to the international system as a whole." [36]

As a novice in the art of promoting socio-economic revolution abroad, the United States found itself at a serious disadvantage, for it lacked adequate experience and instruments to carry out the new policy. The

---

[36] Lagos, *International Stratification*, p. 121.

Soviet Union, however, has had both the experience and instruments; its continuing efforts to subvert established social order provided them. The most valuable of the Soviet instruments has always been the well-organized and disciplined Communist parties, existing everywhere and everywhere involved in revolutionary activity. Their usefulness in the implementation of Soviet foreign policy cannot be overemphasized. The United States, on the other hand, lacked similar instruments within the countries themselves and, on the international level, was confronted with the task of devising such tools as they were needed. Since the matter was an urgent one, the United States decided to inject the revolutionary program of the Alliance into the existing machinery, rather than to create new and specially designed instruments. This decision may have become the ultimate source of all the evils connected with it, for, as we have seen, the machinery in existence was designed for conventional foreign aid programs utilizing the conventional tools of foreign aid— money, men, and materials. What was proposed was something entirely new in foreign relations.

Administration of the Alliance was entrusted to a segment of AID, which, designed to carry out the objectives of the Point IV Program, was an agency definitely not structured to undertake such a dramatic and essentially revolutionary task as was required. Obviously, it was not easy to develop at home a successful diplomacy of social revolution, using as vehicles for execution gigantic and slumbering bureaucratic organisms such as the Department of State and the Agency for International Development. In order to solve the difficulties inherent in administering and implementing the program through multilateral, international bodies, important changes and adjustments may be required in the composition and procedures of the principal institutions. Whatever may be achieved in this respect, international organizations can be only what the member governments want them to be, and success depends ultimately on the action of the governments. Some of these organizations, before being called to play such historic roles as they are now performing, had been little more than polite debating societies. Others of more recent vintage have shown, despite their brief existence, a promising dynamism and imagination. To focus on international institutions as the primary vehicles for action involves certain risks. In the case of the Alliance, the governments have invested greater power in and placed heavier responsibilities upon the inter-American system than ever before, but even so, its role is primarily that of a catalyst. The prime elements are the governments upon whose action or reaction success or failure depends.

By way of conclusion, it may be well to look, if only briefly, into three other factors which will have much to do with the success of our revolutionary diplomacy. The first relates to political problems found in the United States. These problems arise not only from the need of convincing other branches of the government, the bureaucracy, the political parties, and the public of the merits of the new policy, but also from the task of enlightening them about the intricacies of any revolution. "The government of this country faces the dilemma of simultaneously leading a contented people at home, who tend to be conservative because they have a great deal to conserve, and a number of malcontented, allied peoples abroad, who tend to be revolutionary because they have a great deal to change." [37] It will take time, even with today's formidable means of molding public opinion, for the majority of the citizens to become sophisticated in this field. Meanwhile, Congress, with some notable exceptions, will represent the average level of public opinion.

A second problem area concerns the impact of the Alliance for Progress upon the political scene in Latin America. The political parties of the so-called Democratic Left in Latin America are the chosen instruments for implementing the Alliance for Progress. The fact that United States financial support is indispensable in carrying out development programs has created a certain degree of subordination of such groups to Washington. In the interactions of the Left with American leadership, external factors have become a key element within each national political system. The danger is, for instance, that if pledges of the aid that is the base of development programs are not fulfilled in time, the result may be the failure of the social and political policies of a given regime, and eventually the displacement and discredit of political groups which have advocated such policies. The Democratic Left movement is the logical vehicle for the political action of the Alliance, but it is necessary to re-examine whether it is capable of communicating the need for social change to the people.

In general, the Democratic Left relies upon the middle classes of Latin America for the vital roles of leadership, production, and investment in efforts toward social and economic reforms. The capacity and willingness of these classes to fulfill such roles is not beyond doubt. A recent United Nations report states that the prevailing "heritage of social relationships, combined with the primary importance of public employment among the opportunities open to middle-class youth, has contributed to a pervasive reliance on government action for the solution of all problems that inhibit the innovating spirit otherwise to be expected of rising middle classes." Some analysts accuse the middle class of contributing to the frustration of economic development by indulging in self-protective pressures to obtain increased public employment, job security, and legislative safeguards against competition. Traditional upper-class values are blamed for having influenced the rising middle class to avoid the roles most needed for

[37] José Figueres, "The Alliance and Political Goals," in *The Alliance for Progress,* p. 84.

economic growth, as exemplified by the tendency of this class toward luxurious consumption to the detriment of saving.[38]

A third category of problems arises from the newness of the image of the United States as a champion of reform. In the minds of the great Latin American masses, there still persists the impression of the United States as a country interested in financial and military advantage far more than in human welfare. Some Latin Americans believe that the United States is seeking only the guarantee of its national security in order to enjoy the bounty of its economic advancement. They consider the United States to be sympathetic to reactionary, dictatorial, and undemocratic regimes. The stigma of broken promises and domination associated with this image often crops up in the utterances of Latin American intellectuals. It will not be easy to clarify the new image of the United States as a country devoted to freedom and social justice for all men, particularly when our opponents exploit such dissatisfactions to the fullest.

The issues and problems faced by the United States in this new role are innumerable and portend many difficulties. Certain obstacles, previously held to be insuperable, have nevertheless fallen, and despite the dismal prophecies uttered by impatient activists and traditional pessimists, there is solid ground for optimism concerning the outcome of the revolutionary crusade undertaken by the Alliance. If it succeeds—and we cannot afford to let it fail—the United States will have kept faith with its finest and deepest traditions and will once more have served the cause of freedom.

Suggestions for Further Reading

Benton, William, *The Voice of Latin America*. New York: Harper & Row, Publishers, 1961.

Berle, Adolf A., *Latin America—Diplomacy and Reality*. New York: Harper & Row, Publishers, 1962.

Dreier, John C., *The Organization of American States and the Hemispheric Crisis*. New York: Harper & Row, Publishers, 1962.

———, ed., *Alliance for Progress—Problems and Perspectives*. Baltimore: The Johns Hopkins Press, 1962.

Gordon, Lincoln, *A New Deal for Latin America: The Alliance for Progress*. Cambridge, Mass.: Harvard University Press, 1963.

Manger, William, *The Alliance for Progress*, A Georgetown University Symposium. Washington, D.C.: Public Affairs Press, 1963.

[38] This report was prepared by the Bureau of Social Affairs of the United Nations in cooperation with specialized agencies of the world organizations. Quoted in *The New York Times*, April 7, 1963, p. 24.

Matthews, Herbert L., ed., *The United States and Latin America,* The American Assembly Series. Englewood Cliffs, N.J.: Prentice-Hall, Inc., Spectrum Books, 1963.

Perkins, Dexter, *The United States and Latin America.* Baton Rouge, La.: Louisiana State University Press, 1961.

TRANSITIONAL ASIA

AND THE DYNAMICS

OF NATION BUILDING

Lucian W. Pye

Twenty-five years ago, when Whitney Griswold completed his monumental history of American relations with Asia, he concluded that the underlying pattern in these relations was a cyclical rhythm of involvement and withdrawal as Americans vacillated between an intense preoccupation with Asian affairs and a desire to ignore the trans-Pacific world.[1] Since Griswold's conclusion, American involvement in the Far East and in South and Southeast Asia has so expanded as to make the previous periods of our greatest concern with Asia seem almost isolationist.

AMERICAN INVOLVEMENT IN ASIAN AFFAIRS

At present, we transact nearly as much business with Japan every six weeks as we used to transact with all Asia combined. Before World

[1] A. Whitney Griswold, *The Far Eastern Policy of the United States* (New York: Harcourt, Brace & World, Inc., 1939).

LUCIAN W. PYE *is Professor of Political Science at the Massachusetts Institute of Technology. As a senior staff member of the M.I.T. Center for International Studies, he has been the Director of Research on Comparative Asian politics. Before joining the staff at M.I.T. he was a research associate at the Center of International Studies at Princeton University. He is the author of* Guerrilla Communism in Malaya *and* Politics, Personality, and Nation Building. *He is co-author of* The Politics of the Developing Areas, The Emerging Nations, *and* The Role of the Military in Developing Countries, *and editor of* Communications and Political Development.

War II, the American naval presence in Asia was upheld by the Yangtze patrol with its antiquated gunboats, which mounted a few machine guns and a three-inch cannon, and the Asiatic Fleet, based in Manila, which claimed as regular complements a few destroyers and a cruiser. Today the Seventh Fleet, as it moves about the China Seas, holds in check a striking force which is equal to the strength of all American forces in the Pacific at the height of World War II. We once thought of ourselves as intimately involved in the affairs of China, especially with the stationing of the 15th Infantry in Tientsin and with the maintenance of Marine Corps posts in Peking and Shanghai. These, however, were superficial involvements, when compared with the role of our Army advisers in South Vietnam at the present moment.

The picture of increased American involvement is compounded many times over once we turn to such novel departures of policy as economic aid, technical assistance, and the field of cultural relations. The Peace Corps has made it possible to maintain our traditional role of supplying school teachers to the Philippines, even as we move ahead with new commitments in Malaya, Borneo, and Indonesia. And, of course, our whole new concern with India and Pakistan, and with their problems of development and security, represents a quantum leap in our associations with Asians. The same is true with respect to our deep commitments to Korea—commitments which have followed inexorably from the war we fought to defend that country.

Indeed, our earlier history of relations with Asia is hardly an adequate prologue to the deep immersion we now have in Asian affairs. Yet we can still discern something of the rhythmic pattern observed by Griswold. Now, however, the shifts are not in policy concentration, but in public attention. Popular concern with Asian matters still tends to vacillate between moments of vivid awareness, which can reach climaxes of almost frantic anxiety, and periods of general apathy bordering on impenetrable boredom.

For a time after World War II, popular interest and policy concern with Asian affairs paralleled each other in intensity to a remarkable degree. There was not necessarily a congruence in viewpoints; rather, the concern of the two reinforced each other. When the public was searching for the reasons for the loss of China, policy makers were fully appreciative of the importance of other parts of Asia for the next round in the Cold War struggle.[2] At the beginning of the Korean war, popular sentiments supported fully official judgments of the significance of aggres-

[2] Until recently the high emotions generated by the Communist take-over of China made it seem as though policy makers and American public opinion shared little in common. Now, however, as more detailed studies become possible, it is apparent that both did in fact share many weaknesses. See, Tang Tsou, *America's Failure in China 1949-50* (Chicago: University of Chicago Press, 1963).

sion in Asia; and after the war citizens and leaders both wondered if it would not be essential to find less costly ways of dealing with similar problems in the future.

More recently, however, a gap appears to be opening between popular concern and policy involvement in Asia. Possibly the American people have become at last somewhat hardened to the cries of crisis about Asian development, and thus do not sense the same degree of urgency in responding to every turn of events in such distant lands. Having passed through the challenge of Soviet missiles in Cuba, we may have come to feel that it is all too easy to overdramatize the warnings of danger and crisis in Asia. It may also be that the American people feel that they are taking a cue from their leaders: They heard their President tell them that Laos was vital to the security of free Asia, and then they observed him settle on a policy which seemed at best to be only a holding operation that might reduce the sting of defeat when the country eventually fell to the Communists. There has certainly been a breakdown in communications between the inner set of calculations of the Administration's Laos policy and the American understanding of developments in that strange and exasperating land.[3]

The emergence of the spread between popular sentiments and official concerns over Asia has had the immediate consequence of providing our government with a considerably freer hand than it has been accustomed to have in designing and executing Asian policies. In 1963, the government was inwardly concerned with counter-insurgency and the struggle in South Vietnam, while the public, relieved of these responsibilities, was able to focus on matters near home. The gradual acceptance of the idea that the American people do not need to be emotionally mobilized for the conduct of relations with Asia has resulted in increasingly esoteric and involved policies.[4] The public, for example, has certainly not been brought into the Administration's confidence with respect to what precisely is planned to bolster India's defenses, what the expectations are in the Kashmir negotiations which the United States is pushing upon both India and Pakistan, and what the outcome will be of giving any form of aid to Sukarno's Indonesia.

Harassed officials naturally welcome any respite from trying to carry the American public along with every aspect of national policies; and

---

[3] It may be significant that the Chinese reading of the Administration's policies has been essentially the same as the American public's, while the Russians, who have had the benefit of confidential conversations with the appropriate American officials, have a somewhat different and more respectful judgment of our Laos policies.

[4] For a study which reveals how historically the degree of ingenuity of American policy has tended to be in inverse proportion to popular involvement, see Bernard C. Cohen, *The Political Process and Foreign Policy: The Making of the Japanese Peace Settlement* (Princeton, N.J.: Princeton University Press, 1957).

certainly even the most astringent critics must recognize the case for allowing policy makers the necessary freedom to devise ingenious and complex policy maneuvers. It is possibly fortunate that we are now in a period in which Asian policies are not stirring up strong popular emotions. There is little to be said for popular involvement in public affairs if it takes the form of the bitter and heated debates of the 1950's over China policy. Similarly, there is little merit in a government's trying to explain the rationale of its policies to the public if it uses either the naïve and innocently sentimental reasoning or the crudely anti-Communist arguments which have characterized past justifications of foreign aid. Both the American government and certain Asian governments have presented their people with magical and unscientific views of the potentialities of foreign aid.[5]

Eventually, however, public policy must come to rest upon popular sentiments, and it cannot be healthy for the gap in views to persist indefinitely or to expand any further. No matter how clever or ingenious the policy ploys, the work of officials must reflect popular convictions if they are to have sustaining consequences. If American power is to be effectively mobilized in support of our Asian policies, there must be a minimum degree of public understanding of, and sympathy for, those policies.

Sooner or later American leadership is going to have to assume the task of bringing together again the views of the public and of the decision makers. Such a common orientation toward Asian affairs calls for a generally shared understanding of what are the most vitally important features governing political life in the region. During the last decade, however, Asian societies have been undergoing such erratic and unaccountable changes that it is difficult, if not impossible, for people to keep them in perspective.

Countries which seem strongly committed to democratic development and humane socialist values—such as Burma or, even at one time, Indonesia—now appear to be relentlessly moving toward authoritarian rule and economic stagnation. Other countries which appeared to be mired down in corruption and inefficiency—such as the Philippines—have now radically reversed their course and are achieving noteworthy advances. One year the spotlight of crisis is focused on a divided Korea; the next year it is on Laos and Southeast Asia; and then all attention must shift to the problems of India.

The endemic change and uncertainty of Asia has complicated both American policy and our public sentiments. The burden of policy has

---

[5] I have sought to analyze some of the underlying American emotions behind our foreign aid programs in "The Political Impulses and Fantasies Behind Foreign Aid," *Proceedings of the Academy of Political Science*, XXVII, 2 (January 1962), 92-111.

had to center on frantic efforts to cope with the latest crisis, and attention must be constantly diverted from long-range goals. The public constantly discovers that just as it has become responsive and knowing about one set of problems, it can forget about them and start worrying about entirely new ones. The accumulative effect can be a waning of attentiveness and a rising sense of general frustration about Asian problems.[6]

TWO THEMES IN CONTEMPORARY ASIA:
CHANGE AND FRUSTRATION

The two themes which most aptly characterize contemporary Asia are change and frustration. In the immediate postwar world the prospect of change (and even unpredictable developments) was generally welcomed by most Asians and Asian observers as suggesting hopeful prospects for the future of most of the new countries in the region. Now, however, there is hardly a country which is not contending with disappointment, and all the major powers with general Asian policies have found it impossible to realize satisfactorily their prime objectives.

Only a few years ago the general view was that Communist China might well be on the way to surmounting all internal difficulties, and advancing with shocking speed to great power status. Certainly her leaders showed no signs of anxiety or fears of frustration when they boldly proclaimed the Great Leap Forward program in 1958. Within three years, however, her economy slowed to the point of stagnation, and her leaders were experiencing frustration in nearly every sphere of policy.[7]

In India, a steadily rising sense of self-confidence and a belief in the efficacy of democratic measures in speeding modernization received a near-mortal blow when the Chinese attacked the Indian forces and defeated them ignominiously. Indians have had to learn the taste of frustration that invariably follows on living too long with optimistic illusions. Not only was the Indian view of the inherent nature of international politics and Communist state policies shattered, but also India has had to experience the rude discovery that faith in economic development and relative successes with five-year plans are no substitute for national se-

---

[6] Evidence of the tendency of American attention to waver whenever we are called upon to respond over time to an inherently unstable situation is to be found in Hadley Cantril and Mildred Strunk, *Public Opinion 1935-1946* (Princeton, N.J.: Princeton University Press, 1951).

[7] Most of the literature on Communist China in recent years can be readily divided between the categories of "Big China," which stresses the power, either respectfully or fearfully, of Communist China, or "Little China," which emphasizes the weaknesses of the regime. For a balanced and scholarly view, see Allen Whiting, "The Political System of China," in *Modern Political Systems: Asia,* eds. Robert E. Ward and Roy C. Macridis (Englewood Cliffs, N.J.: Prentice-Hall, Inc., 1963).

curity policies. In a matter of a week's time, the actions of Chinese forces in the high Himalayas punctured a decade of hortatory talk about a "race" in development between India and China.

It might seem that prosperous and dynamic Japan might be able to escape from the general sense of frustration of Asia; and, to a remarkable extent, a new spirit of confidence and self-respect has been building up among increasing categories of Japanese society. Yet, even in an industrialized Japan that is realizing European standards and that appears to be doubling its per capita income in less than a decade, there is widespread feeling that the country has yet to find a satisfactory place in the international scene. The feeling persists that the nation has reached a point in development where it is suspended between all normal worlds, and thus the Japanese feel particularly isolated and alone. Japan is neither Asian nor Western, neither fully modernized nor recognizably traditional, neither a developed nor a developing country, neither a have nor have-not nation. Frustration over identifying their own state of development has left the Japanese unsure of their own recent achievements, and they are unable, for example, to appreciate the extent to which they have in fact created a democratic system.

The theme of frustration is possibly most accentuated in Southeast Asia. In the former colonial lands of tropical Asia, independence was generally greeted with inordinately high expectations about the material advances that were believed to be the inevitable accompaniment of the end of foreign domination. Leadership group after leadership group has had to accept new sets of aspirations, while trying not to admit too openly to failures. In Burma, failure and frustration have brought the end of civil government and democratic experiment as the army has imposed an increasingly autocratic system.[8]

A host of reasons underlie the various patterns of frustration which characterize so much of Asia. It would not be possible here even to categorize all the various sources of difficulty in all of transitional Asia. However, a fundamental theme of modern Asian history which parallels the story of increased American involvement in that continent is the steadily increasing difficulties of ruling and maintaining order in Asian societies. A century ago it was possible for a handful of Europeans to control large communities of Asians and to maintain the imperial front of colonial rule. In earlier days extraordinarily inept and short-sighted traditional rulers had relatively little trouble governing their peoples. The reason was that in both traditional and colonial Asia there was little need for government, because the people so completely governed them-

---

[8] For an objective but intimate analysis of the difficulties that have beset economic development efforts in Burma, see Louis J. Walinsky, *Economic Development in Burma, 1951-1960* (New York: The Twentieth Century Fund, 1962).

selves. The disciplines of family life, the dictates of religion and of ancient customs, the unwritten regulations of caste and village community all served to give order and structure to the daily life of Asians. People were thus held in their places by the overpowering pressures of social conventions, and the realm of government was spared the responsibilities of enforcing order or coping with conflicts. Government was the playground of the elite where the few could seek status, prestige, and self-expression without the frustrations of policy issues.

The breakdown of the old order in Asia, which immediately after World War II was heralded as an "awakening," has not been accompanied by the systematic establishment of a new order. Most of the frustrations and difficulties which complicate political life in the separate Asian countries are clearly related to the general problems of nation building. Therefore, in our search for guides for American policy and public thinking about the travails of transitional Asia, it may be well to concentrate on some of these general problems of nation building.

THE PROBLEMS OF NATION BUILDING

In the immediate post-World War II years, Asians shared with Westerners an almost naïve faith in the ease with which modern nations could be formed out of old societies. There were grantedly many statements calling for hard work and sacrifice, but these generally carried all the overtones of mere conventional and highly ritualistic pronouncements. It was nearly universally assumed that nations emerged from nationalism, and the more emotionally dedicated a leadership sounded, the more certain it seemed that a modern nation was being created. At that time few people had given serious thought to the nature of the nation building process. Among Westerners there were no dynamic theories about the processes of political development, for it was generally believed that a people out of their very experience of communal living would readily and spontaneously form themselves into a nation-state.[9] Most Westerners took the fact of citizenship in a nation-state so much for granted that they found it hard to appreciate the extent to which the nation-state in fact is a highly artificial cultural artifact that cannot be created spontaneously and without applied and systematic effort.

Gradually, through observing the frightful difficulties of the Asian peoples in their struggle to build modern polities out of their transitional and tradition-burdened societies, we have come to realize that political development, particularly if it is to point eventually to democratic

[9] For the classical Western views on the origins of the state, see Robert M. MacIver, *The Modern State* (London: Oxford University Press, 1926); and Carl J. Friedrich, *Constitutional Government and Democracy*, rev. ed. (Boston: Ginn & Company, 1950).

practices, must be guided by strategies which rest on an understanding of historical processes. For some time we have been aware that economic development calls for systematic use of resources and carefully worked-out programs and plans. Increasingly, we are coming to realize that we cannot expect economic development efforts to carry the burden of creating new and stable societies.

With every year of experience it seems clearer that the relationship between economic and political development is much more intimate, and probably, if anything, political development must slightly precede economic development for the latter to succeed fully.[10] We have demonstrated our new understanding of this relationship by making far bolder demands for political reforms as a condition for granting economic aid, as seen, for example, in the approach we chose to follow in initiating our big effort in Latin America with the Alliance for Progress. Within Asia the same insights into the political prerequisites of economic development can be observed in our current tendency to concentrate foreign aid in those countries most politically capable of mounting effective development programs. Unquestionably we have made a great advance in the last years by coming to appreciate more fully the importance of political, as contrasted with merely technical, economic development. It cannot be said, however, that we have as yet arrived at any meaningful theories of political development which might be useful in guiding the policies of the new countries of Asia.

Unfortunately, Western social science has only recently begun to confront the serious intellectual problem inherent in arriving at the necessary dynamic theories for illuminating the process of political development.[11] There are many reasons why the social sciences have been so tardy in confronting the problems of social and political development, even though these problems are clearly among the central ones of our age. In part, we have been slow because we have an uncomfortable feeling about any subject which may seem to touch on such concepts as progress, and we have a normative view as to what is "advancement." The social sciences have just emerged from a heroic struggle to escape from primarily normative studies, and we are profoundly anxious about any concepts which might contain hidden normative assumptions that are too similar to those of the old issues.

American political science gained its great strength during recent years by putting aside concern over the ideals of government and by con-

---

[10] For an analysis of the multidimensional aspects of development, see Max F. Millikan and Donald L. M. Blackmer, eds., *The Emerging Nations: Their Growth and United States Policy* (Boston: Little, Brown & Co., 1961).

[11] A pioneering effort in political science which explicitly recognized the phenomenon of development was Gabriel A. Almond and James S. Coleman, eds., *The Politics of the Developing Areas* (Princeton, N.J.: Princeton University Press, 1960).

centrating on explaining the realities of the contemporary scene. Gradually we have moved to the position of being in danger of being the sophisticated rationalizers of why things must be as they are; and as we have gained in wisdom, we have come to increasingly doubt the possibilities of rapid changes, particularly if they seem like reforms and progress. Western social sciences have also been inhibited from thinking about the issues of political development, because we learned fully, but not necessarily well, the lessons of cultural relativism. We are often caught with the feeling that we should not talk about "developed" and "under-developed," and that we have no right even to suggest that other societies should change their ways.

As a result of these and other considerations, Western social science has not been able to be of much help to the leaders of the new countries of Asia that are desperately trying to build up viable and modern societies based on democratic practices. Fortunately, in the last few years there have been some extremely significant changes in the Western intellectual climate, and it is to be hoped that in time we can become more useful to people who want to perform constructive missions. Already many new and promising approaches are being followed in trying to analyze more systematically the problems of nation building.

THE CRISES APPROACH TO POLITICAL DEVELOPMENT

For our purposes of analyzing the problems of nation building in free Asia, it may be helpful at this time to conceive of the process of political development as involving a series of crises, or fundamental problems, which must be dealt with if modernization is to occur.[12] The ways in which a set of five crises are handled and the sequences in which they arise and recur seem to provide a useful basis for understanding the dynamics of political development.

Crisis of Identity. The first crisis in nation building involves a people's gaining a sense of common identity as either subjects or citizens of a common political system. The very identity of the individual must be related to his identification with the nation. His membership in a polity must become the critical factor in helping him to distinguish between what is the "we" and the "they" in his political life.

In Asia the problem of identity is deeply enmeshed in the psychic turmoils associated with breaking from a traditional social and psychological order and becoming associated with modern life. In all the countries of Asia, except Japan and China, the issue of identity is further

---

[12] For the essentials of the "crises" approach to political development, I am indebted to the deliberations of my colleagues on the Comparative Politics Committee of the Social Science Research Council.

compounded by the central role that religion and caste have played in defining the bounds of identity in the traditional order.[13] In most of Asia people tend to expect that they will have a different, not a shared, sense of identity with even their immediate neighbors. In many of these societies people have long been accustomed to living with each other without any assumption that they should have a common sense of community identity.

The process by which these communal differences give way to a national sense of identity will certainly be a major factor in determining the pattern of nation building in each of the South Asian countries. It appeared once that the struggle for independence from colonialism might have been enough to forge new feelings of identity; but now it is clear that in most of the Asian countries there are deeper problems which must be resolved if the crisis of identity is to be effectively met. The most basic of these problems is that of achieving a psychologically satisfying balance between elements of the traditional culture and the dimensions of modern life. How far can a people turn their backs on their own heritage and try to find their identities in the world of the foreigner? What does it mean to a people to have to face the fact that the essences of modern life are so closely associated with those who once conquered, ruled, and humiliated them?

In short, the problem of identity is profoundly compounded for Asian societies because it involves such massive and inescapable issues as the relationship of their earlier identities through religions, with their experiences under colonialism, and finally with their aspirations of a future based on national power and international respect. We could dwell at considerable length on the importance and complexities of the crisis of identity for nation building in Asia. It is my own feeling that it is this dimension of the nation building process which offers the most exciting prospects for research.[14] At the moment, however, our concern is with presenting the entire range of crises which we feel are basic to the nation building process.

Crisis of Integration. The second crisis is closely related to that of identity, but it is concerned with the manner and degree to which the various elements and communities in the nation are interrelated with each other and with the system of national government. At its core the crisis of integration involves the relationship of social structure to the political system. This relationship can be complicated enough in stable

[13] In spite of the manifest importance of religion in Asian culture, there have been exceedingly few systematic attempts to relate religion to modernization and nation building. A noteworthy exception is Robert N. Bellah, *Tokugawa Religion: The Values of Pre-Industrial Japan* (New York: Free Press of Glencoe, Inc., 1957).

[14] I have tried to illuminate many aspects of this problem in *Politics, Personality, and Nation Building: Burma's Search for Identity* (New Haven, Conn.: Yale University Press, 1962).

systems, but in Asian societies it is made far more complex because the social structure is undergoing such radical changes, while the political system has not become fully institutionalized.

This means that many of the problems of integration in Asian countries are still related to traditional aspects of social structure and community life. These aspects involve the problems of relating ethnic minority groups to the national system and of bringing into national life those communities which have long existed in near isolation far from the national capitals. In Burma there is the ubiquitous problem of giving a place in political life to the Shans, Karens, Kachins, Chins, and the other border peoples. In Indonesia there is the problem of the relations between Java and the outer islands. In India the crisis of integration involves the question of linguistic states and the political relationships among the various language groups. These are all problems of integration that are related to the traditional dimensions of the various societies.

There are also in Asia problems of integration with respect to the divisions that are beginning to emerge with modernization and new social structures. Latent interest groups are beginning to take form, and as social change continues, it is certain that there will be increasing pressure to give political articulation to new interests.[15] At present, most of the Asian political systems are not organized to handle and effectively integrate the emergence of new interests. Nationalist parties do exist, but they are often anxious only to communicate with and to control fully the different segments of the emerging social order; they are generally slow to respect the integrity of the special interests of such groups as they are prepared to identify, such as the workers, peasants, students, and women. Indeed, the universal tendency among leadership groups in Asia has been to distrust the emergence of separate interests. Instead of viewing such groups as providing the building blocks for national integration, they tend to see them as a direct threat to national unity.

These anxieties about national unity touch at the heart of the crisis of integration. We would also note that two of the most fundamentally different patterns of nation building are distinguished according to whether the integration crisis is met by efforts at ideological homogeneity or by a pragmatic, bargaining approach among the explicitly recognized special interests within the society. The Asian experience suggests that the attractions of homogeneity are powerful for nationalist leaders, even when their ideological messages are relatively weak and incoherent. At the same time, the trend in Asia seems clearly in the direction of a gradual and steady increase in the emergence of potential interest groups. This

---

[15] For the problems of political articulation and communications in transitional societies, see Lucian W. Pye, ed., *Communications and Political Development* (Princeton, N.J.: Princeton University Press, 1963).

development might suggest that some of the preconditions essential for a pragmatic, bargaining form of democracy are going to be increasingly met in the years to come. Unfortunately, however, the predispositions of the ruling groups in most of the Asian countries suggest that these advantages for democratic development may be ignored, and that we can expect in time increasing tensions between the urge for homogeneity and the demands for special representation. The sum effect would thus be an ever increasing crisis of integration.

Crisis of Penetration. The third crisis of the nation building process involves the ability of the national government to reach out into the society and effect, through formal administration, increasing ranges of social, economic, and political problems. In a modern nation state the formal government must thus be able to penetrate much of the society to carry out public policies.[16]

In the traditional Asian systems government usually involved only the life styles of a relatively small elite. Life within the rural villages was only indirectly influenced by the actions of the governing few. The colonial period usually brought the introduction of the forms of modern public administration. In many Asian countries the most notable political achievement of colonialism was the creation of a civil service tradition. This administrative structure has generally been in the critical super-structure for the building of the modern nation. On the other hand, the colonial administration was only a superstructure, and it did not involve a deep penetration of the society as a whole.

This was particularly the case where the colonial government was primarily concerned with the maintenance of law and order. Formal government only touched the lives of people at the points where tension and conflict among groups might take place. Under colonialism, most of Asia was still ruled by traditional mechanisms of social control; for example, a few Englishmen were able to rule India, because most Indians were still ruled by the dictates of family, village customs, religious conventions, and caste regulations.

The problem of penetration has been greatly increasing in recent years as the old methods of social regulation have been wearing down and losing their ability to give order to social life. More and more formal governments have had to intervene in the life of the community to help create a new sense of order. The rapid pace of urbanization has brought people out of the contexts of their old village systems of social control and has left them insecure and in increasing need of more modern methods of control. Under colonialism the authorities usually penetrated

---

[16] For a discussion of many aspects of the problems of administration in new states, see Joseph LaPalombara, ed., *Bureaucracy and Political Development* (Princeton, N.J.: Princeton University Press, 1963).

at best only the urban communities and hardly touched the lives of the rural masses.

Today the newly independent governments find that there is a great gap between the world of government and the lives of the masses. In part, this is a problem of communications; in part, it is one of expanding the government and moving it away from just the urban centers. The solution to this problem is fundamental in shaping the character of the political processes of most of the new Asian states. At this point, however, we need only point out that the manner in which a government seeks to cope with the problem of penetration can be decisive in determining whether nation building will proceed along democratic or authoritarian lines.

Since there is a very legitimate problem of penetration, some leaders are all too easily impressed with the possible need and the potential efficacy of authoritarian methods. The art of bringing government to the people in a democratic spirit is extremely difficult to learn. In the past Westerners have not been particularly sympathetic about the problems of political tutelage, for the very concept of tutelage is too similar to authoritarian thinking. Yet, if we are to help nations develop, we must seek to understand better the dynamics of this general problem of penetration. To counter authoritarian trends we must learn more about how the process can be effectively met so as to produce the desired democratic results.

Crisis of Participation. The next crisis involves the orderly induction of increasing numbers of people into the political process. In traditional systems those who ruled gained their positions according to ascription considerations and only rarely did new participants enter the world of elite politics. Colonial rule eliminated some participants while it opened the doors to others. Those who received Western education and studied Western law often entered government service, and hence there was some increase in participation according to achievement considerations. The colonial period, however, was mainly characterized by high restrictions on participation.

The nationalist movements of the 1940's represented for much of Asia the first real expansion in participation.[17] New groups began to emerge and to demand a place in the political process. After independence the new leaders often sought to increase national strength and solidarity by mobilizing the entire population. Throughout the 1950's there was a rapid politicalization of life in most of Asia. People were expected to demonstrate at every turn their allegiances to the new governments.

---

[17] A sober appraisal of the role of nationalism and popular participation in shaping Asian politics is to be found in Rupert Emerson, *From Empire to Nation* (Cambridge, Mass.: Harvard University Press, 1960).

These developments have not, however, resolved all the problems of participation. In most of the countries there is still considerable confusion as to the appropriate terms for participation in politics. In some countries the rulers seem to be trying to reinforce restrictions on mass participation. In other cases there has been no orderly pattern of inducting new groups into the duties and responsibilities of citizenship.

The basic issue in the participation crisis is the transition from subject to citizen. In some Asian societies the leaders have tried to keep people as subjects while demanding that they make manifest demonstrations of political support. This is only a modified form of political participation. In other countries, even where there has been a genuine effort to encourage participation in elections, there has been no support for the development of interest groups and voluntary associations which can provide the essential bases for effective citizen participation.

We do not as yet fully understand all the changes in attitude that must accompany the transition from the status of subject to that of citizen. In many parts of Asia there has been a disillusionment over the promises of political participation, and people seem unprepared to make all the necessary commitments prerequisite to effective citizenship. This withdrawal of groups from active participation may give the impression that a country has realized a new degree of stability. It seems, however, that this is likely to be only a temporary illusion, because these people may in time demand readmission as "subjects" in some authoritarian and antidemocratic movement.

In the main, however, the crisis of participation in Asia has been made acute because it has been raised as a major problem before many of the other crises have been adequately resolved. Extensive participation before dealing with the problems of identity and integration has created tremendous uncertainty in much of Asia. This uncertainty has tended to reinforce all the authoritarian inclinations of the leadership elements. It has also resulted in the frustrations which can come from realizing the form, but not the substance, of democracy.

Crisis of Distribution. The final crisis is that of the government's control over the outputs of the political process. What are to be the rewards of the system, and who is to receive them? To what should the powers and the capabilities of government be directed? Who should benefit from public policy?

In the pattern of stable nation building known in the West, the crisis of distribution came at a late stage historically. People became loyal members of national polities before they became concerned over the possibilities of welfare programs. Throughout Asia attention is generally focused on this problem of distribution. New governments have made extensive promises of economic development, and leaders often talk as though the loyalties of their citizens are governed mainly by their expectations of the material returns of public policy.[18]

In part, of course, this is the consequence of being economically poor countries in a world of rich and dynamic industrial countries. Governments in Asia have felt that they cannot delay concerning themselves with programs of economic development. If some of the Asian countries do not soon begin to realize economic growth, they may never be able to do so because of the ominous pressure of population growth.

The distribution crisis is also acute in parts of Asia because colonial governments, paradoxically, often tended to focus efforts on social welfare measures, thus creating populations which came to expect government to provide such services. In a sense, colonial governments tended to exaggerate the distribution problem precisely because they could usually do so little about the crises of identity, integration, and participation. Colonial authorities could not expect their subjects to fully identify with them or to be satisfied with feelings of loyalty to the government. The rationale of colonial rule was generally good government, which meant the preservation of law and order, efficient administration, and the maintenance of advanced public services. At times colonial governments sought to "buy" the consent of the ruled by providing them with various welfare services.

Today some of the new governments also seem to be getting themselves in much the same position of trying to win and hold the loyalty of their peoples by providing the prospects of material rewards. We cannot here deal with all the problems of economic development in Asia except to note that the pace has been exceedingly slow, far from the rate suggested as probable by the leaders a few years ago. It is hard to tell what reactions can be expected if the next decade shows a rate of Asian development no greater than the last. In terms of our analysis we can say that the Asian leaders have, in a sense, been trying to resolve some of the other crises of political development, not on their own terms of identity or integration, but through the distribution crisis. It is hard to say what effect this will have on the total process of nation building, but it does suggest that they may be taking some serious risks in the way in which they are trying to shape their people's sense of loyalty.

The consideration of how the distribution crisis may be used to affect the other crises brings us to the point at which we must briefly look at the interrelationship among these crises. The sequence in which the five are coped with may be critical in determining the pattern of individual national development. The order in which we presented the crises did imply that there might be an ideal historical sequence. In truth, we are

[18] For an excellent study of the relationship of politics to economic development, see Myron Weiner, *The Politics of Scarcity: Public Pressure and Political Response in India* (Chicago: University of Chicago Press, 1962).

not sure that this is the case, but it may be of great significance that in Europe the crises did tend to occur singly in this order. Thus in England, for example, the problem of identity was resolved well before the problems of integration and penetration. The participation crisis occurred in its own context and through gradual stages of expanding suffrage, and only at a late period were the problems of distribution raised as dominant issues.

Throughout Asia all the crises seem to be telescoped in time, and there is little possibility for the orderly and systematic dealing with each in isolation.[19] Although we are far more knowledgeable about social processes, the task of nation building in Asia is certain to be far more complicated than it was in the West. The future of Asia, however, depends fundamentally upon how effectively the nation building process is worked out in the various countries of the region.

THE FUTURE ASIAN BALANCE OF POWER

At the beginning of this essay we introduced the themes of change and frustration in characterizing Asia. We did this largely in terms of the problems of the individual countries. In conclusion, we want to turn to the fact that the most fundamental change in Asia which will determine the future influences of the region in the entire world is at the level of the emerging balance of power among all the Asian states.

The future stability of Asia immutably depends upon the relationships among the three giants of the continent. For the first time in modern history, Asian stability will depend upon a three-way balance of power among China, India, and Japan. The importance of this balance first became clear with the ending of the colonial epic, but it is still extremely difficult to foresee all the problem's possible dimensions, because it has never existed historically.

Before the war, only Japan was a major power. Tropic Asia was a vast expansion of colonial government existing under relatively stable but undynamic conditions. China was weak and internally divided. At the beginning of the postwar epic, the United States felt that the security of the region would depend upon the creation of a strong and independent China, which would no longer be a historic power vacuum area. We also hoped to limit the role of Japan by turning the attentions of the Japanese inward upon their own problems of democratic development. Our hopes for a peaceful Asia were shattered by the emergence of a Communist-dominated China. Suddenly our thinking had to be revised to cope with the problem of a strong and aggressive China.

[19] An insightful essay on the interrelated problems of development is Edward Shils, *Political Development in the New States* (The Hague: Mouton & Co., 1962).

For the past decade of the postwar period, the three-way balance did not begin to take full form. Japan did turn inward and became absorbed with her own phenomenal developments. China likewise was absorbed with her own social revolution. Only India was free to play a larger role, and she too was limited by domestic concerns and by a need to focus on relations with the industrialized world, in the hope of obtaining the best conditions for maximizing foreign assistance for her development plans. During this period the separate countries of Southeast Asia were relatively free from external pressures. Regretfully, it cannot be reported that these countries exploited their opportunities to achieve domestic development.[20]

The key question for the future is whether Chinese influences can be effectively contained, particularly throughout Southeast Asia. The stark fact is that historically whenever China has been united, her influences have always spilled over into the region of Southeast Asia. Today Southeast Asia remains a string of relatively fragile and underpopulated countries along the southern border of a massive and overpopulated China. The hope for the future must be that Indian and Japanese influence, combined with a margin of United States power, can provide the necessary shield behind which the separate Southeast Asian countries can gain their full sense of nationhood. If, in time, the Southeast Asian countries can become a string of vigorously developing independent societies, then the threat of China may begin to recede.

During most of the last decade, China did not press forward in Southeast Asia with maximum effort, yet during this period the image of China as a rising great power became increasingly widespread. Paradoxically, since the internal weaknesses of China were exposed to the view of all with the collapse of the Great Leap Forward campaign and the crises in agriculture, the Chinese have felt compelled to press for more aggressive actions from Laos and South Vietnam to the Indian borders. During most of the decade China was held in check by a strange combination of contradictory policies.

First, the existence of neutralist states and the advantages that China derived from the Bandung Conference encouraged the Chinese to believe that much might be accomplished by blandishments and the appearance of nonaggressiveness. There are few people, including the leaders of the neutralist states, who believe that this was enough to hold China in check. There was the need for the other policy, that of SEATO, and the presence of American power. Although it is conventional in the West to minimize the significance of SEATO, the fact remains that the Chinese were never sure that it would be safe to test by direct action whether SEATO was

---

[20] A useful general study of the foreign relations of these countries is Russell H. Fifield, *The Diplomacy of Southeast Asia 1945-1958* (New York: Harper & Row, Publishers, 1958).

only a bluff; and consequently, the unbelievable occurred when a revolutionary and dynamic China was checked at her boundaries, and she did not succeed in expanding her holdings into Southeast Asia.

In the years that lie ahead, China may appear to be a more slowly and painfully developing giant. Much of the mystique of Chinese development has been lost, and in the future we can expect to see the Chinese grappling with the same kinds of problems which bedevil all poor countries anxious for rapid growth. Out of this prediction we might hope that the countries of Southeast Asia might again gain a respite from the full burden of Chinese pressures. Regretfully, however, it seems that the countries of the region may not be inclined to use the time any more effectively than they did in the first years of independence. We now have, for example, the series of conflicts and feuds among the various Southeast Asian countries: Indonesia opposing the creation of Malaysia; the Philippines laying claims to British Borneo; the Thais and the Cambodians at cross purposes.

In this evolving context it would appear that the United States policy emphasis in Asia should properly be to stress at every turn the need for sober and responsible planning for political and economic development. This should particularly be the case if the free countries in the area are to withstand the shock that would inevitably follow from either further Communist successes in Laos or the detonation by the Chinese of even a primitive nuclear device. More than ever before, the need will be to instill in the leaders and people of free Asia the conviction that they can surmount their past frustrations in development and in time achieve their original ideals of building modernizing and democratic societies. If they are to sustain their faith and not yield completely to authoritarian ways, they must be given the encouragement of knowing that those in the West sympathize with their problems and stand ready to assist where possible.

In the last analysis, the future of Asia, and the key to United States policy in the region, must lie in the problems of nation building. This is the reason why there is urgency in our search for a better understanding of the complex problems of political development. This is also why in Asia there is an extraordinary congruence in the interests of the policy makers and the students of social processes. The mysteries of nation building are a unique intellectual challenge to the scholar, and all the intellectual tools of the social sciences are being tested by the problem. There are possibly few more dramatic cases in which the exciting and legitimate concern of pure scholarship fits so closely with one of the most pressing problems of world affairs.

Suggestions for Further Reading

Almond, Gabriel A. and James S. Coleman, eds., *The Politics of the Developing Areas*. Princeton, N.J.: Princeton University Press, 1960.

Emerson, Rupert, *From Empire to Nation*. Cambridge, Mass.: Harvard University Press, 1960.

Griswold, A. Whitney, *The Far Eastern Policy of the United States*. New York: Harcourt, Brace & World, 1939.

LaPalombara, Joseph, ed., *Bureaucracy and Political Development*. Princeton, N.J.: Princeton University Press, 1963.

Millikan, Max F. and Donald L. M. Blackmer, eds., *The Emerging Nations: Their Growth and United States Policy*. Boston: Little, Brown & Co., 1961.

Pye, Lucian W., *Politics, Personality, and Nation Building: Burma's Search for Identity*. New Haven, Conn.: Yale University Press, 1962.

———, ed., *Communications and Political Development*. Princeton, N.J.: Princeton University Press, 1963.

Shils, Edward, *Political Development in the New States*. The Hague: Mouton and Co., 1962.

Tsou, Tang, *America's Failure in China 1949-50*. Chicago: University of Chicago Press, 1963.

Walinsky, Louis J., *Economic Development in Burma, 1951-1960*. New York: The Twentieth Century Fund, 1962.

Ward, Robert E. and Roy C. Macridis, eds., *Modern Political Systems: Asia*. Englewood Cliffs, N.J.: Prentice-Hall, Inc., 1963.

Weiner, Myron, *The Politics of Scarcity: Public Pressure and Political Response in India*. Chicago: University of Chicago Press, 1962.

* Also available in limited clothbound edition.

* Also available in limited clothbound edition.

The American Assembly Series

* Also available in limited clothbound edition.

* Also available in limited clothbound edition.

Twentieth Century Views*

* Also available in limited clothbound edition.

DATE DUE

MAR 30 '66			
APR 13 '66			
GAYLORD			PRINTED IN U.S.A.